FANNY GINOR ● SOCIO-ECONOMIC DISPARITIES IN ISRAEL

FANNY GINOR

SOCIO-ECONOMIC DISPARITIES IN ISRAEL

DAVID HOROWITZ INSTITUTE FOR THE RESEARCH OF DEVELOPING COUNTRIES
TEL AVIV UNIVERSITY

TRANSACTION BOOKS • RUTGERS UNIVERSITY

ISBN 965-216-000-8

ISBN 0-87855-332-0

University Publishing Projects, Ltd.
Tel Aviv
Printed in Israel, **1979**

CONTENTS

Page

PREFACE 1

Introduction: Concepts and Measurement 7
Forms of inequality; Economic inequality; Income unit; Measurement of inequality; The poverty line; Social justice; Tolerance of inequality; Characteristics of poverty groups.

PART I — *DEVELOPMENTS AND TRENDS*

Chapter 1 — *The Mandatory Period* 23
General developments; Economic growth and the rise in the standard of living; Socio-economic disparities; First family surveys; Distribution of earnings of Jewish wage and salary earners; Income distribution of the Jewish rural and urban population; Socio-economic conditions in the Arab sector; Income distribution of the total population; The second world war period; Housing conditions; Socio-economic differences between the various communities.

Chapter 2 — *Socio-Economic Developments in Israel* 45
The changing demographic base; Economic growth and its social implications; Structural changes and rising capital intensity; The balance of payments problem; The rise in the standard of living; Differences in the standard of living; Employment and labor force participation; Social stratification and social and cultural change.

Chapter 3 — *Income Distribution by Factor Shares* 65
Returns to labor and capital; Capital share and the business cycle; Labor share and inequality.

Chapter 4 — *Development of Income Distribution* 75
Developments over time; Factors affecting income differentials; Employment level; Changes in age structure; Family size; Labor force participation of family members; Educational structure; Occupational structure; The impact of government policy; Redistribution of incomes; Income distribution in the mid-seventies; Analysis of combined impact.

Chapter 5 — *A Historical Aspect* 101
Income distribution of wage and salary earners; Inequality between communities; Regional income differences; Rural-urban differences; The changing pattern of income distribution in the Arab population; Income distribution in the total population.

PART II — *INEQUALITY AND POVERTY IN ISRAEL – AN ANALYSIS*

Chapter 6 — *Factors Affecting Earnings and Income Differentials* 121
The effects of age and education; Life-time income; Income inequality in homogeneous groups; Multiple regression analysis of the family head's earnings.

Chapter 7 — *Determinants of Family Income* 135
Composition of family income; Examination of incomes in all families; Husband-wife families; Family income and the working wife; The wife's earnings; Independent individuals and one-parent families; Determinants of income per standard equivalent adult; Main determinants of family income; Labor force participation of family members; Education, age, sex and occupation; Country of origin, family size and dwelling locality.

Chapter 8 — *Poverty in Israel* 164
Definition of poverty line; Characteristics of poverty groups; Non-participation in labor force; Partial employment, education, age and occupation; Family size; Country of origin; Housing conditions; Causes of poverty and near-poverty; Estimated situation in the mid-seventies.

PART III — *ECONOMIC DEVELOPMENT AND INEQUALITY*

Chapter 9 — *Israel in the World* 179
Income inequality in less developed and developed countries; Comparison with OECD countries; Trends over time; The impact of urbanization; Optimal income distribution.

Chapter 10 — *Income Distribution in the World* 193
The gap between countries; Income distribution in the world; The pace of growth; Causes for differences in the standard of living.

Chapter 11 — *Summary and Conclusions* 205

Appendixes – Tables and Regressions 215
Bibliography 295
Author Index 305
Subject Index 307

LIST OF TABLES

CHAPTER 1

1.1 — Wages and Salaries, 1930 29
1.2 — Income Distribution of Jewish Families, 1930 31
1.3 — Estimated Jewish Family Income Distribution, 1936 (in %) 34
1.4 — Estimated Income Distribution, 1936 (%) 36
1.5 — Estimate of Income Distribution in Urban Population, 1944 42

CHAPTER 2
2.1 — Literate, Aged 14 and Over (in %) 49
2.2 — Economic Growth, 1950-1976 51
2.3 — Infant Mortality Rates and Life Expectancy 56
2.4 — Indicators of the Standard of Living 57
2.5 — Share of Food in Private Consumption in 1973 58

CHAPTER 3
3.1 — Percentage of Urban Families in Lowest and Highest Deciles by Employment Status, 1968/69 66
3.2 — Percentage Shares of Employee Compensation 67
3.3 — Returns to Labor and Capital 69

CHAPTER 4
4.1 — Inequality Index, Unemployment and Economic Growth 77
4.2 — Income Distribution of Employees' Families 78
4.3 — Family Income by Age of Family Head 79
4.4 — Inequality of Gross Money Income per Family and per Standard Equivalent Adult, Jewish Urban Population 81
4.5 — Inequality of Schooling 82
4.6 — Educational Structure of Jewish Population 83
4.7 — Annual Earnings of Employees by Occupation 86
4.8 — Capital per Employed and Educational Level 86
4.9 — Reduction of Inequality by Direct Taxes 92
4.10 — Income Distribution of Urban Population, 1968/69 and 1975/76 96
4.11 — Correlation of Demographic and Other Variables with Inequality Index 97

CHAPTER 5
5.1 — Income Distribution of Wage and Salary Earners 102
5.2 — Women's Earnings as a Percentage of Men's Earnings 103
5.3 — Income and Housing Density in the Jewish Population by Communities 106
5.4 — Urban Family Incomes by Type of Locality 109
5.5 — Income Distribution of Urban Arab Families 114
5.6 — Income Distribution of Total Population 116

CHAPTER 6
6.1 — Estimated Cash Income over Fifty Years, of Families Headed by Persons with 9-12 Years of Schooling 128

CHAPTER 7
7.1 — Beta Coefficients and Percentage Explained 137
7.2 — Results of Regressions on Net Family Cash Income of Husband-Wife Families — Beta Coefficients 142
7.3 — Correlation Coefficients of Years of Schooling of Husband and Wife with Total Family Income 144

7.4 — Regression on "Wife Worked Outside Home" 148
7.5 — Average Monthly Total Family Income, by Family Types 150
7.6 — Regression on Net Cash Income per Standard Equivalent Adult 152
7.7 — Urban Families by Deciles and No. of Earners 155
7.8 — Total Monthly Income by Sex of Family Head 159
7.9 — Family Heads by Country of Origin and Years of Schooling 161

CHAPTER 8
8.1 — Composition of Families 167
8.2 — Causes of Poverty, 1968/69 173
8.3 — Characteristics of Poverty and Near-Poverty Groups, 1968/69 and 1975/76 175

CHAPTER 9
9.1 — Income Distribution in 55 Countries, by per Capita Income 180
9.2 — Inequality of Family Incomes in OECD Countries 181
9.3 — Earnings Differences Between Educational Levels 184
9.4 — Changing Income Inequality During Urbanization 187
9.5 — Income Distribution Compared to Optimal Income Distribution 190

CHAPTER 10
10.1 — Estimated World Income Distribution, 1974 196
10.2 — Estimated Inequality Between Countries by per Capita Income, 1974 197
10.3 — Changes in Income Distribution in the World 198
10.4 — Annual Growth Rate of World Product, Population and per Capita Product 200

APPENDIXES

APPENDIX 0
0A.1 — Income Distribution by Deciles 217

APPENDIX 1
1A.1 — Mortality Rates and Life Expectancy 219
1A.2 — Infant Mortality Rates and Life Expectancy in Egypt, Trans-Jordan and Palestine 220
1A.3 — Income and Expenditure of Jewish Urban Workers' Families, August 1926 221
1A.4 — Monthly Earnings of Jewish Wage and Salary Earners, 1930 222
1A.5 — Income Distribution of Jewish Urban Families, 1930 223
1A.6 — Consumption Expenditure per Member in Collective Settlements 229
1A.7 — Distribution of Income and Living Expenditure in Three Smallholders' Settlements 224

1A.8 — Estimated Distribution of Income in 1936 225
1A.9 — Income Distribution of the Jewish Population, 1936 226
1A.10 — Estimated Distribution of Land Holdings and Income in 1929 in 104 Arab Villages 228
1A.11 — Literacy and Life Expectancy 230
1A.12 —Monthly Income and Expenditure of Jewish Urban Families, January — March 1946 230
1A.13 — Monthly Income by Towns and Communities, Family Survey, 1946 231
1A.14 — Distribution of Family Expenditure by Deciles, 1942 232
1A.15 — Weights Used for Calculation of Inequality Index 233

APPENDIX 2
2A.1 — Annual Rates of Births, Deaths, Natural Increase and Population Growth 234
2A.2 — Gross Reproduction Rates 235
2A.3 — Age Composition 235
2A.4 — Education of Population Aged 14 and Over 236
2A.5 — Net Domestic Product at Factor Cost, by Economic Branch 236
2A.6 — Capital Stock in Fixed Assets 237
2A.7 — Capital-Output Ratios 237
2A.8 — Composition of Domestic Use of Resources (%) 238
2A.9 — Balance of Payments, 1950-1976 238
2A.10 — Families Possessing Durable Consumer Goods by Continent of Birth in 1975/76 239
2A.11 — Housing Density and Family Size 240
2A.12 — Participation in the Labor Force, by Age 240
2A.13 — Employed Persons and Labor Force Participation by Schooling and Sex 241

APPENDIX 4
4A.1 — Income Inequality in Jewish Urban Families and Jewish Urban Employees' Families 244
4A.2 — Income Inequality of Employees by Educational Level 246
4A.3 — Income Distribution of Urban Population, 1968/69 and 1975/76 247
4A.4 — Regression Equations for Inequality Index 248
4A.5 — Correlation Matrix of Explanatory Variables 249
4A.6 — Beta Coefficients (Inequality Index) 250

APPENDIX 5
5A.1 — Educational Capital per Capita 251
5A.2 — Share of Oriental Employees by Occupation 252
5A.3 — Income Distribution Among Kibbutzim 253
5A.4 — Income Distribution in Moshavim 254

APPENDIX 6
6A.1 — Family Income, by Age of Family Head 255
6A.2 — Family Income, by Schooling of Family Head 256
6A.3 — Inequality Indices of the Income of Homogeneous Groups 257

6A.4 — Results of Multiple Regressions on Income from Work by Wage Earning Family Heads 258
6A.5 — Coefficients of Correlation between Continent of Origin and Earnings, and between Continent of Origin and Schooling 259

APPENDIX 7
7A.1 — Composition of Family Income by Employment Status of Family Head 260
7A.2 — Husband-Wife Families with Working and Non-Working Wives 261

Results of Multiple Regressions on Family Income

7A.3 — All Families 263
7A.4 — Husband-Wife Families — Total, Employees, Self-Employed and Not Belonging to Labor Force 264
7A.5 — Husband-Wife Families, Wife Working — Total, Employees, Self-Employed and Not Belonging to Labor Force 265
7A.6 — Husband-Wife Families, Wife not Working — Total, Employees, Self-Employed, and Not Belonging to Labor Force 266
7A.7 — Earnings of Family Head's Wife 267
7A.8 — One-Parent Families and Individuals, Women and Men 268

Results of Multiple Regressions on Income per S.E.A.

7A.9 — All Families 270
7A.10 — Husband-Wife Families 271
7A.11 — Husband-Wife Families with Working Wives 272
7A.12 — Husband-Wife Families with Non-Working Wives 273
7A.13 — Individuals and One-Parent Families, Women and Men 274
7A.14 — Families Whose Heads did not Belong to the Labor Force 275
7A.15 — Employee Families 276
7A.16 — Self-Employed Families 277
7A.17 — Years of Schooling and Labor Force Participation 277
7A.18 — Independent Individuals and One-Parent Families 278
7A.19 — Incomes and Earnings by Occupation 279
7A.20 — Family Income by Continent of Birth and Period of Immigration, by Deciles 280

APPENDIX 8
8A.1 — Scales of Differential Weights for Standard Equivalent Adults 281
8A.2 — Characteristics of Low Income Groups 282
8A.3 — Consumption per Standard Adult, by Deciles of Families, 1968/69 283
8A.4 — Family Heads Not in Labor Force, by Schooling and Age, 1968/69 284
8A.5 — Family Heads Who Worked, by Schooling and Age 285
8A.6 — Family Heads by Country of Origin and Schooling 286
8A.7 — Families by Size and Country of Origin 287

APPENDIX 9
9A.1 — Distribution of Pre-Tax Incomes 288
9A.2 — Distribution of After-Tax Incomes 289

9A.3 — Income Distribution of Households with Heads Aged 25-54 Years 290
9A.4 — Per Capita Distribution of Income 291
9A.5 — Households of Given Size by Decile Shares 292

APPENDIX 10
10A.1 — Annual Growth Rates of Product and Population 1967-75 293

LIST OF FIGURES

CHAPTER 6

6.1 — Graph 1 — Family Income by Age and Schooling
Graph 2 — Family Income of Wage and Salary Earners by Age and Schooling
Graph 3 — Earnings of Wage and Salary Earners by Age and Schooling 125

APPENDIX 0

Figure 0A.1 — Lorenz Curves 218

APPENDIX 4

Figure 4A.1 — Inequality in Jewish Urban Families and Urban Employees' Families 245

PREFACE

This book examines the social and economic disparities of Israel, their causes, their development, and their impact on the country.

The ingathering of the exiles involved the coming together of Jews from all corners of the earth. They had been dispersed for many generations in countries with different cultures, different languages and different outlooks on life. Though they had lived within the spiritual and moral atmosphere of Judaism, the socio-economic environments of their host countries influenced their mentalities, their ways of life, their educational levels and their occupational structures. Their relationships with Christian societies differed from those with Islamic societies — and the changes within these societies differed even more, deeply affecting the Jewish communities.

The formation of an immigrant society in Israel by such disparate groups posed many problems. The relatively rapid development of a diversified economy with modern features gave the groups from modern societies a certain advantage over the others. Social tensions based on feelings of discrimination and deprivation developed as a result of social differentiation in a small country with a very heterogeneous population.

An in-depth analysis of the situation and its historic roots is therefore a timely undertaking. There have been various investigations into income differences and social disparities. Problems of inequality in general, and inequality and poverty in Israel, have been the subject of a number of studies by the author. Part of the results of these studies were published as articles in the *Economic Quarterly*[1] and as research papers of the David Horowitz Institute for the Research of Developing Countries, Tel Aviv University.[2]

This book uses the results of these studies and those of others in its search for the answers to some key questions:

What is the extent of social and economic inequality in Israel today?

What causes are behind this differentiation?

What changes in socio-economic differentiation were brought about by historical developments, economic growth and demographic changes?

In what ways and at what cost can inequality be reduced? How has government policy succeeded in reducing poverty and socio-economic differences?

How do socio-economic inequality in Israel and the problems connected with it compare with the situations in other countries?

An introductory chapter examines some methodological and theoretical aspects of inequality and poverty, and discusses the problems of measurement. The forms of inequality and their social significance, the poverty line and characteristics of poverty groups, and the concepts of social justice and tolerance of inequality are investigated.

The first part of the book shows the trends since the beginning of the Mandatory period (1919). The developments which led to the present social and economic differentiation are analyzed with the aid of economic and demographic data.

Socio-economic differences during the Mandatory period between and within the two main sectors — the traditional Arab sector and the more modern Jewish sector — are investigated in Chapter 1: the extent of the pattern of a dual economy, the mutual influence of the two sectors, the urban-rural differences, the socio-economic differences between the two sectors and between the two main Jewish communities (European and Oriental), and the effect of demographic changes and economic growth on social stratification.

Chapter 2 investigates socio-economic developments in Israel: how socio-economic disparities were affected by rapid economic growth, the rising standard of living, structural changes, capital imports and mass immigration; how the educational level, the structure of the labor force and the employment volume were affected, and how these changes influenced social stratification; what changes occurred within the Jewish population, and how disparities between the two main Jewish communities were affected; how the various developments influenced socio-economic differences in the Arab sector.

Chapter 3 briefly surveys functional income distribution (i.e., the shares of labor and capital in the national income) in order to examine its relationship to socio-economic stratification. The connection of socio-economic differences with returns to physical and human capital is explored in relation to the thesis that income distribution depends considerably on the distribution of physical and human capital.

Chapter 4 examines more closely the impact of various factors on inequality over time. Regression analysis was used in addition to temporal comparisons to find the influence of such factors as the aging of the population, changes in the educational level and the occupational structure, technological advance, unemployment, women's labor force participation, and changes in family size. The impact of government policies on the redistribution of income and on the reduction of social differences was also investigated.

In Chapter 5, a comparison with the Mandatory period aims at clarifying the present situation by revealing its roots. The following questions were asked:

Was inequality in the Jewish sector as small as many assume due to the socialist ideology of the settlers and the workers?

Were the characteristics of inequality in the Mandatory period different from those of today, with regard to differences between Jewish ethnic groups, between occupations, between men and women, between towns and villages, and between regions?

Were the inequalities between the Arab and Jewish sectors in the Mandatory period similar to those between a traditional society and a modern society? What changes have taken place since then?

Can social developments be explained by the theory that inequality rises in the first phases of economic development and declines in the later phases, or were special forces at work? What were the effects of the waves of immigration and of the business cycle?

The second part of the book deals with the various aspects of income distribution in Israel in the beginning of the seventies as the main expression of social and economic disparities.

Chapter 6 inquires into the causes of income differentials. It examines the earnings of employees and of family heads by multiple regression analysis and by comparing homogeneous groups. Explanatory factors include education, occupation, age, employment volume, immigration status, country of origin, sex and region. The issue of lifetime earnings was also explored in this context.

Determinants of family income are investigated in Chapter 7 by statistical analysis and multiple regressions by family types — regular husband-wife families, independent individuals and one-parent families. A special measure (the standard equivalent adult) took into account differences in family size. The importance of the wife's earnings was investigated by separating husband-wife families with working wives from the others, and the motives of married women for working outside their homes were explored.

The characteristics of poverty groups are shown in Chapter 8 by statistical analysis. This, of course, requires a definition of the poverty line. Who are the poor of Israel? Do they include people who work regularly? To what extent are the causes of poverty and near-poverty to be found in the people themselves (old age, mental and physical disability), and to what extent are they found in social and political circumstances such as unemployment, insufficient educational services, overcrowded living conditions, etc.? What policy measures have been taken to improve their lot, and how have they succeeded? How has equality of opportunity (especially for children and youth) improved?

The third part sets the situation in Israel in a world perspective. The questions asked in Chapter 9 are: Is there a pattern of changes in inequality during the process of economic growth? What is the impact of urbanization?

How does Israel compare with other countries, both developed and less-developed? How does income distribution in Israel and other countries compare with an optimal income distribution?

Chapter 10 attempts to estimate inequality in the world. The large and growing gap between the least-developed countries and the developed part of the world is examined, and the causes of differences in the standard of living are briefly reviewed. The main questions: Is economic inequality mainly the result of the distribution of human and physical capital? What measures (both worldwide and within countries) can improve the situation?

A summary and conclusions are given in the last chapter.

The Appendix contains the technical parts such as supplementary tables and regressions.

NOTES

1. Income Distribution in the World (Hebrew), Dec. 1969.
   Factors Affecting Income Distribution in Israel, Fall 1972.
   Social and Economic Disparities, a Historical View (Hebrew), Aug. 1976.
2. The Social Situation in Israel, 1969-73 (written in consultation with Ruth Horovitz), Paper No. 4, Dec. 1973.
   Determinants of Family Income in Israel, Paper No. 10, July 1974.
   Analysis of Low Income Groups in Israel, Paper No. 12, Sept. 1974.
   Inequality and the Poverty Line in Developing Countries, Paper No. 19, May 1975.

ACKNOWLEDGEMENTS

I wish to express my appreciation to Prof. N. Rudi of the University Institute of Technology, Holon, who advised me on the preparation of the regressions in Chapters 6 and 7; and to Ariel Hirt, research assistant, Tel Aviv University, who assisted me in the programming and execution of all regressions. I also wish to thank the Bank of Israel for permitting me to use the survey data for Chapter 8, which were prepared while I was working there; Chana Weinberg, for her assistance in the preparation of the data; and Gideon Burstein, Director of the Consumption Section of the Central Bureau of Statistics, for additional data and explanations.

I am grateful to everyone who read all or parts of the manuscript and made helpful comments: Dr. Ruth Horovitz, formerly with the Ministry of Social Welfare, who read the whole manuscript and whose remarks from the perspective of a sociologist and social worker were much appreciated; Dr. Abba Schwartz, Tel-Aviv University, for his valuable comments on various chapters; Prof. Hans W. Singer and Prof. Emanuel de Kadt of the Institute of Development Studies, University of Sussex, England, whose careful reading and very helpful comments were greatly appreciated; Dr. A.L. Gaathon, formerly with the Bank of Israel, whose extensive knowledge of the Mandatory period made his remarks particularly valuable; Dr. Ruth Klinov-Malul, Hebrew University, Jerusalem, for her very useful and valuable comments; Prof. Y. Hershlag, Tel-Aviv University,for his kind advice and helpful comments, and Prof. E. Marx, Tel-Aviv University, for his valuable remarks. Special gratitude I owe to David Horowitz, first Governor of the Bank of Israel and now the Chairman of its Advisory Board, who stimulated my interest in the subject and encouraged me to engage in its study.

Many thanks go to Lew Golan for his excellent editing of the manuscript. I also wish to thank Gabriela Williams, Secretary of the Horowitz Institute, for her very helpful assistance in the various stages of this study and Ruth Parnas, who typed the text and many tables and appendices through several drafts with great accuracy and patience.

FANNY GINOR

Tel Aviv, January 1979

INTRODUCTION

CONCEPTS AND MEASUREMENT

A clarification of concepts and methods of measurement is essential in this kind of study, although the social stratification of a specific country has its own historical roots and cultural basis.

An introductory chapter cannot pursue in depth the meaning and all of the implications of social and economic inequality, nor can it do justice to the widely ramified literature on the subject. We shall, however, consider some theoretical and methodological aspects relevant to an analysis of the situation in Israel, as well as to socio-economic inequality in a world context.

Inequality

Three forms of inequality can be discerned.[1]

(1) Economic: differences in the level of living.
(2) Social: differences in status and prestige.
(3) Political: differences stemming from distribution of power and participation in decision making.

There are connections between these three forms of inequality. Political power is used to obtain social status and economic advantages. Economic power can serve as a stepping stone to political power; in most societies it enhances social status. Social status may be a precondition to obtaining political power. But there is also a clear distinction among them, and high ranking in one hierarchy is compatible in some societies with low ranking in another. For instance: the high social status of physicians, lawyers and scholars despite their middling incomes; the lower social status of merchants despite their higher incomes; the high prestige of artists and writers despite their relatively low incomes; the high social status of the nobility even after their political and economic decline.

Though all three forms of inequality require investigation, the economic aspects lend themselves more easily to quantification. Attempts have been made to quantify the social and political factors affecting inequality;[2] for a comparison of social changes, such indicators and rankings are useful. However, the interconnections between social, economic and political factors are so complicated and so interwoven with the cultural and historical background of each country, that it is difficult to say how much international comparisons may help to clarify the issues.

The phases of economic development are important to the study of its relationship to changes in inequality. A simple measure is the GNP per capita. More sophisticated and more adequate measures are development indicators such as the one calculated by the U.N. Research Institute for Social Development.[3] Bell and Duloy[4] classified countries according to degree of urbanization, distribution of landownership, and abundance or scarcity of land. However, since these indicators usually show a high correlation with GNP per capita, we have chosen to use GNP per capita in most cases.

Economic Inequality

It is mainly income that determines the command of the individual or the family over goods and services. However, in case of low or no income, a family's wealth or credit can supplement or replace its income through loans or the sale of assets, and capital gains and windfalls can temporarily increase a family's income. Hence, total consumption over an extended period may be a better indicator of the level of living than income,[5] since it reflects not only current income net of taxes but also past savings, windfalls and expectations of future income. Such total consumption should include: (1) The household's purchases of goods and services; (2) Consumption of goods and services produced by the household; (3) Consumption of goods and services taken from the household's own business or received in payment for labor; (4) Use of an owned dwelling, a private vehicle and other durable consumer goods; (5) Consumption of goods and services provided free by the government or non-profit organizations.

Consumption data also permit the assessment of nutritional levels, which help determine a poverty line and evaluate the influence of nutrition on the health of various population strata.

While the level of living is reflected better by consumption data than by income data, an analysis of the latter is required for the following reasons: (1) A considerable part of income is saved over long periods in the highest income brackets; therefore, the distribution of total consumption is likely to reflect smaller overall inequality than does income distribution. (2) Examination of the impact of the tax structure and of social policy measures requires an investigation of income distribution before and after taxes, and with and without social welfare payments and public goods and services. Consumption data are needed to evaluate the impact of indirect taxes. (3) To uncover the causes of poverty, the causes of low or no income have to be investigated. (4) The interconnection between economic growth, structural changes of the economy and society, and institutional changes, on one hand, and changes in social stratification, on the other, are connected with changes in income distribution.

Income data tor such purposes should be as comprehensive as possible. They should include the current monetary income of the family from all sources (wages and salaries, rent and interest, pensions, current income from insurance funds and social payments) as well as income in kind, including goods and services produced by the household and imputed income from owned dwellings and cars. From this gross total income, direct taxes are deducted. To this personal disposable income, we add the value of public goods and services received to arrive at total net income.

Consumption data are said to be more trustworthy than income data, since incomes are usually underreported. The best method for arriving at better income figures is to obtain them within the framework of a consumption expenditure survey. The income data of each household can then be brought in line with consumption expenditure, taxes and savings or dissavings. We prefer such surveys, but had to use income surveys as well in order to view income distribution over time.

Income Unit

When each income recipient is defined as the income unit — as in the case of wage statistics or income tax statistics — the income differentials measured will not reflect differences in the standard of living, since there are families with one, two, or more such income recipients. Even worse, these statistics do not include the total population; families without wage and salary earners (self-employed, employers, and people not belonging to the labor force) are excluded from wage statistics, and families with very low incomes may be excluded from income tax statistics.

The desirable income unit is the consumer unit, in which the level of living is determined by the common income of its members (the household or family). Households differ not only in the number of earners, but also in size. Obviously, households with the same income but of different sizes have different levels of living. Hence, family size has to be taken into account; so does its composition, since the needs of children, women and men are different. Furthermore, economies of scale have to be considered. The U.N. Social Development Division proposed that a poverty budget be based on size-type families representing large groups and significantly varied needs.[6] But this may involve a large number of size-type families — as, for instance, in the U.S.A., where in 1965 poverty lines were drawn for 124 different types of families.[7] In measuring income or consumption distribution, a more general method of taking into account household size and composition is needed — such as income per person with different weights for women, men and children, and the influence of economies of scale.

A recent approach determines equivalence scales in terms of standard persons; it is based on the assumption that households spending the same percentage of their incomes on food enjoy equal standards of living, although differing in size or composition.[8] The question has been raised whether income per standard adult is a proper measure for comparing incomes of families of different sizes in different income brackets. Obviously, the burden of an additional child is not proportional to family income, as may be implied by a fixed standard adult measure; it will be a smaller percentage of family income in the higher brackets.[9] It has, therefore, been proposed that differential scales be devised according to income brackets.

Studies of U.S. and Israeli data show that economies of scale rise with income, when a consumption function is used in which elasticities with respect to family size and income are allowed to vary.[10]

The Israeli study also experimented with different market baskets (on the broader assumption that the same percentage spent on essentials indicates equal standards of living). Economies of scale were considerably greater when clothing and housing were added to the basket. The variable and fixed scales were similar in the below-average income group, and with other consumption functions, they were similar in the lower income groups.[11]

Though the determination of equivalence scales involves certain difficulties, such scales appear to be the best solution. Our analysis uses both income distribution per family and per standard equivalent adult, depending upon the problem being analyzed.

Measurement of Inequality

The method of measurement depends on what we are trying to measure. Are we interested in a summary measure of inequality, or do we need a measure which reflects the whole social and economic stratification? Are we interested in the gap between the low-income groups and a small stratum of the rich and the powerful? Or is our purpose to evaluate the expansion of the middle classes? How important is the inequality between regions, between rural and urban areas or between ethnic groups? Or is the delineation of poverty groups the most important issue?

Income distribution is usually measured by income classes or by fractile groups. Since income classes are defined in national currencies, the first method does not lend itself easily to inter-country comparisons. The classification of households or indivuals into fractile groups (deciles, quintiles, etc.) by ranking their income, consumption expenditure or wealth, permits comparisons between countries and between time periods. Such a ranking preferably should be by income or expenditure per standard equivalent adult The classification gives a detailed picture of the distribution, since each fractile group's share in the total can be calculated; it provides a simple means of identifying economically disadvantaged groups in the population.[12] Lorenz curves can be easily plotted from the data of fractile groups, and the proportions and various indices of inequality can be calculated.

A frequently used summary measure is the Gini Coefficient, which measures the area of inequality of the Lorenz Curve.[13] Though a summary measure of inequality is a convenient tool for comparisons, it should be used carefully. Atkinson[14] showed, in comparing five summary measures, that they embody some value judgment about the distribution. He therefore proposes to include in the index a measure which reflects society's valuation of equality. We have refrained from using such a measure, as this would require a judgment of the valuation of equality by Israeli society.

For certain purposes it may be best to renounce the summary measure. For instance, the Gini coefficient may be the same for two very different distributions: in one distribution, the lowest income groups may have a much lower share of total income than in the other distribution — but the highest income group is less privileged, because the middle classes are better off. (See Appendix, Table 0A.1, distribution D and E). If the poverty line is defined as one-third of the average, more than 30% of the first distribution (D) would belong to the poverty group, whereas in the other distribution (E) there would be no poverty problem. On the other hand, only 35% of total income would have to be transferred in distribution D to obtain equal distribution, whereas 42% would have to be transferred in distribution E.

Likewise, a smaller Gini coefficient does not always signify lower inequality throughout. When two Lorenz curves intersect, although one denotes a lower Gini coefficient than the other, inequality in the lower income groups may have declined while it may have risen in the higher income groups — or vice versa. Only when one Lorenz curve is totally within another one, and there is no intersection, does it denote lower inequality throughout. Thus, the Lorenz curve of distribution C intersects with that of distribution D and E. (Figure 0A.1). Though the Gini coefficient of C is larger than that of D and E, inequality of C is lower in the lower income groups as compared with D, and in the higher income groups as compared with E.

In such cases it is preferable to use income distribution by fractile groups (or the Lorenz curve), since their shares in total income show the form of distribution and permit the delineation of disadvantaged groups. If the poverty group is defined as having income below one-third or one-half of the average, all deciles having less than 3.3% or 5% of total income will belong to it.

The Poverty Line

In order to analyze low income groups ("the poor"), it is necessary to define some kind of poverty line. There are two main approaches to the definition of poverty:

a. The absolute approach, which regards the poverty line as the subsistence level — i.e., the level of living necessary to maintain health and ability to work. Some add minimal cultural requirements to the definition. Thus, Dudley Jackson[15] defines poverty as the failure of needs fulfillment which impairs the ability of the individual or the family to function adequately in society; not only the health and work criteria must be met, but also certain minimum needs necessary for engaging in social life and maintaining a family.

According to this approach, a family is poor when its resources are insufficient to meet minimum needs. This requires the calculation of a minimum living standard for various types of families, which can be adjusted for changes in the general standard of living. J.N. Morgan[16] calculated the welfare ratio of all income groups in the U.S. by comparing income with needs according to a calculated standard family budget. This approach can be simplified by calculating only minimum food requirements for various family types, and determining the share of food in the minimum family budget according to consumption patterns of low-income families.[17] This approach has been criticized as being based upon arbitrary judgments and circular arguments. Furthermore, the assumption that a family budget is used in the most economical way has been criticized as being unrealistic.[18]

b. The relative approach, for which poverty is a relative concept. It maintains that poverty can be understood only as part of a given society, and that the situation of the poor is determined by its distance from the other strata of that society. According to this approach, those belonging to the lowest fraction of the income distribution are the poor. This would mean that a certain percentage at the lower end of the income distribution would constitute the poor, regardless of the degree of inequality and the absolute or relative standard of living. No abolition of poverty would be possible according to this simple, relative concept of poverty. In recent times, this concept has been replaced by one which sees relative poverty only in a too-great distance from the median or average income; relative poverty of this type can be abolished by social policy designed to raise the income of the lower strata above a line not too far below the median or mean income.

V.R. Fuchs defines as poor "any family whose income is less than half the median family income".[19] A preliminary investigation into patterns of poverty in Israel was based on this definition.[20] The poverty line was set at 40% of the median net income per standard equivalent adult, and the near-poverty line was set at a level 35% higher (54% of the median net income).

The absolute and relative approaches may arrive at very different results in measuring poverty. Thus, an attempt to establish a poverty line in rural

Punjab by means of a carefully calculated family budget based on a least-cost diet meeting minimum nutritional requirements and consumption habits led to the conclusion that 18.4% of the population lived below the poverty line.[21] On the other hand, a study of income distribution in Malaysia with two relative definitions of the poverty line estimated the percentage of the population in poverty at approximately 70% (all households with less than average income) by the first definition, and the bottom 40% of households by the second definition.[22] As is well known, the general level of living in Malaysia is considerably higher than that of India, and we might expect a higher incidence of poverty in rural Punjab.

Measuring poverty over time also leads to very different conclusions according to the approach chosen. The absolute approach can eliminate poverty during a relatively short period of economic growth and adequate social policy, if the minimum requirements are determined once and forever.[23] The relative approach requires a much longer period and greater effort, since the poverty line moves upward with the general level of living. But the two approaches are less contradictory than they may appear at first sight. The absolute approach has to take into account the minimum requirements of an existing level of living in a given society (requirements differ according to climate, living conditions and social habits); in a dynamic society, adjustments will be necessary every few years. The relative approach, on the other hand, may give the poverty line a permanent definition as a certain percentage of the median income — but this definition still has to take into account the standard regarded as a minimum in a given society. It seems, therefore, that a combination of the two approaches is needed.

The approach chosen for policy decisions usually takes into account the prevailing views in a society — since the definitions of poverty are based on the views of the various segments of the population, which are influenced by its cultural and social value system.

In traditional societies, the existing social stratification is regarded as part of a permanent and just order. In most societies of this kind, wealth and power imposed responsibilities; the rich were commanded by customs and religion to help the poor. In cultures with a fatalistic view of the world, the fate of the disadvantaged seemed predestined and they had to bear their lot.

In modern societies, these views have undergone important modifications; the following views are generally found:

1. The feelings of deprivation of those at the bottom of the social and economic ladder.
2. The goal of social justice, which gives rise to the striving for more equality.
3. The view that poverty is a defect of the society as a whole, and that the effects of poverty (waste of human resources, crime, juvenile delinquency, etc.) harm the entire society.

4. The two contrasting ideological trends in modern society:
   a. The ideology of equality as applied in equality before the law, in which every citizen has the same rights and the same obligations; and
   b. The ideology of achievement and competition — which results in economic and social inequality, since effort must be rewarded (otherwise, there would be no effort). Sociological theory sees inequality as the outcome of a system of rewards and sanctions necessary for the proper functioning of society.
5. Connecting these two ideologies is the idea of equality of opportunity — i.e., that society has to provide the same starting point and the same conditions of competition for each of its members. These two trends have taken on a special quality in Israeli society under the influence of Jewish ethics and the ideologies of socialism and Zionism. The striving for social equality was relatively strong, and the ideology of achievement was based on the ethos of work; the combination resulted in the formation of special social forms. This ideological background (and the changes occurring within it) are important to the form and content of social policy.

The idea of equal opportunity is anchored in the concept of social justice. J. Rawls bases social justice on two principles: "equal liberty" and "fair equality of opportunity".[24] "First: each person is to have an equal right to the most extensive basic liberty compatible with a similar liberty to others. Second: social and economic inequalities are to be arranged so that they are both (a) reasonably expected to be to everyone's advantage, and (b) attached to positions and offices open to all." (p.60) According to Rawls, the primary social goods are: rights and liberties, opportunities and powers, income and wealth. Equal citizenship is achieved when the above two principles are satisfied, while powers, income and wealth may vary in their distribution.

The first principle (which is first in rank) guarantees the rights and liberties; the second principle requires social and economic policies aimed at maximizing the long-term expectations of the least advantaged under conditions of fair equality of opportunity. This consideration of the least advantaged is most important.

The idea of social justice also gives rise to a generally accepted adequate minimum standard of living below which no member of the society should fall. Such a standard as seen by the majority of the population[25] can serve as a point of departure for determining the poverty line. Instead of a sharp line, a range can be delineated between sufficient and insufficient resources of a household. Thurow speaks of a poverty band "over which poverty shades into economic sufficiency". A "near-poverty" group can also be regarded as such a poverty band.

Tolerance of Inequality

Full equality in all three aspects — economic, social and political — probably cannot be attained. Economic equality is conceivable, as expressed in the slogan of the Israeli kibbutzim: "From each according to his ability, to each according to his needs."[26] However, this kind of equality is apparently workable only in a relatively small society with egalitarian goals controlled by the members' opinions.

When it is recognized that the proper functioning of a society requires a system of rewards and sanctions, this excludes full equality — since rewards, of course, create inequality. In the kibbutzim, the reward of the diligent, the responsible and the talented is the recognition of the other members and the prestige of their positions and their attainments. But the maintenance of the kibbutzim as cells of relative equality requires persistent watchfulness and educational effort.

The hierarchical structure of modern enterprises with great differentiation in responsibility, skills and educational investment, requires differentiation in remuneration. There must be incentives for investing years of study to acquire a profession, and there must be a reward for the ability, effort and responsibility of the manager of a big production plant. There must also be a reward for the risk-taking of the enterpreneur as long as the economic system is based on private initiative and enterprise. Thus, it seems that the complicated and diversified structure of the modern economy with its hierarchical traits requires a system of diversified rewards, meaning a certain degree of economic inequality. The question is what degree of inequality is "acceptable" to the society, as Ian Bowen states it.[27]

Or what determines the degree of inequality with which a society is ready to live? To what extent does the sense of social justice, however vague, affect the degree of tolerance of inequalities, and to what extent is the tolerance determined by feelings of deprivation of disadvantaged population groups?

A surprising result of recent studies is that feelings of deprivation are not correlated to the factual evidence of inequality. Thus, such feelings were voiced more strongly in Israel at the beginning of the seventies, after inequalities in income and education had declined from their peak in the recession years of 1966/67. On the basis of survey results and a historical analysis of England, W.G. Runciman comes to the conclusion that there is a discrepancy between the facts of inequality and the feelings of grievance or relative deprivation.[28] Since feelings of relative deprivation are based on comparisons with reference groups, and these reference groups are taken mostly from the same social group (neighbors, co-workers, etc.), large social inequalities often have small impacts. Hence, according to Runciman, social justice plays "little part in the opinions and feelings even of those whose unformulated claims it would vindicate" (p.285). He further states: "Most people's lives are governed more by the resentment of narrow inequalities, the cultivation of modest ambitions and preservation of small differentials than by attitudes to public policy or the social structure as such". But he admits that at certain times and places, the resentment of inequalities may become stronger than warranted by factual inequalities.

A.O. Hirschman[29] approached this problem from another angle. The degree of tolerance of inequality is very different in different societies, according to habits, religion, etc. Hirschman tries to show that this tolerance changes in the course of development; when the situation of others, especially one's neighbors and colleagues, improves, the hope arises that one's own turn will come sooner or later. This is a period of tolerance for increasing inequality; the period is bound to end when the expectations thus awakened are not satisfied. The recognition of the degree of such tolerance is most important to a successful development policy.

An important point made by Hirschman is that tolerance is usually larger in a unitary society, and smaller in a segmented society. If economic advance becomes identified with an ethnic group or a language group, tolerance for widening inequality declines — and it may even decline for the previously tolerated degree of inequality. The growing sensitivity of Israeli society to inequality in the seventies seems to be connected with its division into ethnic groups.

Characteristics of Poverty Groups

A policy intended to alleviate poverty requires a knowledge of the characteristics of poverty groups and of the causes of their poverty.

Since poverty was defined as a household's insufficient resources or income to meet minimum needs in a certain society, the causes of low income have to be investigated. Income from economic activity flows from work or from ownership of property (physical capital or land). Hence, the distribution of wealth, human capital and ability determines to a great extent the distribution of income. A third kind of income is the income from transfer payments, such as pensions and social welfare payments which are determined by the social and institutional system. There are, of course, additional factors which influence income distribution; these include the degree of economic activity and the employment level in the various economic branches (there may be a considerable difference between the modern sector and the traditional sector, between town and country); the tax structure; the distribution of social services; and the element of luck.

It is important to make a distinction between income differences due to economic activity and income differences due to the social and institutional system, since policy measures designed to raise low incomes will have to be different for the two spheres. Budget constraints may require a choice between investments in employment opportunities, in education, and in social welfare services.

By delineating a poverty line or poverty band, statistical analysis can reveal the incidence of poverty in various population groups — for instance, in the urban and rural population, or in the various regions of a country, or among the families of the employed, the self-employed and those not belonging to the labor force, or among large or small families, among the aged, among children, among the various ethnic groups.

Statistical analysis makes it possible to compare the poverty groups with the other sections of the population, which also indicates the causes of poverty. Regression analysis, too, can provide us with some knowledge of the causes of low income.

The identification of poverty groups and their comparison with the rest of the population serve two purposes. It makes it possible to define the target groups of the policy measures, and it enables us to identify the conditions of poverty which should be altered.

Two sets of policy measures should be distinguished in this connection — those designed to redistribute income by taxes and social payments, and those designed to raise the income of the poorer sections of the population from economic activity within a general rise in the level of living. The first set of measures will be necessary for target groups whose incomes from economic activity cannot be raised because of old age or disabilities. For all other target groups, measures are necessary to raise their incomes from economic activity, though complementary social payments may also be necessary in the short run.

The causes of low income from economic activity eventually stem from insufficient physical and human capital. Since a redistribution of existing physical and human capital is difficult or impossible, the most effective policy would be to direct a greater amount of new physical and human capital to low-income groups through government loans, health and educational services, and vocational training.[30]

It will be important to add an analysis of the nutritional level and of housing conditions of the poor, since these factors have an important influence on labor productivity and on the upbringing of children. Defective nutrition and crowded housing conditions adversely affect health and educational achievement.

To interrupt the vicious circle of poverty, the health and living conditions of the poor have to be improved, and their children will have to be helped to use the educational facilities offered to them. It will, therefore, be useful to examine the effectiveness of health and educational services and the causes of any maldistribution.

NOTES

1. See W.G. Runciman, *Relative Deprivation and Social Justice*, London 1966, pp. 36-52, who distinguishes between class, status and power, going back to Max Weber. We deal here with "man-made" inequality, disregarding the differences in the native properties of people. But these, of course, influence socio-economic disparities in various ways.
2. Adelman, I. & Morris, C.T., *Economic Growth and Social Equity in Developing Countries*, Stanford: Stanford University Press, 1973.
3. McGranahan, D.V. et al., *Contents and Measurement of Socio-economic Development*, Praeger, New York, 1972.
4. Bell, C.L.G. & Duloy, J.H., "Formulating a Strategy". in *Redistribution with Growth,* H. Chenery et al., Oxford Univ. Press, 1974.
5. Milton Friedman, *A Theory of the Consumption Function*, Princeton, 1957. "Definitions and Criteria", *Report of the Committee on Income Distribution and Social Inequality*, Tel-Aviv, 1971.
6. U.N. Social Development Division, *Social Policy and the Distribution of Income*, New York: U.N., 1969.
7. Orshansky, Mollie, "Who is Who Among the Poor", *Social Security Bulletin*, Washington, July 1965.
8. First proposed by Milton Friedman "A Method of Comparing Incomes of Families Differing in Composition". *Studies in Income and Wealth*, Vol. 15, 1952.
9. See also A.G. Gaathon, *Changes in the Consumption of Urban Employee Families between 1959/60 and 1968/69*, Bank of Israel, 1975, who comments on the unproportionally high expenditure for the first child, when the mother is working (p.12).
10. Seneca and Taussig, "Family Equivalence Scales and Personal Income Tax Exemptions for Children", *Review of Economics and Statistics*, August 1971, and Jack Habib and Y. Tawil, "Equivalence Scales for Family Size". *National Insurance Institute*, Jerusalem, 1974. The two functions used in the latter study were a log-linear function ($F=AYb_1Nb_2$) for the fixed scale and a quadratic function ($F=A+b_1Y+b_2Y^2+b_3N$) for the variable scale, where F is expenditure on food, Y is household income and N is the number of persons in the household.
11. Jack Habib, "Horizontal Equity with respect to Family Size". Falk Institute, Jerusalem, 1973.
12. The method is recommended by the Expert Group on "Social Policy and the Distribution of Income in the Nation", New York: U.N., 1969.
13. The area of inequality is the area between the Lorenz curve which denotes actual relative income distribution (the share of each decile of population in total income) and between the diagonal which denotes total equality (when each decile's share in total income is 10%). Total inequality (the total area of the triangle, when total income is concentrated in one hand) is denoted by one, and total equality (no area of inequality) by zero.
14. Atkinson, A.B., "On the Measurement of Inequality", *Journal of Economic Theory*, Vol. 2, 1970.
15. Dudley Jackson, *Poverty*, McMillan Press Ltd., N.Y. 1972.
16. J.N. Morgan et al., *Income and Welfare in the U.S.,* N.Y., 1962.
17. For this approach, see Mollie Orshansky, "Who is Who Among the Poor? A Demographic View of Poverty," *Social Security Bulletin*, April 1966. "Counting the Poor: Another Look at the Poverty Profile," *Social Security Bulletin*, Jan. 1965.
18. M. Rein, "Problems in the Definition and Measurement of Poverty," *Poverty in America*, Ferman, Kornblush, Haber (eds.), University of Michigan Press, 1968.
19. V.R. Fuchs, "Redefining Poverty". in P. Townsend (ed.), *The Concept of Poverty*, London, 1970.
20. R. Rotter & N. Shamai, "Patterns of Poverty in Israel", *Social Security*, Jerusalem, February 1971.
21. Indira Rajaraman, "Constructing the Poverty Line: Rural Punjab 1960-61", Woodrow Wilson School, Princeton, March 1974. Paper 43.

22. Lim Lin Lean, "The Pattern of Income Distribution in West Malaysia 1957-70", ILO, Working Paper WEP 2-23.
23. f.i. The Fifth Five-Year Plan of the Indian Government bases the amounts needed for the abolition of poverty on an absolute poverty line. Hence, after "the abolition of poverty" — i.e., after the calculated requirements have been met — the income share of the 30% of the population with lowest per capita consumption declines from 22% in 1973/74 to 14.4% in 1985/86, as per capita consumption on the average rises. W.v. Urff, "Das Problem der Armut in der Indischen Entwicklungsplanung", *Internationales Asienforum* 5, 1974, p.475.
24. Rawls, John, *A Theory of Justice*, Clarendon Press, Oxford, 1972.
25. Thurow, Lester C., *Poverty and Discrimination*, Washington 1969. He cites this as one of his four bases of definition of poverty. The other three are: (1) a fraction of the income distribution; (2) the relative shape of the income distribution; (3) minimum income level necessary for healthy survival.
26. See Karl Marx, *Critique of the Gotha Programme*, 1875. Marx thought this possible only "in a higher phase of communist society". According to Milton Friedman this is a "Ruskian premise". M. Friedman, "The Distribution of Income" in: *Inequality and Poverty*, E.C. Budd (ed.), New York, 1967. Ruskin proclaimed his economic principles between 1855 and 1870.
27. Ian Bowen, *Acceptable Inequalities*, London, 1970.
28. W.G. Runciman, *Relative Deprivation and Social Justice*, London, 1966.
29. A.O. Hirschman, "The Changing Tolerance for Income Inequality in the Course of Economic Development". *The Quarterly Journal of Economics*, Nov. 1973.
30. See: H. Singer et al., *Employment, Incomes and Equality in Kenya*, ILO, Geneva, 1972; and H. Chenery et al., *Redistribution with Growth*, Oxford, 1974.

PART I

DEVELOPMENT AND TRENDS

CHAPTER 1

THE MANDATORY PERIOD (1919-1948)

Introduction

The Mandatory period was characterized by the development of two distinct sectors: the Arab sector, which was traditional in its main aspects; and the Jewish sector, with modern traits.

In spite of the emphasis of the Jewish national institutions on settling the land, the majority of the Jewish population lived in the towns. There was some increase in the share of the rural population during the Mandatory period — from 18% in 1922 to 25% in 1945 — but some of the larger Jewish villages gradually lost their rural character.

The aspiration to create a modern society along European lines resulted in the establishment of industries, banks and commercial undertakings in the expanding towns. The importance of a well-educated and trained labor force was already recognized, in view of the country's paucity of natural resources.

Modernization of the Jewish sector was not confined to the towns. In order to assure an income sufficient to provide a standard of living acceptable to people from countries with relatively high levels, efficient agricultural production methods were introduced. To compete with the surplus from Arab farms and with cheap imports from neighboring countries, Jewish agriculture was based on modern methods and scientific research.

The Jewish sector developed mainly by means of two exogenous factors: capital imports and immigration. The immigrants were, to a considerable extent, well-educated and trained. Their mentality, living habits, professional knowledge and various skills, together with the inflow of capital, permitted a relatively high standard of living and encouraged the expansion of production.

Socio-economic differences existed between the towns and the rural areas, between the veterans and the newcomers, between the property-less workers, the salary earners, the professionals and the owners of houses, factories and shops. These differences did not vary much in magnitude from those in any small democratic country in a similar stage of development. However, the special conditions under which the Jewish sector developed left their stamp on this area; for example, the competition of cheap Arab labor depressed the wages of the unskilled Jewish laborer, and the historical and cultural backgrounds of the immigrants from so many different countries influenced socio-economic differentiation.

The Arab sector had the traits of a traditional society, since most of the population were farmers involved in subsistence agriculture. The three major sections of Arab society were the village, the town and the Beduin. About 60% of the population lived in the villages; about one-third lived in the towns, including small towns which still retained some rural character; and the Beduin accounted for the remaining 7%.

The feudal regime had been slowly abolished, but some remnants still existed in the Arab rural areas. There was a sharp contrast between the large landowners and the poor fellahin who owned little or no land. The fellahin had to rent land and to hire themselves out in order to make a living. In most cases they were indebted to the big landowners or the money-lenders, since they could not make ends meet from harvest to harvest. The standard of living in the village was low; although there were considerable differences between the more well-to-do and the poorer farmers (especially the landless peasants), the main difference was between the town and the village. The big landowners and the moneylenders lived in the towns, though they remained connected with the villages. Urban occupations yielded much higher incomes than did agriculture; rural income per capita was only 20-25% of that in urban areas.

Though changes in the social and economic structure of the Arab sector were very slow, there was considerable economic growth — and a remarkable rise in the standard of living, which exceeded the rises in neighboring countries. This quicker pace of modernization was brought about by the modern administration of the Mandatory government (which greatly expanded the communications system) and the quickly growing Jewish sector.

The construction of an extensive net of roads was important for the development of all areas of the country. The total kilometers of all-weather roads increased more than tenfold. The expansion of transport, postal, telephone and telegraph services, and the building of a deep-water port at Haifa, greatly facilitated the expansion of trade and the marketing of agricultural produce. The construction of new schools and training of new teachers gradually increased the number of trained and skilled people; the improvement of health services helped to reduce mortality rates.

The quickly growing Jewish urban centers increased the markets for the surplus from Arab farms. Employment opportunities for Arabs developed in the expanding Arab and Jewish citrus groves, and in public works and the civil service.

Economic Growth and the Rise in the Standard of Living

There was a significant rise in the standard of living of all strata of the population. Although national income data are available only from 1936 onwards, other data reflect the rise in living standards before that date.

Total per-capita consumption of commodities rose 96% between 1922 and 1937/38, according to an estimate by the Jewish Agency.[1] The real net national product per capita in the Jewish sector rose by about 120% during the same period, according to Szereszewski.[2] On the assumption that per-capita consumption of commodities in the Jewish sector rose to the same extent as net national product, it can be estimated that Arab per-capita consumption of commodities rose by about 85%.[3]

The rise in the consumption of commodities is a very important indicator of the general rise in the standard of living — especially in the early stages of development, when the share of commodities in private consumption is relatively large, as was the case in the Arab sector. During and after World War II, the standard of living rose further. Real income per capita in the Arab sector is estimated to have risen 48% from 1936 to 1947; that in the Jewish sector 26%.[4] The standard of living of both sectors increased almost three times between 1922 and 1947.

Income per capita in the Jewish sector was two and a half to three times as high as in the Arab sector. But it has to be taken into account that in the Arab sector, prices were lower and the share of children was much larger. If these differences are compensated for, the Jewish standard of living was about twice as high as in the Arab sector — similar to the differences in income per earner, which in 1936 was some 90% higher in the Jewish sector than in the Arab sector.[5]

The faster rise of real income per capita in the Arab sector than in the Jewish sector during the war years has to be attributed to the considerable rise in the relative prices of agricultural products under wartime conditions. Since the rural population constituted about two-thirds of the Arab population, this had a greater effect on incomes in the Arab sector than on those in the Jewish sector. Furthermore, the employment opportunities created by the Allied forces in the country appear to have raised wages in the Arab sector more than in the Jewish sector, in which they were already considerably higher than in the Arab sector.

Other indicators of the rise in the standard of living are the lengthening of life expectation and the decline in mortality rates owing to improved nutrition, better living conditions and improved health services.

Mortality rates declined more than 30% in the Arab population (from 1926/28 to 1938/40) and 36% in the Jewish population. There was a further considerable decline during the war years.

Infant mortality rates declined about one-fourth in the Moslem population, 36% in the Christian population, and 46% in the Jewish population (from

1926/28 to 1938/40). The decline in mortality rates caused a considerable increase in life expectancy at birth. Life expectancy of Moslems rose from 37 years in 1926/27 to 46 years in 1939/41 and to 50 years in 1942/44, and that of Jews from 54 years to 65 years. (Appendix, Table 1A.1)

While the Arabs' decline in mortality rates and increase in life expectancy at birth were evidently the result of the improvement in the standard of living and health services, such changes in the Jewish population originated partly in the great influx of immigrants. Furthermore, the decline in Jewish mortality rates was accompanied by an even greater decline in birth rates, and the rate of natural increase declined from 2.2% in 1923/25 to 1.6% in 1941/43. In the Moslem population there was no decline in birth rates, and the rate of natural increase rose during this period from 2.3% to 2.9%.[6]

Indicators of the standard of living in neighboring countries show a much smaller rise than those for the Arab population of Palestine. Life expectancy at birth increased 15% in Egypt (during the period between World Wars I and II) as against a 27% rise in the Moslem population of Palestine; infant mortality rates declined 5% in Egypt and 18% in Trans-Jordan, but 27% in the Arab population of Palestine. Hence, at the beginning of World War II these indicators showed that the Arab population of Palestine had a higher standard of living than did neighboring countries (Appendix, Table 1A.2). The higher standard of living and better employment opportunities caused Arab migration from neighboring countries to Palestine during the Mandatory period.

Socio-Economic Disparities

One of the outstanding features of the Mandatory period was that modes of life which had changed little in thousands of years — the desert nomads and the subsistence farmers in many parts of the country — coexisted with the modern traits of some of the towns, in which factories were established, elegant shops were opened, houses and hotels with modern comfort were built.

There was a sharp difference in this respect between the Jewish and Arab sectors. The Jewish sector developed along modern lines, and its population (to an increasing extent a population of immigrants) showed the differentiation of a modern society. The percentage of farmers was relatively small (18-20%), although the national institutions directed capital and manpower to settlement of the land. The percentage of skilled workers and well-educated people was relatively large and was rising.

In the Arab sector, the percentage of farmers was relatively high (some 70%);[7] they were to a great extent subsistence farmers; and the share of marketed produce increased only gradually under the influence of the rising standard of living in the expanding towns. The urban population was mainly a population of merchants and artisans, living in traditional extended families.

A small part was well educated and trained, providing doctors and lawyers and some of the employees of the Mandatory government.

Between the two sectors, there was a considerable difference in the pattern of living, in mentality, and in the standard of living (which was about twice as high in the Jewish sector).

However, disparities within the two sectors were even larger. While differences between the urban and rural populations in the Jewish sector were quite small, there were considerable differences between the liberal professions and skilled workers, on one hand, and unskilled workers on the other; and between owners of citrus groves, factories and rented houses, on one hand, and workers, on the other. On the whole, economic inequality appears to have been relatively low in the Jewish sector.

In the Arab sector, there was a very large difference in living standards between the urban and rural populations. While differences within the village were quite moderate, there were large differences within the urban population owing to the greater differentiation in occupations, educational level and property ownership. Because of this and the great difference between town and village, inequality in the Arab sector was quite high.

Thus, the two sectors clearly showed the characteristics of a traditional society (high inequality in the Arab sector) and a more modern society (considerably lower inequality in the Jewish sector).

Though the two sectors developed quite separately, there were connections and influences which affected income distribution. Thus, the low wages of Arab labor depressed the wages of the Jewish laborer — especially in citriculture, the building trade and the government's public works. The incomes of Jewish farmers were depressed by the competition of cheap agricultural products from Arab farms. On the other hand, wages in the Arab sector were raised by the employment opportunities in the Jewish sector and by the government, and the income of the Arab farmer gradually gained from the rise in demand for his produce as a result of rising living standards in both sectors.

We can examine socio-economic differentiation mainly as reflected by income distribution.

First Family Surveys

The first investigation into family budgets was made in 1922 by the British administration in order to construct a cost of living index. Though the investigation was meant to give a picture of standard of living differences of families whose heads were in government employment, it so happened that the family budgets of only 114 Palestinian officials of junior service who were Arabs could be used for this inquiry.

In January 1922, their average monthly salary was 13.80 Egyptian pounds, and the average expenditure for a family of five was LE 20. Some exaggeration of expenditure statements has to be assumed. Furthermore, it seems that other sources of income (savings, property, other family members working) were available to these families to bridge the gap between income and expenditure.

Though this was a relatively homogeneous group, we find a considerable range (5.6 times) among monthly incomes in the 21 budgets for which details were published.[8]

The first inquiry into the living standard of Jewish families was made in 1926. The budgets of 102 employee families who lived in Haifa, Jerusalem and Tel Aviv were investigated. The purpose of this investigation was also to determine the cost of living. The social backgrounds did not vary much (Jewish urban workers' families), and the range of earnings was limited — since the intention was to examine the cost of living of typical workers' families.[9] Earnings ranged from LE 4 to LE 24 per family. No single persons were included in the investigation. In contrast to the results of later studies, there was greater variation in family expenditure than in family income. The Gini coefficient[10] for family expenditure was 0.191; it was only 0.170 for family income. This very low inequality flows from the homogeneous character of the population investigated. (Appendix, Table 1A.3)

The data also permit calculation of the Gini coefficient by standard equivalent adult according to the scale fixed by the Committee on Income Distribution and Social Inequality,[11] which was 0.179 for expenditure by SEA.

Larger families had higher family expenditures (Appendix, Table 1A.3). Hence, the inequality of expenditure per SEA was smaller than that of expenditure per family. Another interesting feature is that the average income of the Haifa families was higher than those of Tel Aviv and Jerusalem families. The value of these data is limited, since the sample was small and was representative of only part of the population.

Jewish Wage and Salary Earners

Data on wages and salaries were assembled in the 1930 census of Jewish wage and salary earners,[12] which comprised 23,830 employed (i.e., some 40% of all Jewish earners).[13]

The wage and salary earners investigated in the census were distributed as follows by economic branch:

Wage Earners	%	*Salary Earners*	%
Agriculture	21.5	Free professions and clerks	22.0
Industry and handicrafts	28.3	Service and household	14.3
Building and transport	13.9		
		TOTAL	100.0

Some 24% of those employed were women. 54% of all employees received daily wages; 37% earned monthly salaries; and 9% received monthly salaries with food.

Table 1.1

Wages and Salaries, 1930
(in % of men's monthly salaries)

Receivers of:	*Women*	*Men*
Daily wages*	44	65
Monthly wages with food	36	49
Monthly salaries	69	100

*Assuming 25 workdays per month

This reflects a significant difference between blue-collar workers (most of whom received daily wages) and white-collar workers whose monthly salaries were considerably higher. Furthermore, whereas blue-collar workers on daily wages could easily be laid off in times of low economic activity, the monthly salaries of white-collar workers provided greater job security.

The difference between men and women was considerable, and was largest between daily wage earners. There were also considerable differences within the various categories. Daily wages ranged from less than 100 mils to over 500 mils; monthly salaries ranged from less than 2 Palestinian pounds to over LP20.

The data of all Jewish salary and wage earners (monthly and daily) have been combined in order to calculate an inequality index (Appendix, Table 1A.4), which was 0.340. This index is relatively high compared with that calculated from the family budget data for 1926. But it has to be taken into account that the earnings of wage and salary earners are those of men, women and youth — whereas family budgets indicate the incomes of family heads, sometimes supplemented by the earnings of a second person. Furthermore, the family budget investigation included only selected families of married employees or workers in regular employment, preferably with children.

The population of the 1930 study consisted, to a great extent, of single persons. 54% of the 23,830 wage and salary earners were single persons, and only 30% had families with children — whereas in the 1926 study there were no single persons, and 89% of the families had children.

The data of the 1930 workers' census gives the most comprehensive picture of earnings distribution in the Jewish population at that time. It includes agricultural wage earners as well as wage and salary earners in the other economic branches. However, the self-employed are not included, and the distribution reflects only the income distribution of earners — not that of families.

The census also reported that housing conditions were quite poor. Only two-thirds of the employees lived in houses; one-third lived in wooden barracks and tents. Average housing density was 2.7 persons per room, and 22% of the employees lived in a density of four or more persons per room.

Jewish Families in the Thirties

In 1930 there was an inquiry into the nutrition standard of families, and data on the incomes of Jewish urban families included in the study were published.[14] Though the study embraced only 74 urban Jewish families, the data are interesting because they show income differences between the various sections of the Jewish population (Appendix, Table 1A.5).

The data show considerable differences in incomes and housing densities between the communities. Average income per Ashkenazi family was 43% higher than the average income of an Oriental family, and income per person was 53% higher. Housing density as measured by persons per room was 40% higher in the Oriental families. The Oriental communities were overrepresented in the sample; they constituted 66% of the sample, whereas they accounted for less than 30% of the Jewish population at the time. The inequality index for all 74 families was 0.195. The data are from low and lower middle income classes. Only families with children were included (family size ranged from 3 to 8); most family heads were wage and salary earners with relatively low incomes. Average family income was LP6.1 compared with an average monthly salary of LP10.4 for men in 1930, according to the workers' census. Since the income of the family head was 80-84% of employees' family income, according to investigations, the difference was even larger. Furthermore, the families in the study were relatively large: average family size was 5.3, compared with 4.2 in the families with children in the workers' census of 1930. Since no families with incomes below LP3 were included, the very poor also seem to have been excluded. 20% of the family heads were unskilled workers, 40% were skilled workers, 32% were clerks, peddlers or small storekeepers, and 8% lived on contributions from Jewish communities abroad.

The investigation into Jewish family budgets by the Jewish Agency in August 1939[15] was more representative. However, since it was intended for a cost of living index, only "employees' families with regular incomes and an orderly household" were chosen for the inquiry.

The sample was relatively small — 200 families in towns, and 37 in two large villages. Average family size was 4 in the towns and 3 in the villages, which was representative. The percentage of families from Oriental communities was on the low side — only 18%, compared with about 23% in the Jewish population. Furthermore, the survey included a relatively high percentage of established settlers; two-thirds of the families had lived in the country more than 6 years.

Evidently, the 1939 family survey gives only a partial picture of the situation. It did not include the very poor and the unemployed (in 1939 there was widespread unemployment), it did not include self-employed, and it did not include employees with higher incomes.

Table 1.2
Income Distribution of Jewish Families, 1930 and 1939
(% of Families)

	Nutrition Survey, 1930	*Cost of Living Survey, 1939*		
Monthly Income LP*		Towns	Moshavoth	Total
up to LP4	4.1	8.4	8.1	8.3
4 — 5.9	47.3	11.5	54.0	18.1
6 — 7.9	25.7	22.5	24.4	22.8
8 — 9.9	10.8	19.9	13.5	18.9
10 — 11.9	8.1	17.5	—	14.8
12 — 13.9	4.0	10.3	—	8.7
14+	. . .	9.9	—	8.4
Average Annual Family Income, LP	73.3	126	86	120
Inequality Index	0.195	0.224	0.180	0.228
Average Annual Income per Person, LP	13.8	31.4	29.2	31.2

*In the 1939 survey, monthly earnings of family head.

The income distribution of the families in the 1930 nutrition survey was similar to that of the employees' families in rural areas in 1939; about three-quarters of their families were concentrated in the two income groups LP4-8. But the income distribution of employees' families in the towns in 1939 showed a much larger spread, with 38% of the family heads earning more than LP10 per month. The data also reflect the differences between town and village, since employees' incomes in villages were only about two-thirds of those in towns; but incomes per person differed less.

Table 1.2 shows that the 1930 survey represents only the poorer strata of the Jewish urban population, while the 1939 survey represents established Jewish wage and salary earners with families and regular jobs. Since real net domestic product per capita in 1939 was 13% higher than in 1930,[16] the average comparable family income of the 1930 survey was about one third lower than that of the urban employees of the 1939 survey, and income per person was only half — thus clearly representing urban lower income groups.

Incomes in Rural Areas

The 1939 survey included agricultural employees' families in large Jewish villages; the 1930 survey of Jewish wage and salary earners included agricultural workers. However, neither survey included self-employed farmers. Some 18% of Jewish earners were in agriculture; in 1939, more than half of these worked in citrus groves and were wage earners, and most of the remainder were self-employed farmers.

Incomes in agriculture were considerably smaller than in the other branches of the economy. Szereszewski estimated that net domestic product per employed in agriculture was about 60% of the average in the Jewish sector in 1922 and 1927, 50% in 1931, and only 43% in 1939.

Income differences in the Jewish farming sector were influenced by the specific kinds of settlements developed by the settlers according to their ideological trends and sociological backgrounds. A short outline of the characteristic features of the main types of settlements is therefore useful.

The kibbutz (collective settlement) is based on common ownership of resources and the pooling of labor, income and expenditure. No wages are paid; every member is obliged to work, and is supplied with the goods and services he needs. The land is allocated to the kibbutz by the national institutions according to the number of settlers. The farm is managed as a large-scale enterprise.

The moshav (cooperative smallholders' village) is also settled on national land. It is composed of individual farms of equal size with the same initial equipment. The size of the farms varies according to region and farm type. The village cooperative handles most economic and social affairs — marketing of produce, purchases of material and equipment, credits, insurance, water supply and mutual aid. In principle, no hired labor is supposed to be employed in either type of settlement.

The moshava (village) is built on private land, and is based on private initiative and private capital. The size of the farms varies. Many single-branch farms have developed in the villages — orange groves, vineyards, poultry farms. Hired labor is employed. Marketing is usually cooperative. Gradually, a number of these villages developed into provincial towns.

In 1936, the kibbutzim constituted 13% of the Jewish rural population; the moshavim, 18%; and the moshavot, 69%. But a considerable part of the population living in moshavot pursued non-agricultural occupations.

Income distribution among collective settlements shows some inequality, although equality reigned within each settlement. Income differences among the farmers in smallholder settlements and especially in villages were greater, and the large citrus grove owners constituted a special class with relatively high incomes.

Consumption expenditure per member (including upkeep of children) in 20 collective settlements in 1929 showed a difference of 51% between the lowest and the highest; in 1937, this difference was 109% for 81 collective settlements. The inclusion of many newly founded settlements in 1937 caused a decline in average consumption expenditure and a rise in the inequality index, from 0.089 in 1935 to 0.122 in 1937 (Appendix, Table 1A.6).

The inequality index shows very low inequality, but it has to be assumed that income differences were considerably greater than consumption differences. In 1957, for example, the inequality index for the distribution of consumption per member among 215 collective settlements was 0.079, but it was 0.180 for income distribution.[17]

Elazari-Volcani gives net incomes and living expenditures by gross income groups for three smallholders' settlements with 177 farms in 1935 and 1936.[18] The inequality index calculated was 0.169 for net income and 0.167 for living expenditure in 1935, and 0.205 and 0.250 respectively in 1936 (Appendix, Table 1A.7).

Inequality increased in 1936 over 1935, while income and the standard of living declined. 1935 belonged to the boom period (1932-35), but in 1936 economic conditions deteriorated owing to political unrest. It is interesting that the decline in average income was accompanied by greater inequality. These were old, established settlements, and the incomes of new settlements were considerably lower. There were also considerable differences in average incomes and living expenditures between the older settlements.

Income Distribution in 1936

L. Gruenbaum (now A.L. Gaathon) estimated income differences between the urban and rural populations in the Jewish and Arab sectors (Appendix, Table 1A.8).

In the Jewish sector, income per capita in the urban population was 40% higher than in the rural population; in the non-Jewish sector, income differences were much larger; and urban income per capita was almost five times as high as in the rural areas.

The data on the various sectors of the Jewish population permit calculation of the income distribution in 1936, though with certain reservations (Appendix, Table 1A.9).

The inequality index calculated for the rural population was 0.317, and for the urban population 0.301. The higher inequality index in the rural population is unusual. The income difference between citrus grove owners and the agricultural workers may be responsible; alternatively, the inequality index in the urban population may be an underestimate. Furthermore, it has to be taken into account that our estimates are based on income per family, and that the average family in the rural areas was smaller than in the urban areas (2.9 as against 3.9). In general, income distribution is more unequal for smaller income units at the same income data. Therefore, it may be assumed that distribution of income by standard equivalent adult would show higher inequality in the urban sector.

The combination of the income distributions in the rural and urban sectors gives an inequality index of 0.320 for the total Jewish population, as shown in Table 1.3.

Table 1.3
Estimated Jewish Family Income Distribution, 1936 (in %)

Decile	Urban Families	Rural Families	Total
1	2.8	3.9	3.0
2	4.8	4.8	4.4
3	6.0	5.9	5.4
4	7.3	6.8	6.7
5	8.3	7.4	8.0
6	9.4	8.3	9.3
7	10.5	9.8	10.6
8	12.0	11.2	12.3
9	15.6	13.7	16.1
10	23.3	28.2	24.2
TOTAL	100.0	100.0	100.0
Average Monthly Income L.P.	15.00	9.78	13.70
Gini Coefficient	0.301	0.317	0.320

Source: Appendix, Table 1A.9

The average income per family according to the above calculation is quite similar to the estimate based on the Gruenbaum estimate of national income (LP14.17 — see Appendix, Table 1A.8), which served as the framework for the above calculation.

Socio-Economic Conditions of the Arab Population

The most outstanding feature of the standard of living of the Arab population was the large difference between the urban and rural populations. The family survey of junior Palestinian officials in 1922 showed an average annual expenditure of LP240, while the 1929 investigation into the standard of living of 104 villages estimated the average annual expenditure of an agricultural family at LP. 27.5.[19] The declaration of the villagers of their cost of living amounted to LP. 38 per family, still only one-sixth of the expenditure of a minor official's family in town. According to Gaathon's estimate, the income of the urban Arab family was almost five times that of an agricultural family. Because of the difference between urban and rural prices, the real income difference was smaller.

The distribution of agricultural holdings is one indicator of the income distribution within the Arab rural population. In 1936, the distribution of land holdings of 322 villages was investigated;[20] it showed very high inequality (0.704). The inequality index was 0.662 for the distribution of owned land and 0.327 for income distribution (Appendix, Table 1A.10) in 1929 in 104 villages, on the basis of data of the Johnson-Crosbie report.

According to our estimate, income distribution was much more equal than the distribution of owned land, which is a generally observed phenomenon. There was a considerable income difference between the various villages, especially between the poorer mountain villages and the more comfortably situated villages of the plains and the valleys, as reflected in the data of the Johnson-Crosbie report.

For income distribution in the urban Arab sector, we have only the investigation of Arab civil servants in 1922 up to the outbreak of World War II, and the estimate of income per earner in the various economic branches in 1936 by Gruenbaum-Gaathon. According to this estimate, income per family in construction was twice as high as in agriculture; in industry, commerce and transport about four times as high; and in the other branches, even higher.

A combination of the estimated income distribution in the Arab rural sector and estimated income per family by economic branch in the urban areas yields an inequality index of 0.469 for the total Arab population. Obviously, income distribution by economic branch underestimates income distribution in the urban sector, since there was a considerable spread of incomes in each economic branch. During the war years, additional surveys allowed for an estimate of income distribution in the Arab urban sector; we translated this income distribution into 1936 values, and calculated income distribution in the Arab sector.[21] The inequality index thus calculated was 0.520 (Table 1.4).

Income Distribution of Total Population

If we divide the population into three parts — the 40% with the lowest incomes, the 20% with the highest incomes, and the 40% with medium incomes — we obtain the following income distribution in 1936, on the basis of the above estimates (Table 1.4).

Table 1.4
Estimated Income Distribution, 1936 (%)

Population Group	*Jewish Population* Urban	Rural	Total	*Arab Population* Urban	Rural	Total	Total Population
Lowest 40%	20.9	21.4	19.5	16.4	20.3	11.3	11.0
Middle 40%	40.2	36.7	40.2	35.9	38.0	30.1	36.2
Highest 20%	38.9	41.9	40.3	47.7	41.7	58.6	52.8
TOTAL	100.0	100.0	100.0	100.0	100.0	100.0	100.0
Inequality index*	0.301	0.317	0.320	0.401	0.327	0.520	0.479

*Calculated on the basis of deciles.

Inequality in the Arab population was higher in the urban sector than in the rural sector, a well-known phenomenon in less-developed countries. In the urban sector there is a greater differentiation of occupations and skills, which leads to a greater spread of incomes. The interesting feature is the much greater inequality in the total Arab population than in either the urban or rural sectors, because of the large difference between urban and rural incomes. There was also a considerable difference between the Christian and the Moslem communities in this respect. The percentage of Christians was much higher in the urban population than in the rural population; the average income and educational level were higher in the Christian population than in the Moslem population.

The Jewish sector showed relatively low inequality. Its most outstanding feature was the large share of the middle classes in total income. The middle 40% had 40% of total income in the Jewish population, while the middle 40% of the Arab population had only 30% of the income.

Table 1.4 reveals the large difference in income distribution between the Jewish and Arab sectors. The relatively modern Jewish society had low inequality; the traditional Arab society was characterized by high inequality, and especially by a large income difference between the rural and urban population (which is consistent with the findings of S. Kuznets and others).[22]

M.S. Ahluwalia[23] classified as highly unequal those countries in which the 40% of the population with the lowest income have less than 12% of the income; those where the share is between 12% and 17%, moderately unequal; and where the share is 17% and above, low inequality is indicated. According to this classification, the Arab sector was highly unequal — while the Jewish sector had low inequality. The total population also had high inequality, though the inequality index for the whole population was smaller than that of the Arab sector.

The considerable income difference between the Jewish and Arab sectors was accompanied by a much greater difference in the percentage of literate persons among the population. According to the 1931 census, 93% of all male Jews were literate, compared with only 30% of male Arabs. During the Mandatory period, literacy increased in the Arab sector. The number of Arab pupils tripled between 1925/26 and 1944/45, whereas the Arab population increased only 67%. Within the Arab sector, the Christian population had relatively high literacy; 72% of all males were literate, against only 25% of Moslem males. The difference between Moslem and Christian women was even larger. Differences in the standard of living were also reflected in the differences of life expectancy at birth; Table 1A.11 (Appendix) shows the difference between Christians and Moslems within the Arab sector, and the difference between the Arab and Jewish sectors.

THE SECOND WORLD WAR PERIOD

During the war, the shortage of shipping space and imported goods, combined with the scarcity of locally produced goods, caused a rise in prices.

Consumer prices rose two and a half times by the end of 1944, and an additional 10% by the end of 1946. This led to various surveys — partly in order to revise the cost of living index, and partly to examine the nutritional situation of the population. Some of these surveys give data on income distribution.

A standard of living survey in 1946 gives a comprehensive picture of the economic situation of Jewish urban families before the establishment of the State, including families of the self-employed. But the principle that family heads should be regularly employed, married and with children seems to have influenced the choice of the families for this survey, too. No single persons were included, and only two of the 913 families covered were two-person families; the other families had children, and average family size was 5 (compared with 4 in the 1939 investigation, and an average of about 3.9 in the Jewish urban population) (Appendix, Table 1A.12).

The inequality index of the 1946 survey was similar to that of family surveys in 1939 and 1930. The data for 1946 also show income differences between the Ashkenazi (European) and Oriental communities. These differences were smaller than in the 1930 survey, but the difference in family size was greater. Hence, the income per family of Oriental communities was 22% smaller than that of Ashkenazi families, but income per person was 46% smaller. Housing density was much greater (66%) in the Oriental communities. In this survey, income differentials were larger than expenditure differentials; the inequality index for incomes was 0.229, and for expenditures 0.198.

Family income was highest in Haifa and lowest in Jerusalem. Oriental families were somewhat overrepresented. They constituted 35% of the sample, while Oriental communities accounted for only 22% of the Jewish population in 1946 (Appendix, Table 1A.13).

Income differentials between the various occupations show that the highest family incomes were in the liberal professions and in transport (bus drivers). 42% of all family heads were laborers; their family income was somewhat below the average. The self-employed (tradesmen and artisans and some of the liberal professions) were in the higher income brackets. The percentage of family heads from Oriental communities was relatively high in the occupations with lower incomes, and relatively low in the occupations with higher incomes, especially in those which required a relatively high level of formal schooling (Appendix, Table 5A.1).

How far is this survey representative of the total Jewish population? Pensioners, jobless persons and single persons were not included. Only 3% of the families had monthly incomes of less than LP15. Thus, the lowest income groups were not included — and neither were the high-income groups. Net domestic product per capita in 1946 in the Jewish sector was LP189.5 (according to Szereszewski), while the survey showed an income per head of only LP100. It seems that in the main, middle and lower middle income groups were represented.

Income distribution by expenditure per capita reflects larger income differentials when the inequality index is calculated on the basis of persons as income receivers (with a Gini coefficient of 0.287); but on the basis of the family as the income receiver, the Gini coefficient is even lower — 0.166.

A 1943 investigation covered 14,000 Jewish blue-collar workers in industrial enterprises (i.e., clerks, administrative and technical personnel were excluded). Considerable differences were found between male workers, female workers and youth. Weekly earnings of female workers in May 1943 amounted to only 59% of those of male workers, and the earnings of youths came to only 45%.

The inequality index was 0.193 for male workers and 0.236 for all workers — i.e., much smaller than that of all Jewish employees in 1930. But the 1943 data reflect only the income distribution among industrial blue-collar workers, whereas the census in 1930 embraced all Jewish wage and salary earners.

Wage differentials in 1943 were quite considerable between male and female workers; between skilled, semi-skilled and unskilled workers; and between industrial branches. There was a 50% range between the lowest and highest earnings for male workers between industrial branches, and a 70% range among female workers. In each industrial branch, a wide distribution of earnings was found. Weekly earnings of unskilled workers were about 60-70% of those of skilled workers in the same industry. Apart from differences in skill, there were differences in hours worked per week. A very large part of the workers in the lowest income brackets worked only part-time (less than 24 hours per week), and a considerable part of those in the highest income brackets worked overtime (57 hours and more per week). Part of the income differentials between male and female workers is explained by the fact that more female workers worked part-time.

A wartime survey[24] inquired into the nutritional situation. Although the investigation covered 1370 family budgets and four collective settlements with 1390 inhabitants, the economic situation was reflected only in the more detailed investigation into 179 budgets of families in the three large cities (77 Arab families and 102 Jewish families). Since income data received were unreliable, only expenditure was given. The distribution of family expenditure according to this investigation showed an inequality index of 0.229 for Arab families, of 0.221 for Jewish families, and of 0.222 for all families. (Appendix, Table 1A.14).

Inequality was similar among Jewish and Arab families. They belonged to similar income categories, and only expenditure per person was 25% higher in the Jewish families because of smaller family size.

This was the expenditure distribution of urban families in low and lower middle income classes, especially in the Jewish population. Though the intention was to include broad sections of the population, the data on occupation show that most family heads were laborers, small artisans, peddlers, etc. Most were wage and salary earners, but there were also a few small self-employed. The family size among the Jewish families was far above the average, and the percentage of Oriental Jews was also much higher than that in the Jewish urban population (42%, compared to 22%).

Housing density was very high: Jewish families lived 4.3 persons per room, and Arab families lived 4.1 persons per room in 1943.

The same families were investigated again in 1943, and we compared the expenditures of the Jewish families in 1942 and 1943. Average monthly expenditure per family rose 63%, and the inequality index declined from 0.221 in 1942 to 0.184 in 1943 (i.e., 17%). It may be that this relatively large rise in the family expenditure of the poorer sections of the population (annual expenditure per person was LP49.5 in early 1943 in these families, compared with a net national product per capita of LP119 at the beginning of 1943) indicates an improvement in their relative situation.[25]

The comparison of Ashkenazi families with families from Oriental communities shows that the average family expenditure of the latter was 12% smaller in 1942 and only 7% smaller in 1943; however, expenditure per person was 37% smaller in 1942 and 36% smaller in 1943, because of the great difference in family size.

The Vickers Report also included the results of a special study of unskilled labor in 1942 which embraced 126 Arab and 114 Jewish families.

Their average expenditure was lower than that in the general survey and family size was larger. Inequality was low in these homogeneous low-income groups; the inequality index was 0.163 in the Arab group, and 0.136 in the

Jewish group. This study in the main seems to reflect the economic situation of the poorer population in the towns — large families of unskilled workers with low earnings.

In 1944, the Government statistician estimated the national income by communities, and brought indicators of income distribution within the Arab and Jewish sectors (such as the distribution of land holdings and the distribution of assessable income of taxpayers).[26]

The tax data for 1944 covered only a small part of the population. Individual taxpayers constituted about 15% of Jewish earners, and only about 4% of Arab earners. The Gini coefficient was 0.327 for Arab taxpayers, 0.313 for Jewish taxpayers, and 0.315 for all taxpayers.

Can the data of the various family and other surveys in connection with the national income estimate be used to estimate income distribution in the Jewish and Arab sectors? We made an attempt to calculate such an income distribution for the urban population.

Very useful for our calculation was the estimate of income distribution by broad social categories in 1944, by the Statistical Department of the Jewish Agency.[27]

According to the estimate for the Jewish population, per capita income of the new settlers from Europe was 50% higher than that of the old Yishuv and Oriental communities. In the Arab population per capita income in the urban population was twice that of the rural population. This difference was much smaller than before the war, since farmers' incomes rose in relation to other incomes during the war.

The Jewish Sector

Income distribution in the Jewish urban population can be estimated on the basis of the 1946 family survey (the most comprehensive at that time) and tax data. A combination of these data yields an inequality index of 0.254. But obviously, the lower income groups are missing in this combination, and inequality in the Jewish urban population is estimated to have been considerably higher.

The addition of low income groups (on the basis of the Vickers investigation of Jewish families in 1943, of unskilled workers' families in 1942, and the survey of industrial workers in 1943) gives a more comprehensive picture of the income distribution of Jewish urban families. (For weights, see Appendix, Table 1A.15). The distribution thus calculated showed an inequality index of 0.324. It must be assumed that inequality was higher; the highest incomes are missing in this combination because of underreporting to the income tax authorities (income tax was newly introduced), and the poorest sections of the population were underrepresented in the various surveys.[28]

Income of the Jewish rural population was considerably smaller than that of the urban population in pre-war days (some 60% of the average); this changed during the war, and income per employed in agriculture was estimated to have been above the average.

Income differences within the agricultural sector appear to have been larger than during the pre-war period because of different adjustment capabilities to changing market conditions — although the drastic decline in the income of the citrus sector reduced one of the factors of inequality.

While there may have been some rise in inequality in the rural and the urban sectors during the war, the fact that income differences between the urban and rural sectors disappeared may have reduced total inequality in the Jewish sector.

The Arab Sector

Two sources of data are available for income distribution of the Arab urban population — the income tax data of 1944, and the Vickers survey. Arab taxpayers constituted only about 11% of Arab urban earners, and the 75 Arab families for whom details of expenditure are available in 1942 and 1943 are not representative of the total urban population. But it can be assumed that they were representative of the lower and middle classes in the towns. The study of unskilled labor in 1942 furnishes additional data for the lower income groups, while the tax data reflect the incomes of middle, upper middle and higher income groups.

Hence, we made an attempt to calculate income distribution in the Arab urban population on the basis of these data. (For weights, see Appendix, Table 1A.15). The inequality index was 0.401.

Some indicator of income distribution in the Arab rural sector is the distribution of Arab land holdings. A survey of social and economic conditions in five villages in 1944 showed the distribution of holdings possessed by resident villagers.[29] The inequality index was 0.576 — considerably smaller than that for the distribution of holdings in 1936 in 322 villages, which was 0.704. The survey states that the five villages in 1944 constituted a "carefully selected sample of typically sized villages in respect of area and population" and that "abnormally rich and poor villages were avoided". All five villages were in the Ramleh area. This explains the lower inequality index of the distribution of land holdings in 1944.

When considering the inequality index of land holdings, it has to be taken into account that a considerable part of the rural population was working for wages in the military camps, in the towns, or on large farms, and that others with small land holdings rented land from the large landowners. Hence, it must be assumed that income distribution in rural areas was considerably less unequal than the distribution of land holdings, as in the pre-war period.

The better employment opportunities in 1944 (compared with pre-war conditions) must have raised relative incomes of the poor farmers who had to work for wages in order to supplement low farm incomes. On the other hand, the relatively high agricultural prices raised the incomes of farmers with relatively large holdings. It is difficult to assess any changes in rural income distribution, but it may be assumed that the changed conditions increased differentiation. However, there is no doubt that the difference between rural and urban incomes declined during the war because of the rise in the relative prices of agricultural produce. According to Loftus, income per employed in agriculture was about two-thirds of that in the other branches of the Arab sector in 1944, compared with 26% in 1936 according to the Gruenbaum estimate. This reduction in the difference between rural and urban incomes as a result of wartime conditions must have reduced inequality in the total Arab sector.

Our data make it possible to only estimate income distribution in the urban population in 1944 (Table 1.5). As indicated above, this estimate seems to be on the low side. The relatively large weight of the Jewish population in the total urban population (about half), combined with a relatively small difference between average incomes in both urban sectors, contributed to the relatively low inequality index of 0.37 in the total urban population. The share of the lowest 40% of the total urban population in total income was 17.4%, which also indicates relatively low inequality.

Table 1.5
Estimate of Income Distribution in Urban Population, 1944.

Decile	*Jewish Population*	*Arab Population*	*Total Population*
1	3.3	2.8	3.0
2	4.6	3.9	3.8
3	5.5	4.6	4.8
4	6.5	5.1	5.8
5	7.8	6.1	7.0
6	9.1	7.5	8.6
7	10.1	9.7	10.7
8	11.8	12.6	12.1
9	14.8	15.5	15.1
10	26.5	32.2	29.1
TOTAL	100.0	100.0	100.0
Gini coefficient	0.324	0.401	0.367

NOTES

1. *Palestine Facts and Figures.* Economic Department of the Jewish Agency, 1947.
2. Szereszewski, R., *Essays on the Structure of the Jewish Economy in Palestine and Israel*, Falk Institute, Jerusalem, 1968.
3. During this period, the Jewish share of the total population rose from 11% to about 30%.
4. Gaathon, A.L., "Erez Israel" *Hebrew Encyclopaedia*, vol. 6, 1957.
5. Gruenbaum, L. (now A.L. Gaathon), *National Income and Outlay in Palestine*, 1936. Jerusalem, 1941.
6. The Christian rate of natural increase declined somewhat owing to declining birth rates, from 2.0% to 1.8%, but Christians constituted only about 10% of the Arab population.
7. Including nomads.
8. Investigation of Cost of Living, *Palestine Commercial Bulletin*, No. 23-24, 1922.
9. Report on Investigation of Cost of Living of Jewish Workers' Families, Aug. 1926. *Palestine Zionist Executive Statistical Bulletin*, No. 14, Jerusalem.
10. The Gini coefficient is an inequality index between zero and one; zero indicates complete equality and one indicates complete inequality. (see Introduction).
11. Report of the Committee on Income Distribution and Social Inequality, Tel Aviv, 1971.
12. Census by the Jewish Agency and the Histadrut. Published in *Commerce and Trade*, Sept. 1931 (Hebrew monthly).
13. 66,700 in November 1931, according to the Government census.
14. J. Kligler, A. Geiger, Sh. Bromberg, D. Gurevitz, "An inquiry into the diets of the population of Palestine," *Commerce and Industry*, No. 20-21, October 1931. In this survey, oriental families were subdivided into Sephardim, Yemenites and other Oriental Communities. There were considerable differences in mentality and living habits among these communities, but the main distinction was between the European and the Oriental communities.
15. D. Gurevich, A. Gertz, "Survey of the Standard of Living", Department of Statistics, Jewish Agency for Palestine, Jerusalem, 1940.
16. Szereszewski R., *op. cit.*
17. J. Simchoni and Sh. Shmueli, "Inequality in Communal Settlements 1957-68". Economic Training Unit, 1974.
18. I. Elazari-Volcani, "Planned Mixed Farming", Rehovot, 1938.
19. *Report of a Committee on the Economic Conditions of Agriculturists in Palestine*, W.J. Johnson and Crosbie, Jerusalem, 1930.
20. Published in P.J. Loftus, *National Income of Palestine, 1944.* Jerusalem, 1946.
21. For a detailed description of the 1944 distribution in the Arab urban sector, see Table 1.5 and the text before.
22. S. Kuznets, "Economic Growth and Income Inequality", *American Economic Review*, March 1955. F. Paukert "Income Distribution at Different Levels of Development", *International Labour Review*, Aug.-Sept. 1973.
23. M.S. Ahluwalia, "Income Inequality: Some Dimensions of the Problem", H. Chenery et al. (eds.), *Redistribution with Growth*, Oxford, 1974.
24. W.J. Vickers, *A Nutritional Economic Survey of Wartime Palestine*, Department of Health, Jerusalem, 1944.
25. It is not clear whether this rise was greater than the average rise in incomes. Net national product per capita rose 67% from 1941 to 1942, but only 24% from 1942 to 1943. (Prices rose 46% from 1941 to 1942, and 22% from 1942 to 1943). As the survey was conducted in the early months of each year, and the rise in expenditure may have lagged after the rise in incomes, the 63% rise in expenditure may well be near the average.
26. J.P. Loftus, *National Income of Palestine, 1944*, Government Publication, Jerusalem, 1946.

27. Alon Statisti, January-June 1946, p. 101, Jewish Agency, Department of Statistics, Jerusalem.
28. The Vickers survey seems to have included very poor sections of the population, but reflects only expenditures; incomes were lower in the lowest brackets, according to incomplete data.
29. Government Department of Statistics, Special Bulletin No. 21, 1945. Table on distribution of land holdings published in *National Income, 1944,* Appendix II.

CHAPTER 2

SOCIO-ECONOMIC DEVELOPMENTS IN ISRAEL

The development of the economy after the establishment of the State of Israel was, basically, a continuation of the development of the Jewish sector. In many ways, however, the establishment of the Jewish state also marked a new beginning.

After decades of Mandatory restrictions the gates were opened to mass immigration. During the three and a half years from May 1948 to the end of 1951, 687,000 new immigrants entered the country — more than the 650,000 Jews who had lived in Israel at its inception. Independence also permitted new policies in the economic field, in order to build an expanding economy that could absorb the large numbers of immigrants and bring full employment and a rising standard of living for everyone.

The war of independence, the great waves of immigration, and the severance of the economy from the Sterling bloc created grave economic problems. These included an increasing deficit in foreign current accounts without a parallel rise in capital imports; strong inflationary pressures; high unemployment; and a shortage of housing. Government expenditures soared, the tax system was inefficient, the Sterling balances (which were the main foreign currency reserves) were blocked, and capital imports were low. This led to deficit spending and inflation.

Rationing and price controls were introduced (the so-called austerity regime) to overcome shortages and to provide adequate nutrition to all strata of the population at reasonable prices.

The influx of mass immigration changed the social structure of the country in two ways. The demographic and ethnic structures of the newcomers were different from those of previous waves of immigration, so the population became more heterogeneous in its ethnic composition, its educational level and its cultural background. Furthermore, the available capital was insufficient to finance a crash program of housing construction and the expansion of production,[1] and there was still a world shortage of essential materials and equipment owing to the reconstruction work in Europe. Thus, many of the newcomers could be provided only with temporary housing — in tents, wooden huts and tin shacks in immigrants' camps and *maabarot.*[2] Those living in immigrants' camps (about 90,000 at the end of 1949) were supplied with food, medical and other services by the Jewish Agency; those living in transit camps and *maabarot*, most of which were established later near urban centers and agricultural settlements, gradually found jobs and were integrated into the economy. At the end of 1951, 230,000 people lived in *maabarot* and transit camps, and about 26,000 in immigrants' camps; this means that about 18% of the total Jewish population and 37% of the immigrants who had arrived since the establishment of the State lived in temporary housing in crowded conditions.

Many of those who lived in crowded, low-standard temporary housing found only low-paying jobs because of their lack of training and experience. Together with those who lived in old, dilapidated houses and had only temporary or low-paying jobs, they joined the low-income groups at the lower end of the social ladder. Only slowly and gradually could they be moved into better houses, and be integrated into permanent, better-paying jobs. Some of the many children who spent their formative years under these conditions became the problematic youth of later years.

The large influx of immigrants from the traditional societies of North Africa and Asia (10% of all immigrants came from those countries before 1948, and about 50% after 1948) proved to be one of the important elements in the developing social fabric. They greatly strengthened the traditional elements in Israeli society, such as the extended family, and had relatively high birth and death rates, a low educational level and lack of vocational training. It proved difficult to integrate these immigrants, who were unaccustomed to modern production methods and to the mentality of modern life. But most of them were quick to learn and to adjust, and after a difficult initial period they were gradually integrated into economic and social life. The ensuing greater differentiation in education and occupations must have contributed to an increase in economic and social disparities.[3]

As the economy expanded, the standard of living of all strata of the population rose. The traditional sectors underwent a process of modernization — slower among Arabs, more rapidly among Jews.

Mortality and birth rates declined, life expectancy lengthened, educational level rose and skills increased. But despite some decline in economic inequality after its rise during the recession in 1966 and 1967 (as reflected in income distribution and housing conditions), feelings of deprivation became stronger and more outspoken, and the public became increasingly concerned with socio-economic disparities.

This led to the government's greater emphasis on social targets in the seventies. More measures were taken to improve the situation of disadvantaged population groups. Priority was given to education, since it was regarded as an investment in human resources — not only for promoting economic growth, but also as an instrument for reducing socio-economic disparities and the tensions arising from them.

Economic growth and full employment remained the government's foremost development goals; the importance of integrating economic and social policies were recognized, and some progress was made. After the October War of 1973, the cost of security became greater than ever; as a result the balance of payments and inflationary pressures became the central economic problems. Though it thus became necessary to impede the rise in private consumption, the improvement in the standard of living of the poorer strata — especially large families — became even more important. The marked decline in income inequality in the mid-seventies can be partly attributed to the government's social policy.

The Changing Demographic Base

The total population of Israel rose four and a half times, from about 800,000 in May 1948 to about 3.65 million at the end of 1977. Of these, 84% were Jews; the non-Jews were mainly Arabs. The Jewish population increased 4.7 times. 56% of Jewish increase stemmed from immigration,[4] while the three-fold growth of the non-Jewish population was due mostly to its high natural increase.

The Jewish birth rate rose considerably during the early fifties because of the mass immigration of people with traditionally high birth rates; it declined during the late fifties and the beginning of the sixties, and rose slowly in the early seventies. In the non-Jewish population, the most striking feature is the declining death rate; the birth rate, after an initial rise, shows only a small declining trend. Hence, the non-Jewish rate of natural increase rose from 3% at the end of the Mandatory period to over 4%, declining in the seventies to 3.8%. The Jewish rate of natural increase rose from 1.9% at the end of the Mandatory period to 2.6% during mass immigration, but later declined to 1.6%; in the seventies it rose to 1.8%. Population growth was very high during mass immigration, and declined in later years as immigration declined (Appendix, Table 2A.1).

The bulk of the Jewish immigration arrived during the first three and a half years after the establishment of the State, when the Jewish population grew an average of 24% per year (88% of the additional population were immigrants), compared with an average annual growth of 3.1% during the 25-year period 1952-1976. The percentage of the non-Jewish population declined from 18% in 1948 to 11% in 1951; it rose to 15½% in 1976, owing to the higher birth rate and to the addition of the East Jerusalem population after 1967.

The composition of the Jewish population was greatly changed by immigration after the establishment of the State. Immigrants from Asian and African countries had constituted only 10% of all immigrants during 1919-48, but were 48% of all immigrants during 1948-76. This, together with the higher reproduction rates of the Oriental communities, raised their share in the Jewish population from 22% at the end of the Mandatory period to about 53% at the end of 1976.

Gross reproduction rates by mother's continent of birth reveal divergent trends (see Appendix, Table 2A.2). Those of Jewish mothers born in Asian and African countries declined significantly from a high of 3.0 in 1951-53 to 1.8 in the mid-seventies, reflecting the social and cultural influences of the society surrounding them. Reproduction rates of Israeli-born mothers and mothers from Europe and America, which were much smaller throughout, rose somewhat in the late sixties and seventies after a previous decline.

There was a great difference in this respect between Moslems and Christians. The reproduction rate of the Moslems which was spectacularly high (about 4) was twice as high as that of the Christians. There has been a declining trend for both since the mid-sixties; it was more pronounced among the Christians.

The different birth rates of the Arabs and Jews were reflected in the different age compositions of the two groups. The share of children among non-Jews (49%) was much higher than among Jews (30%) at the end of 1976, and the share of those of working age (15-64) was smaller (47%) among non-Jews than among Jews (61%) (Appendix, Table 2A.3).

Age composition changed with changing birth and death rates. After mass immigration, the share of children reached a high of 34% in the Jewish population and then declined; the rising life expectancy and the declining birth rate are reflected in the rising share of older people. In the non-Jewish population, there was no rise in the share of the old; the share of children rose as a consequence of declining infant death rates.

Birth and deathrates of the Jewish population were similar to those in Southern and Eastern Europe. The Arab birth rate was among the highest in the world, and the death rate among the lowest; hence, the Arab rate of natural increase was exceptionally high.

Birth rates and age composition influence family size and the percentage of earners. Average family size in 1976 was 3.5 in the Jewish population and 6.4 in the non-Jewish population (including singles). A similar difference, though much smaller, is found between the average size of Jewish families in which the family head was born in Asia or Africa (4.5) and those in which the family head was born in Europe or America (2.7).

35% of the Jewish population were in the civilian labor force, compared to only 20% in the non-Jewish population owing to the difference in the shares of the population of working age. The difference in labor force participation becomes much smaller when the civilian labor force is compared with the population aged 14 and over; then its share was about 49% in the Jewish population, and 39% in the non-Jewish population. The higher labor force participation of Jewish women mainly was responsible for the difference.

35% of Jewish women aged 14 and over were in the labor force in 1976 compared with only 8% of non-Jewish women.[5]

More than three-quarters of the Jewish population was urban at the establishment of the State; in spite of the settlement of a considerable number of new immigrants in rural areas, the urban share rose from about 77% in 1951 to 91% in 1976.

Urbanization of the Arab population was even more pronounced; its urban share rose from 26% in 1951 to 61% in 1976. The addition of the East Jerusalem population in 1967 raised the urban share considerably. An additional factor was the transformation of large villages into urban localities as they lost their rural character.

The educational level rose considerably, after an initial decline because of mass immigration. The percentage of literate Jews declined from over 90% at the end of the Mandatory period to 83% in the beginning of the fifties, then rose to 91% in 1972 and 93% in 1976. Among non-Jews the increase in literacy was spectacular — from an estimated 26% at the end of the Mandatory period to 48% in 1961, 64% in 1972, and about 77% in 1976(Table 2.1 and Appendix, Table 2A.4).

Table 2.1
Literate, Aged 14 and Over (in %)*

	Jews			*Non-Jews*			*Total Population*
	M.	F.	Total	M.	F.	Total	
1931 census (Pal.) aged 7 and over	93.4	78.7	86.1	29.7	7.4	18.7	31.4
1961 census	92.8	82.9	87.9	68.0	28.5	48.3	84.1
1972 census	94.1	87.1	90.8	77.8	48.8	63.5	87.6

*Literate:one who knows to write a simple letter.
Source: Statistical Abstract of Palestine, 1937/38.
Statistical Abstract of Israel, 1976.

The greatest increase in literacy was among non-Jewish women; still, half of them were illiterate in 1972 and 36% in 1976. Most of the illiterate are older people; because of compulsory education, most of the younger people are literate.

The number of Jewish pupils rose seven times from 1948/49 to 1976/77, while the Jewish population grew four times; the number of Arab pupils increased 14 times, while the Arab population increased three and a half times. The much quicker expansion of the Arab educational system was caused partly by the Arabs' greater increase in the share of children; the main cause however, was the introduction of compulsory education, and the lengthening of the period of schooling. In the Jewish educational system, the extension of the period of schooling was the most important factor. The number of pupils rose from 16% to 30% of the total Jewish population, and from 7% to 29% of the Arab population.

The educational level rose significantly between 1961 and 1976 (Appendix, Table 2A.4). The percentage of Jews with less than 5 years of schooling declined from 20% to 11½%, and that of Arabs from 63% to 35%. The share of Jews with more than 12 years of schooling rose from 10% to 17½%; that of Arabs, from 1½% to 4%. The Jewish population shows a considerable difference according to continent of birth; the comparison with the second generation is important. Those with more than primary education accounted for 39% of those born in Asia or Africa, but 73% of those born in Israel whose father was born in Asia or Africa. However, while the percentage of those receiving secondary education more than doubled, the percentage of those receiving university education did not rise — and the difference between those born in Asia or Africa and those born in Europe or America widened in this respect in the second generation.

Educational level by age also reflects the expansion of the educational network. In 1976 in the lower age groups (14-17 and 18-34), almost none of the Jewish population had less than 5 years of schooling, compared with 32% of those aged 65 and over and 21% of those aged 55-64.

SOCIAL IMPLICATIONS OF ECONOMIC GROWTH AND TRENDS

Economic Growth

Estimates of the national product at constant prices are available from 1950. The impact of mass immigration in 1948 and 1949, together with the influence of the War of Liberation, may have caused some decline in per-capita national product in 1949 compared with that at the end of the Mandatory period. From 1950 onwards, economic growth was quite high — apart from two interruptions during the recessions in 1953 and 1966/67, and the latest stagnation in 1975/76.

During a period of 26 years, from 1950 to 1976, the national product rose nine times — an average of 9% per year. The per-capita national product grew at an annual rate of 4½%.

The quick rise was the result of the great increase in the capital stock and in the labor force. Since the capital stock rose more quickly (11% annually) than the number of employed (4% annually), capital per employed rose at an annual rate of 7%. The product per employed rose at an annual rate of 4½%, and total productivity (taking into account the increase in capital input) rose

3% per year (Table 2.2). The quality of the labor force also improved, though only after an initial decline. Educational capital per employed declined in the first half of the fifties due to mass immigration by some 7%, but rose in the sixties (from 1961 to 1972 by 22%), and with increasing pace in the seventies (see Chapter 4).

Table 2.2
Economic Growth, 1950-1976
(IL at 1970 prices)

	1950	*1962*	*1976*	*Index 1976 (1950 =100)*	*Average annual rate of growth (In %) 1950-76*	*Jewish sector 1922-47*
Average population, thousands	1,267	2,288	3,533	279	4.0	8.3
Gross national product, IL mill.	2,925	9,853	26,582	909	8.8	13.5
GNP per capita, IL	2,309	4,306	7,528	326	4.6	4.8
Private consumption per capita, IL	1,655	2,874	4,506	272	3.9	
Number of employed persons, thousands	419	788	1,187***	283	4.1	
GNP per employed, IL	6,979	12,758	22,394	321	4.6	
Capital stock*, IL mill.	5,620	25,930	87,108	1,550	11.1	11.4
Capital stock per employed, IL	13,413	32,906	73,385	547	6.8	
Capital/output ratio	1.9	2.6	3.3			
Productivity (product per unit of input)**					3.1	

*At the beginning of year
**Ratio of labor to capital, 4:1
***Including employed from the administered territories (66,000)

Source: Statistical Abstract of Israel, 1977; Annual reports, Bank of Israel; A.L. Gaathon, Economic Productivity in Israel, New York, 1971. R. Szereszewski, *op. cit.*

As capital intensity grew, the capital/output ratio rose from 1.9 in 1950 to 2.6 in 1962 and 3.3 in 1976. Though there was almost full employment in 1976 (the unemployment rate was only 3½%), the productive capacity of the capital stock was not fully utilized — which it had been in 1950. The increase in the effective capital/output ratio, therefore, was smaller than the above figures indicate.

Very few countries showed such high economic growth rates during a prolonged period; these include Japan and some oil producers. Some countries had a similar or higher per-capita growth rate, due to smaller population growth (Appendix, Table 10A.1 and Table 10.4).

Structural Changes

Structural changes in the economy usually influence social stratification. In particular, the decline in the share of agriculture and the increasing industrialization and urbanization affect the standard of living and inequality.

The share of agriculture in the domestic product rose in the first years, then declined steadily while there was a modest rise in the share of industry. The share of trade, finance and personal services declined; the share of public services rose, indicating the increase in social services (Appendix, Table 2A.5).

These changes at current prices were partly the result of changes in the relative prices in the different branches. The prices of the net product (value added) of industry and agriculture declined in relation to those of the other sectors, because of the comparatively greater increase in productivity in industry and agriculture. A comparison at constant prices reveals that the share of agriculture remained almost constant, while that of industry rose considerably — showing the steady advance of industrialization. During 1958-65 the share of agriculture at current prices declined from 13% to 8½%, but remained 13% when calculated at constant prices; the share of industry rose from 21.6% to 24.2% at current prices, but to 32.6% at constant prices.[6]

The share of agriculture in the labor force showed a more pronounced decline than in the national product at current prices, while the rise in the share of industry was a little more restrained. The share of agriculture declined from 21% of Jewish earners in 1936 to 18% of all employed in Israel in 1955, and to 6½% in 1976; the share of industry rose from 20% in 1936 to 25% in 1976. The decline in the share of agriculturists was accompanied by further urbanization of the population. Industrialization and the advance of technology in all economic sectors created greater differentiation in the labor force, which influenced income differences.

The structure of the capital stock also underwent changes connected with the rise in the technological level of the various branches, with the degree of utilization, and with changes in capital intensity. The share of agriculture declined spectacularly from 33% of all fixed assets (excluding housing) in 1950 — when there was underutilization of capital in agriculture due to lack of skills — to 11% in 1976, while the share of industry was maintained at about a fifth of the total. The biggest rise occurred in the shares of public services, transport and communications, reflecting the expansion of the infrastructure on a modernized basis. (Appendix, Table 2A.6).

The Jewish sector during the Mandatory period had a very low share of capital assets for the infrastructure, and a very high share for housing. Since part of the capital stock in transport, communications and public services belonged to the government sector, it was not included in the Jewish sector. But even so, the shares of those branches were relatively low.

Housing constituted 55% of the capital stock of the Jewish sector in 1937, but 37-40% after 1950. The continuing high share of housing was caused by the need to provide housing for the new immigrants and by the government's social policy aimed at improving the housing conditions of the lower income groups. As a result, housing density declined significantly in recent years.

The share of housing in the capital stock has an important influence on the productivity of the total capital stock, owing to the high capital/output ratio of the housing sector. A comparison shows that capital/output ratios excluding the housing sector were about 35% lower than those including the housing sector (Appendix, Table 2A.7).

There was a steady increase in the capital/output ratio up to the sixties, owing to the rise in capital intensity in all branches. Changes in the composition of the capital stock (decline of agriculture and rise of services) and some increase in its utilization led to a decline in the capital/output ratio (i.e., a rise in the productivity of capital) at the beginning of the seventies. In 1975 and 1976, the capital/output ratio rose again — as a result of rising capital intensity and of lower utilization due to slower business activity.

Capital per employed in all branches except housing rose five and a half times during the 26 years from 1950-1976, reflecting the great increase in capital intensity during this period.

The increase in capital intensity was accompanied by a rise in total productivity, a rise in the educational level of the labor force, and an increase in the share of skilled and professional workers.

The pace of the rise in the standard of living was determined mainly by the growth of GNP per capita. Additional factors were changes in the import surplus, which increased total resources for domestic use; the share of private consumption in these resources; and the proportion of public consumption devoted to social services.

Table 2.2 shows that the annual rise in private consumption per capita (3.9%) was less than that of GNP per capita (4.6%). The main reason for this was that total resources for domestic use increased considerably less than the GNP because of the decline in the share of the import surplus. This development was especially pronounced between 1950 and 1966; the share of the import surplus in resources for domestic use declined from 32% to 13%, reflecting less dependence on capital imports.

The trend changed in 1967 due to rising defence requirements (and, to some extent, to expanding social services) after the Six-Day War. The share of the import surplus rose, and total resources for domestic use rose more than did the national product. But private consumption rose even less, because of the great rise in the share of public consumption from 20% in 1966 to 29% in 1970, and to over 30% after the 1973 War. (Appendix, Table 2A.8)

A comparison with the Jewish sector in 1936 is interesting. Private consumption in 1936 accounted for a very high share of total resources (62%) compared to 48% in 1976, while public consumption was only one tenth of that (6%). Although public consumption is admittedly underestimated,[7] it still must have constituted a very small part of total resources. This changed dramatically after 1948, when the Israeli government took on the responsibilities of internal and external security, immigrant absorption and social services. The high investment share in 1936 reflects the Jewish economic development and integration of immigrants in the thirties. (Immigrants constituted about 8% of the Jewish population in 1936, and approximately 15% in the three preceding years which were years with high immigration.)

The Balance of Payments Problem

Capital imports were an important factor in the rapid growth of the economy. During the Mandatory period, capital imports constituted a major part of investments in the Jewish sector; there was a relatively large import surplus which created a structural dependence on capital imports. This dependence grew after 1948. Economic policy was designed to reduce this dependence on capital imports, and eventually to abolish it. During the fifties, the share of the import surplus in total resources for local use (at constant prices), which indicates the degree of dependence on capital imports, declined from 30% to 16%, since exports increased more quickly than imports. After some rise in the early sixties, the import surplus declined further in the mid-sixties. Due to the greater defence requirements after the Six-Day War, the share of the import surplus rose, and after the Yom Kippur War in 1973, there was another sharp rise to 23-24% (Appendix, Table 2A.9). In 1976 and 1977 the import surplus again declined to less than one fifth of resources for local use as exports increased at a quicker pace than imports.

The large rise in imports and exports in the seventies was due partly to price increases. Import prices (in dollars) rose 90% from 1971 to 1976, and export prices rose 65%. Imports for security purposes accounted for about half of the import surplus in most of the years since 1967, while they constituted only 25% of the import surplus in 1966.

The import surplus was met by capital imports and foreign currency reserves. A very important factor in Israel's capital imports were unilateral transfers, which do not create indebtedness. In the beginning of the fifties, Israel suffered from an acute shortage of foreign currency. Only 43% of the import surplus could be paid by unilateral transfers in 1950-52, while the import surplus supplied 29% of the resources for domestic use; exports covered only 16% of imports. Economic growth and economic policy measures, including a gradual change in the exchange rate, succeeded in improving the balance of payments. As new sources of capital imports became available (German reparations, U.S. food surpluses, U.S. aid, Israel bonds), the share of unilateral transfers rose to 70-80% of capital imports in most years, and long-term loans covered most of the remainder.

Currency reserves, which were at a low of $27 million in 1953, were raised to $626 million in 1965. After 1967 and 1973, unilateral transfers, though rising considerably, could meet only about half of the rapidly increasing import surplus — so foreign currency indebtedness grew considerably, from $1.2 billion in 1965 to $9 billion at the end of 1976. Foreign currency reserves in 1976 were only $1.2 billion, and debt servicing amounted to 1.3 billion dollars (of which $645 million went for interest payments) i.e., 27% of total exports.

The problem of the balance of payments deficit — always one of the central economic problems — became more urgent, and in October 1977 a new economic policy was initiated to improve the situation. Its most important feature was a considerable devaluation of the Israeli pound, combined with some liberalization of foreign currency restrictions.

Improvement in the balance of payments had been a high priority goal since the fifties. World-wide inflationary pressures and the Government's deficit spending affected the balance of payments negatively in the seventies. Social benefits and social services increased more than taxes did thereby adding to inflation. Hence, there was a conflict between the goals of improving the balance of payments and reducing social disparities. Inflation also had a negative influence on social stratification, and special measures were taken to prevent deterioration in the situation of the lower income groups.

A further connection between the balance of payments and the social situation are two components of capital imports which had a direct impact on the standard of living and socio-economic disparities: direct investments by private investors, and personal restitution payments from Germany.

Tax concessions and other privileges offered to foreign investors attracted people with means who were used to high incomes and to a high standard of living. Though the main goal of this policy was to increase capital imports and to provide employment in development towns for new immigrants, the concessional loans and capital grants by the government must have increased the concentration of wealth in the highest income groups.

The personal restitution payments from Germany considerably raised the standard of living of the families receiving them. On the average, they doubled their incomes which, in most cases, were above average before the receipt of these payments.

Rise in the Standard of Living

The rapid pace of economic growth resulted in a remarkable increase in the standard of living. The rise in the standard of living varied according to the pace of economic activity, but its changes were also influenced by changes in taxes and subsidies. In the recession year of 1953, there was no rise in per-capita private consumption, and it even declined somewhat in 1966 and 1967. After the recessions, it rose 12% in 1954 and 8% in 1968. Its average annual rise over the 26 years was about 4% (Table 2.2).

The great rise in the standard of living was reflected in demographic characteristics such as rising life expectancy and declining infant mortality. Jewish infant mortality rates had risen sharply from 36 out of 1000 live births at the end of the Mandatory period to 52 in 1949, owing to mass immigration; however, they quickly declined to 32 in 1955 due to the impact of local health services and then gradually to 18 in the seventies (Table 2.3).

Table 2.3

	Infant Mortality Rates (per 1000 live births)		*Life Expectancy at Birth* (in years)			
Year	*Jews*	*Non-Jews*	*Jews* M.	*Jews* F.	*Non-Jews* M.	*Non-Jews* F.
1944/45	36.0	95.3	64.1*	65.9*	50.3*	51.6*
1949	51.7	...	65.2	67.9	...	...
1955	32.4	62.5	69.4	72.1	...	...
1960	27.2	48.0	70.7	73.5	69.0	69.9
1965	22.7	43.4	70.5	73.2	70.5	72.1
1970	18.9	41.0	69.9	73.3	69.7	73.2
1975	17.9	39.5	70.9	74.5	68.2	71.5
1976	...	...	71.6	75.4	68.8**	72.0**

*1942/44 **Average 1973-76

Source: Statistical Abstract of Palestine, 1944-45.
Statistical Abstracts of Israel.

Among non-Jews, infant mortality rates declined steadily from 95 at the end of the Mandatory period and 62 in 1955 to 39 in the seventies.

Jewish life expectancy at birth was about 65 years at the end of the Mandatory period; it rose to about 72 years in the sixties, and remained at that level. Among non-Jews, there was a spectacular increase from about 51 years at the end of the Mandatory period to 70 in the seventies. The low mortality rates and relatively long life expectancy in the non-Jewish population were undoubtedly attributable to improved health services and better living conditions.

From 1950 to 1976, the standard of living as reflected in per-capita private consumption rose almost threefold. The share of food in consumption expenditure declined by one-third, and the consumption of animal protein rose by one-half. The percentage of families possessing electric refrigerators, washing machines, TV sets, private cars, etc., grew constantly (Table 2.4).

Table 2.4
Indicators of the Standard of Living

	1950	1960	1970	1976
Private consumption per capita at constant prices, Index	100	153	232	272
Percentage of food in consumption expenditure	38.5	36.7	28.6	26.5
Consumption of animal protein per capita, gr. per day	32.2	34.0	44.3	49.4
Percentage of families possessing durable goods:				
Gas range	14.6*	59.3	85.8	49.2
Gas/electric range and oven			5.0	51.8
Electric refrigerator	2.4	46.8	88.9	99.0
Electric washing machine	6.9**	15.8	42.8	74.6
Radio	54.7*	78.7	89.9	84.2
TV set			49.7	89.5
Private car		4.1***	15.4	31.2
Telephones per 100 inhabitants[1]	2.1	5.5	17.4	24.6
Number of persons per room (Jewish families only)	2.44**	2.34	1.53	1.27

*1955 **1957 ***1962
[1]In 1970, 35% of all families had a telephone; in 1976, 59%.
Source: Statistical Abstracts of Israel, Family Survey 1975/76.

In the seventies, Israel's standard of living compares well with those of some European countries, such as Greece, Ireland, Italy and Finland. The percentage of food in private consumption expenditure is an important indicator (Table 2.5).

Among the twelve countries chosen for comparison, only Greece and Ireland had a lower GDP per capita than Israel's — but five countries had a higher food share in consumption expenditure. Israel's food share ranges with Norway and Belgium, whose per-capita income was about two-thirds higher than Israel's. To some extent, the large subsidies on essential food items in Israel were responsible for its relatively low share of food in consumption

Table 2.5
Share of Food in Private Consumption in 1973 (%)

Country	*Share of food in private consumption** %	*GDP per capita* US$	*Energy Consumption per capita in 1974, kg. of coal equivalent*
Greece	34.3	1,816	1,828
Finland	28.0	3,703	4,899
Ireland	27.8	2,144	3,569
France	25.7**	4,797	4,389
Norway	23.8	4,842	4,979
Israel	23.4	2,883	2,868
Belgium	23.0	4,662	6,253
Sweden	21.7	6,185	6,110
Netherlands	21.3	4,435	6,090
Denmark	19.5**	5,481	5,547
United Kingdom	19.0	3,088	5,778
Canada	16.8	5,412	11,237
U.S.A.	15.1	6,167	11,960

* Excluding alcoholic beverages and tobacco. which distort the picture owing to different tax policies.
** Excluding non-alcoholic beverages as well.
Source: U.N. Yearbook of National Accounts Statistics, N.Y. 1974.
U.N. Statistical Yearbook, N.Y. 1975.

expenditure. Israel had the second lowest energy consumption per capita after Greece, indicating its lower stage of industrial development compared to most of the countries in Table 2.5.

The various countries' price policies, food subsidies, farm supports, import policies and eating habits may explain the deviations from the negative correlation between the share of food in consumption and per-capita income such as the relatively low share in the United Kingdom and the relatively high share in France.

Differences in the Standard of Living

Did the great rise in the standard of living benefit all strata of the population? There is evidence that the standard of living of the new arrivals during the first years of the State was lower than that of the Jewish population before 1948, and that there was some decline in the average standard of living in the first year after the establishment of the State.

In the first period after the establishment of the State, the capital at its disposal was insufficient for immigrant absorption, and the economy was suffering in the aftermath of the War of Liberation. Consequently, there were considerable differences in the level of living, especially in housing, particularly between the new immigrants and the established population. But, as always in such cases, some of the newcomers had the professional skills or private means to quickly improve their situation, whereas the economically weak strata of the established population also suffered (along with the other newcomers) from the adverse economic conditions such as unemployment, rising prices, etc.

The possession of durable consumers' goods in 1975/76 shows no significant difference for most items among the Jewish population by continent of birth or by period of immigration. In the possession of only two items — the telephone and the private car — the percentage of families from Asian and African countries was significantly smaller (Appendix, Table 2A.10). It seems that with the general rise in the standard of living, the possession of most durable consumers' goods became so widespread as to be no longer indicative of differences in the standard of living. According to these indicators, non-Jewish families show a lower standard of living, similar to that of the Jewish population at the end of the sixties. (see Appendix, Table 2A.10 and Table 2.4).

Food consumption according to income groups has been calculated for 1968/69 by deciles based on consumption expenditure per head — which gives a stratification of families similar to that of net income per head, at least for the lower income strata. A comparison of food intake per unit (taking into account differences in food requirements by age and sex) by deciles shows a steady rise in nutrient intake from decile to decile, with the lowest three deciles being below the national average. A comparison with internationally recommended food intakes shows that on the whole, food intake was quite satisfactory even in the lowest deciles; the exceptions were the intake of calcium and vitamin A which were unsatisfactory (less than 80% of recommended allocation) in the two lowest deciles, and those of iron and thiamin, which were unsatisfactory in the lowest decile. Intake of calories and animal protein were satisfactory even in the lowest decile.[8]

Differences in food expenditure per head were much more pronounced between the deciles than were differences in nutrient intake per unit. While food consumption expenditure per head in the highest decile was three-and-a-half times as high as in the lowest, differences in nutrient intake were much smaller; the ratio moved between 1.4 and 2.6.[8]

Housing density is an important indicator of living conditions. It was about 2.5 persons per room in the Jewish population at the end of the Mandatory period. After an initial rise in the early fifties it declined to 2.4 in the late fifties and to 1.3 in 1976 (Table 2.4).

The difference in housing density between the various population groups was still quite significant in 1976. The average housing density of families from Asian and African countries was 1.6 persons per room; in families from Europe and America, 1 person per room; in Israeli born Jewish families, 1.3 persons per room. In non-Jewish families, the average density was 2.8 persons per room. Differences were larger within the groups than between the groups. To some extent the differences in housing density between the groups are explained by differences in family size; the average number of rooms per family was quite similar in all groups (Appendix, Table 2A.11); in all groups, density was higher in the larger families.

Price fixing and rationing during the austerity period of 1949-1951 attempted to halt the rise in prices and even to reduce the prices of some essential goods. But this period of restrained inflation ended in 1951, as inflationary pressures grew stronger in an atmosphere of relative prosperity. The percentage of unemployed declined from 14% in 1949 (including potential workers living in the immigrant camps) to 8% in 1951.

The increasing shortage of foreign currency and rising inflationary pressures caused the Government to initiate its "New Economic Policy" at the beginning of 1952; the devaluation of the Israeli pound was combined with various anti-inflationary measures. This policy, designed to stabilize the economy and to reduce the balance of payments deficit brought about a recession and a considerable increase in unemployment (which rose to 11% of the labor force in 1953). New immigrants were particularly affected by the recession, since a considerable part of them had not yet obtained permanent jobs.

Social and economic differences must have been deepened by the substandard housing and widespread unemployment among newcomers in 1949 and again during the recession, while part of the established population was improving its living standard during the prosperity years of 1950/51.

The question is whether these differentials widened, were maintained or declined in subsequent years.[9]

Employment and Labor Force Participation

The level of employment is an important factor in income distribution. Inequality rose in years of high unemployment, and declined in years of prosperity. While unemployment affects the low income groups in particular, high prosperity may add to inequality in the high income groups. Unemployment rates were as high as 10 and 11% in depression years, and declined to 3% and less in years of prosperity.

The percentage of earners in the Jewish population declined considerably, from 42% in 1947[10] to 37% in 1955, due to changes in the age structure of the population (the share of children up to 15 years of age rose from 29% to 34%). The decline in labor force participation, together with the considerable increase in large families, contributed to greater inequality of incomes. Labor force participation rates were also influenced by the working of women, by the duration of schooling and military service, and by the demand for labor.

Labor force participation (civilian labor force as a percentage of the population aged 14 and over) declined from about 54% in 1955 to 48% in 1976. The participation of males declined from 80% to 65% because of aging of the population, longer schooling and military service (Appendix, Table 2A.12). Participation of women rose; although prolongation of schooling caused a decline in women's youngest age groups (14-17 and 18-24; see Table 2A.12), their participation in other age groups rose.

The expansion of education contributed to a steady rise in the quality of the labor force. In 1965 only 48% of those employed had post-primary education; in the course of a decade, the share rose to 65% (Appendix, Table 2A.13).

It is interesting that among employed persons the proportion of girls receiving post-primary education exceeds that of boys. And the percentage of employed with secondary and university schooling is higher among women than among men (76% and 59%, respectively in 1976). The reason is the strong correlation of labor force participation with the level of education among women; no such correlation exists among men (see labor force participation by schooling, Appendix, Table 2A.13). 66% of all women with some university schooling were in the labor force in 1976, compared with 36% of all women with some secondary schooling and 17% of all women with primary schooling or less. Median years of schooling of employed women were 11.7 in 1976, compared to 10.2 for employed men. Since income from the wife's work is an important element in many families' incomes, the higher labor force participation of women with higher educational levels increases inequality — especially among employees' families, in which labor force participation of married women is relatively high (see chapter 7).

The share of employees among the gainfully employed rose steadily from about 63% in the early fifties to 76% in 1976. This continuing trend (from some 60% in the thirties in the Jewish sector) is related to the structural changes which occurred in the economy during its process of modernization:

1. The decline in the share of agriculture contributed to the rising share of employees, since it has a relatively large share of self-employed. The share of agriculture in the labor force declined because of the spectacular increase in the efficiency of production methods in agriculture, and its share in the national product declined mainly because of the decline of the relative prices of agricultural products. To some degree the quicker rate of growth of other branches, especially of industry, was also responsible for the declining share of agriculture.
2. With growing modernization, large economic units increased at the cost of smaller units. Supermarkets replaced many small grocery stores; industrial

plants developed out of small workshops in which the owner had worked alone or with one or two assistants.

3. Large companies managed by employees took the place of small enterprises managed by their owners.

Social Stratification and Social and Cultural Change

Social ideologies among Jews prior to the establishment of the State aimed at an open, more or less egalitarian and mobile society. Connected with these ideologies were the spirit of pioneering and the ethos of work, which led to special value patterns in the occupational sphere; manual labor (especially agricultural labor in collective and cooperative settlements) was regarded as superior to most occupations.

After the mass immigration of the early fifties, changes occurred in the stratification of Jewish society. The steady rise in the standard of living and the growing occupational diversification of an industrializing society — together with greater educational differences — increased income differentials. Value patterns regarding occupations changed decisively; manual labor shifted to the lower end of the scale, the free professions came to the top, and white collar workers in general rated higher than members of agricultural settlements.[11] The coincidence of educational and occupational stratification with ethnic differences became important, as the proportion of the oriental communities greatly increased.

Although there exists a considerable amount of social mobility and there are no well defined social classes, social differences are quite marked. At one end of the scale, there is a considerable number of unskilled workers partly with large families, and people unable to participate in the labor force for various reasons; at the other, a class of industrial and commercial entrepreneurs (still small at present) has come to the fore.

Israel's Moslem population is, on the whole, less mobile than are the Jewish, Druze and Christian populations. Traditionally, class differences within the Moslem sector loom larger.

In sectors of the Jewish, Arab and Druze populations, in which patriarchal family patterns and the extended family system prevailed, there have been radical changes in the roles of youth, the aged and women. The institution of the extended family has started to disintegrate and the authority of parents, husbands and community elders is no longer uncontested. Younger leadership has come into being, in which women often have some share — although not proportional to their share of the population. In parliament and some central bodies (for example, the Histadrut), youth and women are considerably underrepresented.

The status and situation of the aged vary greatly in different population groups. The general trend is to ensure as much as possible their community participation and their right to live an independent life. On the whole, Israel's society tends to be child-centered. There has been a growing awareness of the influence of the socio-cultural and educational environment of young children on their future development, and growing concern with the position of disadvantaged children — many of whom are members of large, often multiproblem families.

Most traditional communities (especially those in urban areas) tend to adopt western living habits, such as buying ready-made goods, and acquiring radio and television sets, cars or motorcycles, etc; some orthodox Jewish groups, however, do not avail themselves of radio and television programs, and make every effort to preserve their own life style.

Television programs are broadcast in Hebrew and Arabic; radio programs are broadcast in Hebrew, Arabic and a number of European languages as well, and certainly serve as an integrative factor. However, there is no intention to eliminate the differences between value systems — but, rather, to preserve them. Since many Israeli citizens have adopted only the outward trimmings of modern living, without the western values that stand behind it, they are encouraged to value their specific cultural heritage and their own life styles in order to strengthen their feelings of belonging.

During mass immigration, there was a tendency to force quick acculturation; however, this policy was modified when the authorities realized that it led to a loss of orientation and actually obstructed integration. Now, knowledge and appreciation of the cultural heritage of Israel's different cultural and ethnic groups are promoted through instruction in schools, exhibitions, concerts, dance and theater performances.

While Israeli society has not been immune to the rebellion of youths and to the emergence of subcultures, it appears to have been affected much less than have most western societies. Community cohesion and community control are fairly strong, especially in smaller towns and rural areas. Except for some groups which adhere strictly to their religious and cultural tradition, Israeli society has been rather permissive towards new life styles so long as they do not affect the fabric of the society. There have been practically no student revolts; the greater maturity of Israeli undergraduates — most of whom come to the university after having completed their national service — may partly account for this. Problems of drug addiction have arisen, but they have not assumed the alarming proportions as in some other countries. There has been an increase in juvenile and adult delinquency, and the rise in crimes in recent years has caused growing concern.

A committee was appointed to examine the situation. Its report (February 1978) regards lack of values and feelings of deprivation among the main causes of the growth of crime in recent years. It emphasizes that the school and the family are the basic factors in the education of the young and the formation of their personality, and that it is necessary to create for all children suitable homesurroundings and educational standards which succeed to inculcate values and the motivation to study and to work.

It must be assumed that this report will increase the priority rating of the improvement of social conditions.

NOTES

1. See F. Ginor, *Twenty Years of Israel's Economy*, Rivaon le Kalkalah, No. 57/58, Aug. 1968.
2. Settlements of a temporary character.
3. See: S.N. Eisenstadt, R. Bar Yosef, Ch. Adler (ed.), *Integration and Development in Israel*, Jerusalem, 1970; S.N. Eisenstadt, *The Israeli Society*, Jerusalem, 1967; Segre V.D., *Israel – A Society in Transition*, Oxford, 1971; Weintraub D., *Immigration and Social Change*, Jerusalem, 1971.
4. After deduction of emigration.
5. F. Ginor, "Structural Changes in A Developing Economy: the Case of Israel". *Weltwirtschafliches Archiv*, No. 1, 1970.
6. L. Gruenbaum, op. cit., Statistical Abstract No. 28, 1977, p.314.
7. Based on the value added of Jewish government employees. Services supplied by the government to the Jewish sector are estimated to have been larger (see R. Szereszewski, op. cit., p.6). Furthermore, services supplied by the national institutions are included in private consumption.
8. Sara Bavly, *Level of Nutrition in Israel 1968/69*, Jerusalem 1972.
9. Chapters 4 and 5 deal with this question.
10. According to Jewish Agency statistics.
11. See M. Lissak, "Patterns of Change in Ideology and Class Structure in Israel" in *Integration and Development in Israel*, S.N. Eisenstadt, R. Bar Yosef, Ch. Adler (ed.), IUP, Jerusalem, 1970, p. 156/157.

CHAPTER 3

INCOME DISTRIBUTION BY FACTOR SHARES

The functional distribution of income is the income to the factors of production — i.e., the returns to labor (wages and salaries and remuneration of self-employed labor) and to capital (profits, rent, interest and dividends). According to Marxist doctrine, the private ownership of capital goods is the main cause of social and economic gaps. We should therefore expect the main social gaps to exist between the capitalists (the owners of capital goods) and the workers.

In modern societies there is no strict division between capital owners and capital-less workers. Income and labor surveys divide the population into wage and salary earners, the self-employed, and those not working. All these categories own capital assets, especially if housing is included. Even business capital, though concentrated more among the self-employed, is also owned by the other categories. The difference between the average incomes of wage and salary earners and the self-employed is relatively small; on the other hand, there is a large difference between these two categories and those who do not work. The average income of a wage or salary earners' family in 1968/69 was more than twice as high as that of a family whose head was not in the labor force (mostly pensioners and disabled persons); that of the self-employed's family was about two and a half times as high. The difference declined somewhat in 1975/76, since the relative incomes of families whose heads were not working had risen (Table 3.1). Because of their smaller family size, however, the difference in per capita income was only 30-40%. Furthermore, inequality of incomes among the self-employed was greater than among wage and salary earners (23-25% in the sixties), but even greater among the non-working (36-47% greater than among wage and salary earners).[1] The non-working constituted 20% of all families in 1975/76, the self-employed 12%, and wage and salary earners about 68%. Consequently, the income gap between the economically active and economically non-active, and the larger inequality within the latter category, contributed more to total inequality than did income differences between wage and salary earners and the self-employed.

Table 3.1
Percentage of Urban Families in Lowest and Highest Deciles of Gross Family Income by Employment Status, 1968/69.

Employment Status of Family Head	*Lowest Decile*[2]	*Highest Decile*[2]	*Average*	*Average Family Income (Index) 1968/69*	*1975/76*
Employees	27.8	69.0	64.4	228	208
Self-employed	4.7	28.3	16.8	262	236
Not working	67.5	2.7	18.8	100	100
TOTAL	100.0	100.0	100.0	212	190

Table 3.1 shows that more than two-thirds of the family heads in the lowest decile did not work, compared with only 3% in the highest decile. Hence, 36% of families whose heads were not working were in the lowest decile, compared with only 4% of all employees' families and 3% of all families of self-employed.

Income stratification depends greatly on the distribution of educational capital, work experience and personal talents, in addition to wealth (see Chapters 6 and 7); consequently, division of income into remuneration of labor and capital is only partly indicative of general inequality. Changes in wage differentials may have a greater impact on general inequality than do changes in the shares of capital and labor in the national income.

In spite of the rise of the percentage of employees from 63% in the total labor force in 1952 to 76% in 1976, the share of the employees' compensation in the net domestic product rose only little, moving between 58 and 62% during that period. This points to a rise in the share of the remuneration of capital in the NDP, connected with the great rise in capital per employed over the period (see Chapter 2), and some rise in the rate of return to capital.

In a comparison with 17 other countries, Israel was the only country in which the percentage share of employee compensation remained almost the same over a period of 13 years (1960-73). The average rise was eight percentage points; in some countries it was 10-13 percentage points. The two countries with a very small rise (two percentage points) were Canada and Jamaica; and both already had a relatively high share in 1960 compared with their GDP per capita and their percentage share of employees (Table 3.2). In 1960, Israel's share of employee compensation was also relatively high; it was similar to that of a number of countries whose GDP per capita was considerably higher. But in 1973, its share was relatively low.

In 1976, wage and salary earners constituted 76% of all gainfully employed in Israel, but employee compensation was only 62% of the net domestic product. However, this does not mean that the remaining 38% was received by employers and self-employed, who represented only 24% of the gainfully employed (which would have meant that average income per employee was about half the average income of employers and self-employed). As Table 3.1 shows, the actual income difference between these two categories was much smaller — family income of the self-employed was only 13-15% higher than that of employees.

Table 3.2
Percentage Shares of Employee Compensation

Country	*Employee Compensation % of NNP*		*GDP per capita in US$*	*Employees as % of employed*
	1960	1973	1973	1974
Sweden	67	79	6.185	91
U.S.A.	71	75	6,167	90
West Germany	60	69	5,671	86
Denmark	59	71*	5,481	83
Canada	69	71	5,412	89
Norway	65	76	4,842	83
France	58	67	4,797	80
Belgium	57	66	4,662	81
Netherlands	57	70	4,435	...
Japan	50	60	3,782	68
Austria	59	67	3,752	80
Finland	57	67	3,703	78***
United Kingdom	74	79	3,088	88**
Israel	58	58	2,883	74
Ireland	56	64	2,144	66**
Jamaica	57	59	871	44***
Costa Rica	55	59	798	73***
Egypt	42	49**	225**	54§

*1972 **1971 ***1973 §1966

Source: U.N. Yearbook of National Accounts Statistics, 1974
Yearbook of Labour Statistics, ILO, 1975.

Returns to Labor and Capital

Before analyzing the functional distribution of income for these differences, the returns to labor and to capital have to be calculated.

The compensation of employees plus the remuneration for labor by the self-employed constitute the total remuneration of labor. The remainder of the national income represents returns to capital.

Returns to labor declined from 85-90% of the NNP in the early fifties to 70-75% in the first half of the seventies, and rose to 82% in 1976. (See Table 3.3). The influence of the business cycle is clearly discernible; the share of profits was smaller in recession years, and higher during prosperity. Thus, in 1967 (a recession year), the percentage of employees among all employed declined because of high unemployment — but the share of their compensation in the net national product rose, as did the share of the remuneration of labor, while the share of returns to capital declined. The rise in the share of labor in 1976 can also be attributed to the slowdown of economic activity. Per capita product did not rise in 1975, and declined 1.3% in 1976.

Capital Share and the Business Cycle

In spite of the strong fluctuations caused by the business cycle, a rising trend is discernible in the share of the returns to capital. This resulted from the increase in capital intensity in all branches of the economy. Gross capital stock per employed (at constant prices) rose five and a half times from 1950 to 1976.

The rate of return to capital reflects mainly the fluctuations of the business cycle — declining to 5% in recession years, and rising to 10-12% in years of prosperity. However, it appears that it rose somewhat in the seventies. Real wages and salaries per employee rose about two and a half times.

How does the functional distribution of income indicate the distribution of income between workers and capitalists, between farmers and townspeople? As already pointed out, there is no clear-cut distinction in this sense between the income of wage and salary earners and that of employers and self-employed. Some managers of large enterprises are employees, as they receive a monthly salary; but they may also own stock in the enterprise, and thus receive part of the returns to capital. The majority of wage and salary earners are home owners, and as such receive part of the returns to capital. A number of wage and salary earners own also stocks and bonds, and receive dividends and interest. On the other hand, some self-employed own little capital and pay interest on loans, and most of their profit consists of remuneration for labor.

A considerable part of the population receives transfer incomes, and their share in total income is not included in the functional distribution. Some 20% of the family heads in the family survey 1975/76 did not belong to the labor force; half of the total incomes of these families consisted of pensions, allowances and supports. Hence, changes in the functional distribution of income will have little direct influence on their share in total income, though there may be some indirect influences via the interest received by pension funds and pensioners on their investments.

Furthermore, total returns to capital include the public sector, in which the returns are usually relatively low — since capital stock in this sector includes hospitals, schools, roads, harbors, railways, etc. It may therefore be more meaningful to calculate the rate of return to capital in the business sector.

The Institute for Research on Output and Income calculated the shares of the remuneration of labor and capital in the business sector. The share of the remuneration of capital in the net product was somewhat smaller than in the total economy; but the rate of return to capital was considerably higher, and the fluctuations caused by the business cycle were stronger. The movements of the business cycle are indicated by the unemployment rate and the percentage change of per capita product (Table 3.3).

Table 3.3
Returns to Labor and Capital

Year	*Share of Returns in NNP*				Real Wage Index	*Rate of Return to Capital (%)*		% of unemployment	% change in GNP per capita
	to Labor in %*		*To Capital in %*						
	Total Economy	Business Sector**	Total Economy	Business Sector**		Total Economy	Business Sector**		
1952	85		15		100	8		8.1	−2.6
1955	90		10		119	5		7.4	10.0
1960	84		16		142	7		4.6	3.9
1965	83.6	88.8	16.4	11.2	192	6.6	6.4	3.6	5.5
1967	87.5	93.3	12.5	6.7	209	4.6	4.2	10.4	−1.0
1970	77.6	80.7	22.4	19.3	228	9.4	12.5	3.8	5.3
1971	75.8	76.4	24.2	23.6	237	10.3	15.8	3.5	6.5
1972	71.5	72.7	28.5	27.3	239	12.1	18.5	2.7	8.7
1973	72.7	73.4	27.3	26.6	254	10.8	16.5	2.6	1.9
1974	70.3	71.6	29.7	28.4	248	10.4	16.4	3.0	3.7
1975	72.8	74.2	27.2	25.8	248	8.7	13.5	3.1	−0.2
1976	81.6	86.9	18.4	13.1	250	5.3	6.2	3.6	−1.3

*Calculated for self-employed according to average wages and salaries per employee.
**From 1971 share in net domestic product.

Remark: Estimates for 1952, 1955 and 1960 have been made on a somewhat different basis than the estimates for 1965 and later, and are therefore not strictly comparable.

Source: Statistical Abstracts of Israel; Reports of the Institute for Research on Income and Output.

The share of labor (including the labor component of self-employment) was estimated at 73% of the GNP in the United Kingdom for 1950-1969, and 80% of the national income in the U.S.A. in 1960-65.[3] In both countries, calculations were made for a longer period — showing a rise in the labor share from the beginning of the century (from 55% in the U.K., from about 70% in the U.S.A.). This rise paralleled the rise of the share of employee compensation, which is the main component of the labor share; however, the rise was somewhat smaller, since the share of the labor remuneration of the self-employed declined owing to their decreasing share in the labor force.

The share of wages in employee compensation declined, and the share of salaries rose,[4] reflecting the increase in the relative importance of white-collar workers. The rising share of labor in national income over long periods in industrialized countries is shown by S. Kuznets for the United Kingdom, France, Germany, Switzerland and the United States.[5]

The trend in Israel contrasts with this, although during a relatively short period (23 years). The elasticity of substitution between labor and capital[6] was below one in the above industrialized countries; thus, the share of capital in the national product declined. In Israel, we found an elasticity of substitution above one.

As may be seen from Table 3.3, only a slight upward trend in the rate of return to capital in Israel is discernible; the fluctuations were caused mainly by the business cycle, while wages and salaries per employee in real terms rose about two and a half times. At the same time, capital per employed rose more than four times.

According to our calculation,[7] the elasticity of substitution was greater than one over this period. Since the ratio of the rate of return to capital to the wage rate declined less than capital per employed rose, the elasticity of substitution was greater than one, and the share of capital in the net product increased.

Some authors have compared returns to physical capital with those to human capital as a basis for priority decisions in investment policy. Psacharopoulos[8] calculated a social rate of return to investment in education for 30 countries, including Israel. His calculation for Israel is based on the data of R. Klinov-Malul[9] for 1957/58. The rate for Israel was 9.6 compared to 13.6 for the United States, 12.4 for Canada, 7.8 for Denmark, 4.6 for Great Britain — but 21.9 for Mexico, 17.2 for India, and 12.7 for the Philippines. The rate of return to physical capital in Israel is estimated at 6-7% for the whole economy in 1957/58, and 8-9% for non-residential investments.[10]

According to Psacharopoulos, the rate of return to physical capital was higher than to human capital in the developed countries; in the developing countries, the reverse was true, indicating that investment in human capital should receive priority in developing countries. In Israel in 1957/58, the rate of return to human capital was higher than that to physical capital according to the above figures, indicating that Israel belonged to the category of developing countries. Psacharopoulos based his calculations on rates of return in manufacturing industries or for non-residential investments. The rate of return to capital in the business sector in Israel appears to have been higher than that to human capital. As the rate of return to physical capital has been rising and the rate of return to human capital appears to have declined somewhat (owing to the great rise in the educational level), the rate of return to physical capital is estimated to be higher than that to human capital in the seventies, reflecting Israel's resemblance to developed countries in this respect now.

The distribution of income by factor shares is not parallel to the distribution of income between wage and salary earners and self-employed, and does not take into account those not belonging to the labor force; nevertheless, it has some implications as to the size distribution of income within the population.

In a very general sense, it can be maintained that income distribution is a function of the distribution of physical and human capital in the population, even for those no longer belonging to the labor force — since the size of pensions is a result of the previous level of income, and the income from property in old age is connected with the ownership of wealth and the accumulation of savings from income over a lifetime.

Since the distribution of wealth is more highly concentrated than is the distribution of human capital, a high share of capital remuneration (relative to the share of employers and self-employed among the total gainfully employed) may indicate relatively high inequality. Income from property has more weight in the higher income brackets, and property seems to be the main source of income of those with the highest incomes. Furthermore, also human capital seems to be concentrated more in the wealthier part of the population.

Only partial data on the distribution of wealth in Israel are available. The savings surveys of 1963/64 and 1964/65 assembled data on wealth without commercial assets — i.e., the value of homes owned, of liquid assets and of liabilities. The inequality index was relatively low (0.48), apparently because of the lack of commercial assets. Housing constituted 79% of net wealth.[11]

The family survey 1975/76 gives data on holdings of securities by the families. In an ordering of the families by net income per standard adult, the inequality index for securities' holdings was 0.516, while the index for gross total family income (including computed income) was 0.251. This is only an indication of the distribution of wealth, probably on the low side, as real estate, commercial assets and homes are not included.

The inequality index of wealth in Great Britain was 0.70 in 1965 and 0.65 in 1970, about twice the index for income.[12] In Great Britain, the top 5% owned 56% of total personal wealth in 1968, but the top 5% of income units received only 18% of total pre-tax income in 1967. In Israel, the top 5% of families received 16% of total pre-tax income in 1968/69 and 15% in 1975/76. They owned 28% of total securities in 1975/76. A considerable part of the income in this group was income from property, which is not reflected in the securities' holdings. The rise in the share of capital in the NNP (from about 15% in the fifties and early sixties to about 25% in the early seventies) may have contributed to a rise in the concentration of wealth, and thus may have been a factor increasing inequality.

Labor Share and Inequality

In general, it may be maintained that an increase in the labor share indicates a decline in inequality. But, as we have seen, the share of labor in NNP rose in years of recession, when unemployment was high, and inequality also rose. Though there may be some decline in the share of the highest income groups in total income during periods of recession, due to the lower profit share, inequality increases in the lower income groups in times of unemployment.

The figures available to us reflect very clearly the influence of the recession in 1966/67, whereas the general trend is less evident. The share of labor in the NNP rose from 84% in 1960 and 1965 to 88% in 1967. In that year the full impact of the recession became evident. The rate of unemployment rose to over 10% (from 3½% in 1965), real wages per employee declined somewhat (from 1966), and the rate of return to capital fell to a low of 4-5% from 7% in 1960 and 1965. The inequality index of the urban population rose about 18% from 1965 to 1967. (Table 4.2)

The rise in economic activity after 1967, as expressed in the decline of the unemployment rate, was accompanied by a decline in the share of labor in the NNP, a rise in the rate of return to capital, and a rise in the real wage per employee. Income inequality declined to its previous level. In 1972, the rate of return to capital reached a peak of 12% (18% in the business sector), while the share of labor in the NNP had declined to 72% with an unemployment rate of 2.7%. Up to 1975 the share of labor moved between 70 and 73%, and the rate of return to capital declined somewhat, while the inequality index fluctuated around the same level.

In 1976, the economic slowdown became more pronounced. The share of labor rose to 82%, and the rate of return to capital fell to a low of 5-6%. However, the unemployment rate remained relatively low (3½%), and real wages (which had declined somewhat after 1973) started to move upward again.

The inequality index declined considerably in 1975 and 1976, after a small rise in 1974. Government policy had restrained the rise in real wages after 1973 to combat inflationary pressures arising from the large rise in defense expenditure. An adverse impact on income distribution was prevented by social policy measures, and the inequality index declined (see Chapter 4).

NOTES

1. In 1963/64. See report of the Committee for the Examination of the Distribution of National Income in Israel, 1966, Table 25, p. 80. Similar differences were found in 1968/69.
2. Lowest decile: 10% of the population with the lowest incomes.
   Highest decile: 10% of the population with the highest incomes.
3. A.B. Atkinson, *The Economics of Inequality*, Oxford, 1975, p. 162/163.
4. According to data available for the U.K., Feinstein C.H., *Changes in the Distribution of National Income in the U.K. since 1860,* 1968, see Atkinson.
5. S. Kuznets, *Modern Economic Growth*,New Haven, 1966, p. 168/169.
6. Elasticity of substitution is defined as the proportionate change in the ratio of capital to labor associated with a proportionate change in the ratio of return to capital to wage rate.
7. Capital per employed rose 350% from 1952 to 1975, the rate of return to capital rose 9%, and real wages per employee rose 148%. The proportionate change in the share of capital at the end of the period (from 15% to 27.2%, i.e. 81.3%) can be calculated as follows:

   $$(1 - \text{share of capital}) \times \left(1 - \frac{1}{\text{elasticity of substitution}}\right) \times \text{percentage change in capital per employed}$$

   (see Atkinson, op. cit., p. 171).

   $$0.85 \times \left(1 - \frac{1}{1.376}\right) \times 350 = 81.3$$

   A calculation for the period 1952 to 1976 yields a lower elasticity of substitution, but still greater than one (1.078); for the period 1955 to 1976, it is even higher (1.58).
   According to the neo-classical theory, factor shares are determined by the value of their marginal product and the supply of capital and labor under conditions of perfect competition. The bargaining power of the labor unions, monopolies and the intervention of the government are apt to influence factor shares.
8. G. Psacharopoulos, *Returns to Education*, N.Y., 1973.
9. R. Klinov-Malul, *Return on Investment in Education in Israel*, Falk Institute, Jerusalem 1966.
10. Report of National Income Committee, 1966, p. 192.
11. Savings Survey 1964/65 CBS, Special Series No. 239, Jerusalem, 1967. See also: Habib J., Kohn M., Lerman R., "The Effect on Poverty Status in Israel of Considering Wealth and Variability of Income" *Review of Income and Wealth*, March 1977.
12. A.B. Atkinson, op. cit.

CHAPTER 4

THE DEVELOPMENT OF INCOME DISTRIBUTION

Several consumption surveys of Jewish urban employees' families were made between 1950/51 and 1975/76. Developments in this major share of the Jewish population (55-56%) can indicate trends in the total Jewish population.

The surveys clearly show growing inequality during the 18-year period from 1950/51 to 1968/69, but a decline in 1975/76 to the level of 1959/60. (Table 4.1). Investigators and politicians alike concluded that inequality increased mainly because the Jewish population became more heterogeneous after mass immigration. Is this conclusion justified?

Analyzing the distribution of income over a certain period of time is difficult when the data from various years are not strictly comparable. Although the consumption surveys focus on the same segment of the population, differences in coverage and survey methods ask for caution. In particular, we must examine how representative the first survey in the series is.

Appendix 4A.1 shows that the relatively low representation of the first survey (1950/51), the gradual increase of the population represented in later surveys, and the gradual improvement of survey methods impaired the comparability of the consumption surveys between 1950/51 and 1968/69. The two last surveys in the series (1968/69 and 1975/76) are fully comparable.

The savings surveys and income surveys can be regarded as a combined series, because their methods were similar. Since they embraced a wider spectrum of the population than did the consumption surveys, and had higher comparability among themselves, they apparently reflect historical development more consistently than do the consumption surveys.

While the consumption surveys show increasing inequality up to 1968/69, no such trend is visible in the savings and income surveys, especially since 1957/58.[1] A comparison with our estimate of income distribution in the Jewish urban population in 1944, before the establishment of the State (an inequality index of 0.324) indicates a much smaller rise in inequality since then than that reflected in the consumption surveys. We believe that the rise in inequality occurred mainly in the beginning of the fifties as a consequence of mass immigration and a high rate of unemployment.

Factors Affecting Income Differentials

Analysis of family incomes showed that the main factors explaining individual income differences were the educational level, the volume of employment, the number of earners in the family, and the earner's age and occupation.[2]

Government policy affects income distribution not only by influencing these factors, but also through various measures such as taxes, subsidies and social benefits. Other factors include the government's credit policy, inflationary pressures and wage policy. Furthermore, wage differentials are determined to a considerable extent by the bargaining power of the unions and the conditions in the labor market.

The effect of the various factors on income distribution over time is examined below.

Employment Level

The most marked feature of the savings and income surveys was the considerable rise in inequality in the recession year of 1967, and the subsequent decline in inequality as economic activity rose (Appendix, Fig. 4A.1). This influence of the business cycle on inequality can be seen from a comparison with unemployment rates (Table 4.1).

The inequality index peaked in 1967, when unemployment was at its height and there was a decline in national product per capita. In years with low unemployment and relatively high economic growth (1971 and 1972), the inequality index was low. 1975-1977 seem to be somewhat exceptional; although a relatively low inequality index was matched by low unemployment, there was no economic growth and per-capita GNP declined.

An increasing portion of the decline in inequality during the seventies may be attributed to social policy measures. Transfer payments from the National Insurance Institute alone more than doubled from 1972 to 1976 (at constant prices);[3] this does not include other transfer payments from the Ministry of Welfare and the municipalities. Old age pensions and children's allowances were linked to the average wage; the total population was gradually included for children's allowances; and compensation was paid to the needy for the rise in the cost of living.

There was a strong correlation between the inequality index of employees' families and the rate of unemployment from 1957/58 to 1974.[4] The correlation coefficient was 0.905; the changes in the rate of unemployment explained 82% of the changes in the inequality index of employees' families. According to our data, an additional one per cent of unemployment raised the

Table 4.1
Inequality Index, Unemployment and Economic Growth

Year	*Inequality Index of Income and Savings Surveys*** Urban Employees' Families	Urban Families	% of un-employment	Annual Change in GNP per capita (at constant prices) %
1957/58	0.311*	0.355*	6.3	3.0
1963/64	0.309*	0.364	3.4	6.2
1965	0.304*	0.355*	3.4	5.5
1966	0.326*	0.371*	7.4	−1.6
1967	0.359	0.418	10.4	−1.0
1968	0.327	0.385	6.1	10.5
1969	0.314	0.384	4.5	10.3
1968/69***	0.314	0.371	5.3	10.4
1970	0.305	0.378	3.8	5.5
1971	0.293	0.362	3.5	6.9
1972	0.298	0.374	2.7	8.5
1973	0.300	0.373	2.6	1.8
1974	0.315	0.386	3.0	3.7
1975	0.289	0.360†	3.1	−0.2
1976	0.281	0.350†	3.6	−1.3
1975/76***	0.276	0.334	3.3	−0.7
1977	0.290	0.341†	3.9	−1.2

*Jewish population only.
**Gross Cash Income.
***Family Consumption Survey. †calculated by income groups.
Source: C.B.S. Statistical Abstract 1977; Annual Report 1977, Bank of Israel.

inequality index of employees' families by seven points. The equation is

$$GE = 0.280 + \underset{(0.001)}{0.007}\, u$$

where GE represents the inequality index of employees' families, and u the unemployment rate. The negative correlation between the inequality index of employees' families and GNP growth per capita was −0.448. But this did not add to the explanation, because the negative correlation between the unemployment rate and the growth rate was −0.503.

The unemployment rate influenced the inequality index of the total urban population to a lesser degree; the correlation was only 0.570, explaining only 32% of the changes in the inequality index. An additional one per cent of unemployment raised the inequality index of all urban families by 4 points.[5] Economic growth added little explanation.

The influence of business fluctuations on inequality was also shown by L. Soltow in his study of eight Norwegian cities covering a period of over 100 years.[6] From the middle of the nineteenth century to 1920, the inequality index declined by about half. In the Depression of the thirties it rose 10% to 60% in different cities; the declining trend resumed in the fifties and sixties. The influence of the business cycle in the U.S. is also shown by L.E. Metcalf.[7]

Since unskilled and casual workers are hit the hardest by unemployment, the income of the lowest groups declines the most during a depression. The decline in profits, which may be substantial during a depression, affects the highest income groups. Therefore, the gain may be greatest in the shares of the upper income groups, and less in the highest income group. We have no details on the income distribution of the total urban population[8] over the entire period, so we can only assume that this may have been the case in Israel; the fluctuations in the inequality index were smaller for the total urban population than for employees. In the employees' population, the highest income group was the main gainer (Table 4.2).

Table 4.2
Income Distribution of Employees' Families
(% of total income)

Year	*Lowest 20%*	*Lowest 70%*	*Highest 20%*	*Highest Decile*	*% of unemployment*
1957/58*	6.6	48.4	38.9	23.0	6.3
1963/64*	7.2	48.4	39.0	23.4	3.4
1967	5.7	44.6	42.7	26.9	10.4
1970	7.6	48.6	38.6	23.2	3.8
1975	8.0	50.0	37.3	22.1	3.1
1975/76*	8.1	51.2	36.0	20.8	3.3
1977	8.1	49.6	37.7	22.3	3.9

*Consumption Surveys.
Source: C.B.S., Statistical Abstracts.

The influence of unemployment is most marked in the two lowest deciles. Their share declined drastically in 1967, when unemployment was at its peak, and rose as unemployment declined. The share of the lowest 70 per cent also declined; the two highest deciles gained, with most of the gain falling to the highest decile. Table 4.2 reflects also the improvement in income distribution in the seventies when the share of the two lowest deciles was higher than in 1963/64, though the unemployment rate was similar. The small rise in unemployment in 1977 was accompanied by a slight increase in inequality. However, the income share of the two lowest deciles was maintained due to social policy.

Changes in Age Structure[9]

Two important changes took place in the age structure of the Jewish population: a decline in the percentage of persons of working age, and a rise in the percentage of the old (Appendix, Table 2A.3).

The percentage of persons in working age declined from 67% at the end of the Mandatory period to 61% at the beginning of the fifties, due to the rise in the share of children (see Chapter 2). In the sixties, the share of children started to decline. The share of old persons more than doubled between 1950 and 1976. Changes in age structure affected income distribution by raising the proportion of families without earners and by influencing family size.

The age-income profile also underwent some changes, as shown in Table 4.3.

The increasing weight of the lowest and highest age groups must have increased income inequality. As the percentage of heads of households aged 65 and over rose from 10% in 1957/58 to 17½% in 1968/69, there was a great increase in the share of families whose heads did not belong to the labor force: 10% of all urban families belonged to this category in 1957/58, but 19% in 1968/69 and 20% in 1975/76. The average income of this category was less than half the average in 1968/69 and somewhat more in 1975/76 (Table 3.1).

Table 4.3
Family Income by Age of Family Head
(% of average)

Age of Family Head	*Savings Surveys* 1957/58	1963/64	*Family Expenditure Surveys* 1968/69	1975/76
18 — 24	63	66	70	65
25 — 34	99	109	107	105
35 — 44	121	119	114	121
45 — 54	118	114	119	116
55 — 64	90	92	101	97
65+	61	62	56	63
TOTAL	100	100	100	100
Inequality Index			0.111	0.109

The inequality index of family income by age groups in 1975/76 was quite similar to that in 1968/69, though income differences between age groups changed. Most important was the rise in the relative income of the highest age group to which 17% of family heads belonged.

Using standardization of ages, the Committee on Income Distribution and Social Inequality tried to assess the influence of the aging of the population on inequality. It found that the index of inequality of income per family would have been 0.353 in 1968/69 if the age composition of household heads had remained as in 1957/58. The actual inequality index in 1968/69 was 0.373, so the changes in age composition raised inequality by 6%.

Family Size

Any measurement of inequality by income per family is affected by changes in average family size and the distribution of family size. Changes in age composition and in the birth rate affected family size considerably. Average Jewish family size (including singles) declined from 3.8 in the fifties to 3.5 in 1976. The percentage of large Jewish families (six or more persons) increased to 15.3% in 1960, and declined to 13% in 1976.

As the standard of living rose, more university students and old parents could afford to live separately; consequently, the percentage of singles almost doubled during the nineteen years from 1957 to 1976, rising from 7½% to 14%, and the percentage of two-person families rose from 20% to 24%. Inequality measures of income distribution per family will therefore show a rise in inequality, even if no actual deterioration occurred — since total income is distributed among more and partly smaller units.

This distortion of the picture is prevented when income distribution per standard equivalent adult is measured.[10] According to this measure, the inequality index shows a very small rise from 1957/58 to 1968/69, and was 13% lower in 1975/76 than in 1957/58 — i.e., it declined more than did inequality of income per family (Table 4.4).

The data for employees' families show that the decline in inequality of income per SEA was stronger than that per family, following the same trend as all urban families. Inequality of income per SEA was higher than per family in employees' families, but lower in all families from 1968/69, since they included families with non-working heads, and among them many small units.

Changes in family size led to a rise of 7% in the inequality index from 1957/58 to 1975/76.[11]

In order to calculate the total impact of changes in age composition and family size on inequality, standardization of ages would have to be used for a comparison of income per S.E.A. Such a calculation has not been made;

Table 4.4
Inequality of Gross Money Income per Family and per Standard Equivalent Adult, Jewish Urban Population (Gini Coefficients)

Year	*All Families*				*Employees*			
	Income per family		*Income per SEA*		*Income per family*		*Income per SEA*	
	Inequ. Index	Ratio of highest to lowest decile	Inequ. Index	Ratio	Inequ. Index	Ratio	Inequ. Index	Ratio
1957/58	0.355	15.3	0.367	13.9	0.311	9.9	0.351	...
1963/64	0.361	16.7	0.369	13.5	0.309	9.0	0.346	10.5
1968/69	0.373	17.9	0.372	12.3	0.313	9.9	0.342	9.8
1970	0.373	...	0.368	...	0.304	7.6	0.332	7.7
1973*	0.373	...	...	...	0.300	7.6	0.324	8.2
1975*	0.360	...	...	...	0.289	7.4	0.324	...
1975/76*	0.334	12.4	0.319	8.8	0.276	6.7	...	...

*Including Arab families
Source: C.B.S.; Report of the Committee on Income Distribution, 1971.

consequently, we can only assume that changes in age composition and family size composition raised inequality by 7-13%.

Labor Force Participation of Family Members

The number of earners in the family, and their duration of work during the year, determined the level of family income to an important degree (see Chapter 7). Two important changes affected income distribution: a doubling of the percentage of families whose heads did not belong to the labor force, and an increase in the labor force participation of women from 26% in 1955 to 32% in 1976. The first was, to a considerable extent, the result of the aging of the population and the increasing tendency of old persons and university students to live in separate households (which were taken into account in the above calculations). But the rise of women's labor force participation was an additional factor in inequality.

The average number of earners in employees' families rose from 1.3 in 1959/60 to 1.5 in 1968/69 and 1975/76 as the percentage of working married women rose from 22% in 1955 to 33% in 1976. The income of the wife's work was an important factor of income inequality. The average income of "husband-wife" families in which the wife worked was 57% higher than that of such families in which the wife did not work. The 1968/69 survey also showed that husbands of working wives earned, on the average, 22% more than husbands of non-working wives (Appendix, Table 7A.2); this constituted part of the income difference between these two categories of families.

Regression analysis showed that the wife's schooling explained 21% of income differences of all families, with each year of her schooling adding 3% to family income.[12] The high explanatory power was due partly to the correlation of the wife's educational level with that of her husband, and partly to its correlation with labor force participation. Since women's educational level and labor force participation have risen steadily, this must have been a factor in increasing inequality.

The earnings of married women increased income inequality of all families in 1968/69 by 7%.[13] Since the contribution of married women's earnings to family income rose, it must be assumed that the influence of this factor on inequality also increased. (In employees' families, the average contribution of the family head's wife to total money income rose from 10% in 1967 to 13% in 1976,[14] and it must have been lower in the fifties).

Educational Structure

The most important factor in the income distribution among employed persons is the educational level, which determines occupational status (Chapters 6 and 7). The steady expansion of the educational network and the general rise in the educational level (Appendix, Table 2A.4) should therefore have reduced income differences to some extent.

Two trends are apparent over the last decade: a decline in educational inequality, as measured by years of schooling (Tables 4.5 and 4.6), and a decline in income differences by educational level (Appendix, Table 4A.2).

Table 4.5
Inequality of Schooling

	Labor Force			
	1961	1965	1976	Change in %
Average Years of schooling	8.1	8.2	9.9	+22
Inequality Index	0.278	0.267	0.221	−21

Source: Statistical Abstracts, Labor Force Surveys, Population Census 1961. See also Appendix, Table 2A.13.

We do not have comparable figures for the fifties. The available data, however, show a considerable decline in the educational level of the Jewish population in the fifties in the wake of mass immigration. The percentage of Jews aged 14 and above with more than 8 years of schooling declined from 44% in 1948 to 32% in 1954, and the share of those with less than 5 years of schooling rose from 24% to 37%. The inequality index of education rose 25% during that period. (Table 4.6).

Table 4.6
Educational Structure of Jewish Population Aged 14+ (%)

Years of Schooling	1948*	1954	1961	1976	Change from 1954 — 1976 %
0	8.0	15.0	12.6	7.2	−52
1 — 4	15.8	21.7	7.5	4.4	−80
5 — 8	32.5	31.1	35.4	25.8	−17
9 — 12	36.0	27.0	34.6	45.2	+67
13+	7.7	5.2	9.9	17.4	+235
Average	7.4	6.2	7.6	9.1	+47
Change (%)		−16	+22	+20	
Inequality Index	0.303	0.379	0.303	0.237	−37
Change (%)		+25	−20	−22	

*Calculated in 1954 on the basis of persons who immigrated before 1948.
Source: CBS, Special Series No. 66; Statistical Abstract, 1977.

Table 4.6 shows the steady decline in educational inequality after the fifties. In 1961, the inequality index was back down to its level of 1948 but there were more persons with no schooling at all, and the share of university trained persons was higher. There is some evidence that the educational level of the economically active population declined somewhat from the fifties to the mid-sixties. The average educational level of employees declined 5% between 1957/58 and 1963/64, according to the savings surveys; Baruch shows that the educational capital per 25-65 year old in the labor force declined 5% from 1950 to 1954, and an additional 2% by 1956 — where it remained until 1961.[15] Educational capital per head of those aged 14 and more rose 2% from 1961 to 1965 and from 1965 to 1971 — 19%.[16]

The educational level of the total Jewish population measured by years of schooling rose from the mid-fifties to the mid-seventies 47%, and the inequality index declined 37% (Table 4.6). In the non-Jewish population, average years of schooling rose 78% between 1961 and 1975, and inequality of schooling declined 36%.

The rise in educational inequality in the first half of the fifties would have increased income inequality even if income differentials between educational levels had remained the same. But these increased since the technological advances increased the demand for qualified manpower, while the share of those with higher education declined — thus increasing the impact of greater educational inequality on income differentials.

The increase in relative incomes of employed people with higher education is indicated by the rise in the relative incomes of engineers, physicians, lawyers and accountants between 1950 and 1957. While average nominal wages and salaries per employee rose 3.6 times, and national income per employed increased 4.3 times, the income of engineers and physicians rose about 5½ times, and those of lawyers and accountants approximately 6½ times.[17]

Income inequality by educational level seems to have risen somewhat from the late fifties to the mid-sixties, and to have declined slowly in the late sixties. From then on it declined more quickly up to 1976. (Appendix, Table 4A.2).

Income inequality by educational level started to decline in the mid-sixties, although the decline in educational inequality had begun earlier. The demand for qualified manpower rose more quickly than the supply up to the mid-sixties; from then on, supply grew more quickly than demand. Tinbergen sees the impact of these factors on inequality as "a 'race' between supply (by education) and demand (by technological development) which determines the changes in relative scarcity of any type of manpower."[18] He maintains that the rise in the percentage of university-trained manpower is the most important indicator of the increase in supply of qualified manpower; doubling of the percentage of university-trained manpower would reduce income inequality by one-half in the Netherlands and Norway, according to his theory.

In Israel, income inequality of employees by educational level declined 36% from 1968 to 1976, and the percentage of university-trained employees rose by about 50%. However, total inequality of employees' earnings declined only from about 0.36 to 0.34. Though the percentage of university-trained persons tripled during the last twenty years (Table 4.6), income inequality of urban families did not decline until the mid-seventies — when it dropped below the level of 1957/58, partly because of government policy.[19]

The fact that income inequality declined only little in the wake of the great decline in educational inequality and the spectacular rise in the percentage of university-trained manpower must be attributed to changes in other factors — such as age structure, family size, growing participation of women in the labor force, inflation, restitution payments and capital imports, capital accumulation, etc., as well as to the quick pace of technological advance, which raised the demand for qualified manpower, and to the bargaining power of certain groups of qualified workers.[20]

Changes in Occupational Structure

Wage differentials by occupation and within occupations are determined primarily by educational differences — and by age differences (work experience). The occupational structure becomes more differentiated with technological development, but the impact on income inequality depends on the changes in the supply side — as well as on the institutional framework of the labor market, the power of the labor unions and government policies.

An inquiry[21] showed that wages and salaries would have been higher in 1963/64 had the same age and educational structure prevailed as in 1957/58, as well as the same composition of country of origin and year of immigration; changes in these factors led to a decline in average wages for all employees, as well as for each of the four occupational groups. On the basis of this material, we calculated that income inequality by occupational groups rose 7½%, but that it would have remained the same if the demographic changes had not occurred. Though the average educational level of the family heads in the survey declined, it declined only among skilled and unskilled workers; it remained the same for liberal and technical professions, managers and clerks. Average age rose among blue-collar workers, but remained about the same among white-collar workers.

Earnings of skilled and professional workers rose more than the average, those of unskilled workers rose somewhat less, and those of the unprofessional white-collar workers rose considerably less than the average. This indicates that in the mid-sixties the supply of skilled manpower (blue and white-collar workers) had risen less than demand — i.e., technological development was faster than the rise in the educational and occupational levels of the employed.

The figures in Table 4.7 reveal the trend of income differentials by occupations — although they are not strictly comparable, since the 1957/58 and 1963/64 figures are earnings of heads of income units, while the later figures are earnings of all employees.[22] Furthermore, the classifications of occupations were different, and we had to combine subgroups into the four categories for 1968, 1972 and 1976.

Income differentials by occupation rose until the late sixties; from then on, they declined considerably. Within the four categories, there were large differences between subgroups; however, inequality calculated by more occupational groups shows a much smaller decline from 1972 to 1976.

The decline in earnings differentials by occupation from the late sixties may indicate that the quality of manpower improved more than was required by technological development. The government's social policies, as well as the strength of the labor unions also influenced earnings differentials. Thus, the large rise in children's allowances in recent years must have reduced income differences between occupational categories.

Using capital per employed to indicate technological advance, and the

Table 4.7
Annual Earnings of Employees by Occupation
(% of average)

	Head of Income Unit				Employees					
	1957/58		1963/64		1968		1972		1976	
Occupation	%		%		%		%		%	
Unskilled workers	20.1	70	21.6	67	19.1	66	18.5	68	18.3	69
Skilled workers	41.5	95	43.3	100	43.1	93	38.9	97	31.5	98
Clerks	21.9	123	18.3	109	21.6	121	23.9	114	27.7	109
Professional and technical workers	16.5	135	16.8	150	16.2	146	18.7	133	22.5	117
Total	100.0	100	100.0	100	100.0	100	100.0	100	100.0	100
Inequality Index	0.120		0.129		0.138		0.112		0.085	
Inequality Index of 9-groups							0.139		0.122	

Source: CBS: Employee Earnings (1968, 1972, 1976)
Savings Surveys, Ch. Levi op. cit. (1957/58, 1963/64)

Table 4.8
Capital per Employed and Educational Level[23]
(Change in %)

Period	*Capital per Employed*	*% of those with 13+ years of schooling*	*Average years of schooling*	*Educational capital per head*[24]
1948*—1954	+ 52	−32	−16	− 5**
1954 —1961	+ 62	+90	+22	− 2
1948 —1961	+147	+29	+ 3	− 7
1961 —1965	+ 27	− 4	+ 1	+ 2
1965 —1970	+ 30	+30	+ 6	+10
1970 —1975	+ 30	+40	+10	+ 8***

*1948 calculated in 1954 on the basis of persons who immigrated before 1948.
**1950-1954 ***1970-1972.

Source: CBS; Statistical Abstracts: Capital per Employed: Annual Reports, Bank of Israel;
A.L. Gaathon, *Economic Productivity in Israel*, Praeger, 1971.
J. Baruch, Bank of Israel Bulletin No. 25, 1966.
Z. Hercovitz, Educational Capital in Israel, 1961-72, Falk Institute, 1976.

percentage of university-trained persons, average years of schooling and educational capital per head to indicate the supply of qualified manpower, we can see that the latter declined in the face of rising demand, up to the mid-sixties (Table 4.8).

The gap between technological advance and the supply of qualified manpower in the fifties and the beginning of the sixties must have influenced wage differentials considerably; this seems to have been the most important factor in the rise in income inequality at that time, as also revealed in regression analysis (Appendix, Table 4A.3). It is difficult to quantify this interplay of technical advance and educational improvement. In the late sixties, some balance was achieved; in the seventies, occupational income differentials indicate that educational improvement surpassed technical advance.

On the basis of the savings surveys data, Ch. Levi[25] showed that the educational level of employees declined somewhat from 1957/58 to 1963/64, and that the relative earnings of professional and technical workers rose after the influence of age, education,[26] country of origin, and year of immigration had been taken into account. This supports the view that up to the mid-sixties, technical advance outpaced educational improvement.

S. Amir[27] calculated that changes in the distribution of education of employees raised average real income by 2% between 1961 and 1968/69. We may therefore assume that the turning point was in the mid-sixties. In the late sixties, the high unemployment rate and other factors seem to have counteracted the excess rise in the educational level, but in the seventies the impact of this excess became important.

The Impact of Government Policies

One of the declared goals of the Government, especially in recent years, has been to reduce socio-economic gaps — mainly by raising the absolute and relative standards of living of low-income groups. Various committees were set up to examine the situation and to devise solutions. One of the most important such committees was The Prime Minister's Committee on Children and Youth in Distress, which summarized the findings of its ten working groups in June 1973. Its special area of concern stems from the fact that a considerable number of large families belong to the lower income groups and live in crowded conditions, and thus the second generation is being caught in the vicious circle of poverty.

Government policies influence socio-economic gaps in two ways: directly by redistributing income through taxes, subsidies, social services and social payments; and indirectly by measures designed to insure economic growth and full employment.

Economic and social development are considered necessary to achieve security, national unity, absorption of new immigrants and a fair standard of living for all. Hence, since the establishment of the State, the government has directed sizeable amounts into investments through its development budget (in addition to investments by the national institutions, which had made large investments during the Mandatory period in the settlement of new immigrants — especially in agriculture). In order to increase investments and capital imports, a special law offered tax concessions, government loans under favorable conditions and other privileges to foreign investors.

Investments in development towns created new jobs for new immigrants and reduced unemployment, thereby contributing to a decline in inequality — although there remained a considerable income difference between the new towns and the other areas of the country. On the other hand, the privileges granted to private investors widened the socio-economic gaps, since they increased the accumulation of wealth and incomes in the higher income brackets.

One of the most important long-term measures for quickening economic growth and increasing equality of opportunity was the rapid expansion of education and occupational training. Education was also regarded as the best means for unifying a population with different cultural, ethnic and social backgrounds. National expenditure on education rose rapidly over the years, increasing from 5% of the GNP in the fifties to 6% in 1962/63 and 8.8% in 1974/75. The public sector financed 83% of the total expenditure on education.

The 1949 Law of Compulsory Education provides free compulsory education for one year of kindergarten and eight years of primary school, later extended to nine years; in 1973, a tenth year was added. The remaining years of secondary school education were covered by a system of graded tuition fees, with a high percentage of pupils (in 1971/72, 56% of all Jewish and 60% of all Arab pupils) being completely exempt from paying fees. All post-primary education in development towns was free. From 1978/79 all secondary education will be free.

For a number of years, there have been cultural enrichment programs and other special arrangements for children from deprived homes. These include a prolonged school day, supervised homework, individual coaching and special residential schools and boarding departments for intellectually well-endowed children, to enable them to receive a secondary and higher education.

A large-scale educational reform is being introduced by stages. It provides, inter alia, for new patterns of socio-cultural integration through new comprehensive schools and the mixing of secondary school pupils from different socio-cultural strata. The system is being converted to six years of primary school, three years of middle school and three years of high school or other post-primary education.

All adult education programs have been considerably extended, especially those for members of the armed forces and young recruits to national service.

The army plays a major part in many educational programs. Gifted ex-servicemen and women from development areas and deprived neighborhoods who have not been able to complete their secondary education, are eligible for special courses to prepare them for a university education.

As a result of the expansion of educational services, the educational level rose gradually over the years. This was an important factor in the technological advance of the economy. However, the expansion of education apparently contributed to greater equality only in recent years, after it overtook technological development in the mid-sixties (Table 4.8).

Disadvantaged population groups profited less from the expansion of education, especially of higher education, than did the middle and higher income groups, because of low aspirations and difficult home conditions. Thus, in spite of government intentions, the integrating and equalizing influence of education remained quite modest.

The expansion of health services was another factor that increased equality. They expanded proportionately more than the population increased — because of the aging of the population and the effort to improve the quality of the services. Health services are provided by public clinics and hospitals, non-profit institutions, and the various sick funds which insure approximately 90% of the population. National expenditure on health rose from about 5% of the GNP in 1962/63 to 6.3% in 1975/76. The public sector financed 47% in 1974/75, and the various sick funds and other non-profit institutions 36%.

The number of hospital beds per thousand of population rose from 5.6 in 1950 to 7.1 in 1965, then declined slightly to 6.9 in 1976. To promote delivery under hygienic conditions with medical attention, the National Insurance Institute pays maternity allowances only to mothers who deliver at a hospital. As a result, the percentage of births in hospitals rose over the years: 100% of all Jewish births took place in hospitals in the seventies; for non-Jews, the 1976 figure was 98%, compared with 55% in 1960, 81% in 1965 and 91% in 1970. The network of mother and child health centers run by the Ministry of Health was considerably expanded, especially in rural areas and in Arab and Druze villages. In 1975 there were 778 centers, compared with 589 in 1960.

All health services and geriatric medical services have become more community oriented. Increasing stress is placed on preventive activities, on ambulatory care to enable the patient to remain in his home surroundings, and on medical and supplementary home care services.

The number of inhabitants per physician declined from 438 in 1952 to 337 in 1974. While this ratio is very favorable in comparison with other countries, it should be noted that a comparatively high percentage of Israel's physicians are engaged in research, health administration and medical instruction. Moreover, since physicians tend to congregate in or near the major teaching hospitals, there is a shortage of physicians in some development towns and the more outlying areas.

A high percentage of Israel's population is medically insured, but not all of those insured are fully covered. Among those not insured at all are some at the lower end of the social scale — especially among the aged. (Social welfare bureaus arrange insurance for their clients who are not insured). A governmental health insurance scheme is scheduled to be introduced; it will be operated through existing medical facilities and sick funds (at least in its initial stages).

Social transfer payments guarantee a minimum income to those who do not receive adequate income from work because of temporary interruption (unemployment, birth, work accident, sickness) or because of physical or mental disabilities or other reasons; and to those with large families and low incomes.

The National Insurance Institute provides old age, widows' and orphans' pensions; maternity benefits; children's allowances; allowances and rehabilitation services to victims of work accidents and industrial diseases; supplementary benefits to the aged who have no other income; and unemployment insurance. It also provides pensions and rehabilitation services for physically and mentally disabled persons.

The problem of large families in distress received special attention in the wake of the report of the Prime Minister's Committee on Deprived Children. In 1972, child allowances were raised considerably.

Among the most dramatic changes in social transfer payments have been the linking of all national insurance pensions to the average wage, with adjustment for rises in the cost of living; extension of the scope of insurance and range of clients; and a general easing of eligibility requirements for old age pensions.

The National Insurance Institute, which bases many of its activities on the findings of research, supports a number of pilot projects. These include a day center for the aged, nutritional guidance to mothers, counseling and part-time employment for pensioners, and preparation for retirement (in 1972, a Society for Planned Retirement was formed). Most of these projects are carried out through other bodies, or jointly with other bodies.

The total expenditure of the National Insurance Institute on benefits rose spectacularly from 1½% of the GNP in 1960/61 to almost 6% in 1975/76. The number of recipients of benefits more than doubled between 1965 and 1975, and allowances were increased with the aim of raising minimum income to 40% of the average national wage. To finance this expansion, the maximum income on which contributions are levied was raised, and the rates of contributions were raised.

By transferring some administrative functions to the National Insurance Institute and by automating welfare payments, the Ministry of Social Welfare and the local welfare bureaus have been able to devote more time to planning and to intensify their services — especially to large and multi-problem families. Pamphlets inform clients and potential clients of their rights and of procedures for obtaining aid. The Ministry provides, inter alia, services for child and youth welfare, the aged, the blind and the retarded; vocational rehabilitation of the physically handicapped; correctional services; and community work services. Most of these have increased their activities; the specialized medical services have become more family centered and community oriented.

Based on recommendations of an interdepartmental committee, a joint fund of governmental and other public bodies has been established to plan and develop services for the aged: multifunctional community services; improvement and expansion of residential homes and special housing facilities (such as protected housing units within community settings); and the promotion of local action through the establishment of local committees for the care of the aged.

The Social Services Section of the Jewish Agency's Immigration and Absorption Department provides reach-out services to immigrants of all ages at their port of arrival. Residential absorption centers and Hebrew courses at kibbutzim or in urban areas help newcomers adapt themselves to the country, and provide a stepping-stone to paid employment — along with educational and vocational counseling, training and work placement.[28]

Redistribution of Incomes

The government's policy is to redistribute incomes by taxes, subsidies and transfer payments. The progressive character of the direct taxes and compulsory loans (and to some extent of the subsidies) and the expansion of old age pensions, grants and other payments to the needy, assure a certain redistribution. Indirect taxes (levied to a considerable extent to raise government revenue) had a regressive character inspite of heavier taxes on luxury goods. Taxes and compulsory payments took 57% of the national income in 1976, compared with 30% in 1949, 38% in 1960 and 44% in 1970.[29]

Direct taxes reduced income inequality 10-12% and the ratio of the highest decile to the lowest decile 15-18% in the fifties and 25-28% in the sixties and seventies (Table 4.9). Figures for 1950 show that direct taxes reduced income inequality of employees' families only 7%, and the ratio of the highest to the lowest decile only 8%. They reduced the income inequality of that part of the population 12-14% in the later fifties and the sixties, reflecting the improvement of the tax system.

The ratio of the highest to the lowest decile declined more than did general net income inequality (Table 4.9), reflecting the growing progressiveness of direct taxes. Direct taxes increased their share in total taxes from about 17% in 1950 to 26% in 1960, 39% in 1970 and 48% in 1975.

Net indirect taxes (including subsidies) raised the income inequality of employees' families in 1959/60 by 5%; direct and net indirect taxes together reduced family income inequality 8% (compared with a 12% reduction by direct taxes only). The regressive character of net indirect taxes was still evident in 1968/69; however, they were progressive in relation to consumption expenditure, and they were also somewhat progressive for income per standard equivalent adult. Net indirect taxes were 4.5% of consumption expenditure in the lowest decile, 6% in the second lowest decile, and 10.4% in the highest decile.[30] The inequality index of consumption per SEA was reduced by 6%. In 1974 the impact of indirect taxes on consumption was similar.[31]

Table 4.9
Reduction of Income Inequality by Direct Taxes

	All Urban Families					
	Gross Cash Income		*Net Cash Income*		*Change (%)*	
	Gini Coeff.	Ratio of highest to lowest decile	Gini Coeff.	Ratio of highest to lowest decile	Gini Coeff.	Ratio
1954*	0.298	9.1	0.265	7.7	−11	−15
1960/61**	0.371	20.5	0.334	16.9	−10	−18
1963/64	0.364	17.9	0.317	13.4	−13	−25
1968/69	0.371	17.5	0.327	12.6	−12	−28
1975/76	0.334	12.4	0.296	9.2	−11	−26
	Income per Standard Equivalent Adult					
1963/64*	0.369	13.2	0.323	10.4	−12	−21
1968/69*	0.372	12.5	0.328	9.4	−12	−25
1975/76	0.319	8.8	0.287	6.9	−10	−22

*Jewish families only.
**All income units, including rural (tax data).
Source: Committee Report 1966; Committee Report 1971; Statistical Abstract, 1972. CBS, data of family survey 1975/76.

Social transfer payments are included in the families' income according to the definitions of the various family surveys, and the inequality index reflects their influence. Allowances and supports constituted 75% of the gross money income of the families in the lowest decile, 30% in the second lowest decile, and only 2% in the highest decile in 1975/76. A calculation by us of the inequality index when allowances and supports are excluded shows that these reduced inequality of family income by about 9% in 1968/69[3] and by 12% in 1975/76, and inequality of income per SEA by 13.8%.

A study[33] showed that public expenditure on education, health and welfare services (not including transfer payments) reduced the inequality of gross income per family by 7% in 1968/69, but that of net income by only 5%. Because of the high correlation with family size (public expenditure on social services was only 8% of the net income of a family without children, but 67% of that of a family with 6 children), the inequality of net income per standard equivalent adult was reduced to a much greater extent — by 11%. The substantial rise in public expenditures on social services after 1968/69 is estimated to have increased their influence on income distribution.

A calculation made by us, combining the results of the various 1968/69 and 1975/76 investigations (impact of direct and indirect taxes, social benefit payments and social services) shows that the whole system of taxes and benefits reduced the inequality of income per standard equivalent adult by about one-third.[34]

Other government measures which affected income distribution to some extent were the setting of minimum wages and the continuance of rent controls on old apartments (built before 1947). The setting of minimum wages is estimated to have had a positive influence on equality; the influence of rent controls is not clear, since some of the landlords were in lower income brackets than were some of the tenants.

Inflation

The Israeli economy experienced inflationary pressures of differing strength over the years, and various measures for linking wages, salaries, pensions, bonds and loans to the price index were introduced. To what extent did price increases and the linkage system influence income inequality?

The extent of inflation is reflected in the following data: The average annual increase in the cost of living index was 12.3% from 1948 to 1976. There were years with low price rises (about 2% in 1959/60 and in the late sixties), and years with very high price rises (58% in 1952, about 40% in 1974 and 1975, 31% in 1976 and 35% in 1977).

The influence of price changes on the consumption of families in seven different income groups was examined for the 1963-1971 period. The average price of the consumption basket of the highest income group rose 66%, and that of the lowest income group 58%; the average price rise was 62%.[35] Subsidies restrained price increases on essential goods, and indirect taxes were levied mostly on luxury goods — so the lower price increase of the consumption basket in the lower income groups was apparently the result of government measures.

During 1971-75, the lower income groups suffered more from price increases than did the higher income groups. From January 1971 until April 1975, the consumers' price index rose 170% — but prices of the consumption basket of the lowest decile rose 178% and that of the second lowest decile 176%, while the consumption basket of the highest decile rose only 163% and that of the second highest 165%.[36]

Over the entire period 1963-1975, price increases were somewhat higher for the lower income groups, indicating some unfavorable influence of inflation on equality.

The linkage system and the government's credit policy apparently had quite different influences on income distribution. The linkage of wages and salaries to the cost of living dates from the Second World War period. The cost of living allowance was paid on a basic salary up to a certain ceiling. The definition of the basic salary and the ceiling changed with rising prices.

The ceiling and the computation of the allowances on a basic salary maintained real incomes of employees in most income groups, apart from the highest. Because of its exemption from income tax, it raised the real net incomes of the middle income groups more than those of the lower income groups — and may have maintained the incomes of the higher income groups.

The cost of living index therefore increased net wage differentials in most years, apart from the early fifties and the early seventies. From 1975, the allowance became subject to income tax, and its influence on net wage differentials may have been neutral.

The 70% linkage introduced in 1976 and the abolition of the income tax exemption reduced the capacity of the allowance to maintain net real earnings. Since the strong workers' organizations are intent on maintaining net real earnings as well as differentials, wage disputes have become more frequent.

The linkage of government bonds to the cost of living index resulted in considerable rates of savings in the higher income groups. Therefore, the accumulation of wealth did not suffer from inflation; to some extent it actually profited from inflation — since government loans and mortgages (which previously were linked to the cost of living index) were increasingly being granted without linking. The government's practice of linked borrowing and unlinked lending led to substantial deficits which reinforced inflationary pressures.

The Committee on Income Distribution devoted a special chapter of its report to the influence of the government's credit policy.[37] Some long-term loans were partly linked to the price index, but the real interest paid was very low. Between 1949 and 1953, the real interest on development loans was even negative (about 10%), since development loans (and mortgages) were unlinked. During 1954-61, the average real interest was about 3%. The subsidies inherent in these loans were calculated at 63% of the loans in 1949-53, and at about 30% in 1954-61. Short-term bank credit under privileged conditions (partly from public funds) also improved the relative position of farmers, factory owners, building contractors, etc.

Since most of the development loans were given to those already possessing wealth, this must have contributed to the accumulation of wealth under inflationary conditions. The abolition of linkage on mortgages and development loans (though these were made at higher interest rates) must also have accelerated this trend.

It is not clear whether mortgages from public funds increased the inequality of wealth; many went to new immigrants, large families living in crowded conditions, and young couples. Publicly financed housing accounted for over one-third of all housing erected. The mortgages from public funds constituted 20% of the total investment in housing in 1974, and about 10% in previous years.

In 1976, about 71% of all households owned their dwellings — compared to an estimated one-third in 1948 and 59% in 1966. Mortgages from public funds were an important source of financing for these dwellings, and made possible the wide dispersion of dwelling ownership.

Income Distribution in the Mid-Seventies

During the seven years from 1968/69 to 1975/76, income inequality declined about 10%. The most important change was the rise of the income share of the lowest twenty percent of families. Their share in gross monetary income rose by 19%, and in net monetary income by 18%. To some extent this was caused by the decline in unemployment, but mostly the rise in the educational level and social benefit payments were responsible.

Table 4.10 shows that the income shares of the two lowest deciles rose at the expense of the two highest deciles, and that the income shares of the middle income brackets also rose. Income inequality of employees' families declined more than did that of all families, indicating the decline in income differences by occupation (Appendix, Table 4A.3).

The distribution of net income per standard equivalent adult shows a smaller gap between the lowest and the highest fifth of the population than net income per family (a ratio of 4.8 compared to 5.5 in 1975/76), though the inequality index was similar. This is the result of the considerable social benefits conferred on large families (children's allowances). Inequality measured by income per SEA reflects the social situation better than the per family income measure (see Introduction). The distribution of net total income per SEA among families (last column of Table 4.10) may be regarded as the best indicator of family income distribution in 1975/76. According to this distribution, the income of the highest fifth of the population was only three times that of the lowest fifth, and the income of the lowest decile of families was 44% of the average. This reflects a decline in the proportion of families in poverty to below 10% (see Chapter 8).

Analysis of Combined Impact

We used a multiple regression analysis[38] to examine the combined impact of the above variables (apart from government policy) on income inequality. The explanatory variables used were: 1) the ratio of capital per employed to the percentage of the labor force with post-secondary education (13 years and

Table 4.10
Income Distribution of Urban Population 1968/69 and 1975/76
(% of Income)

% of Population	*Income per Family*				*Income per SEA**		
	Gross Monetary Income		*Net Monetary Income*		*SEA Income*		*Family Income*
	1968/69	1975/76	1968/69	1975/76	1968/69	1975/76	1975/76
20 lowest	4.7	5.6	5.6	6.6	6.8	7.8	10.5
60 middle	52.6	54.9	55.5	56.8	52.9	54.4	56.6
20 highest	42.7	39.5	38.9	36.6	40.3	37.8	32.9
Inequality Index	0.371	0.334	0.327	0.296	0.328	0.297	0.224
Ratio of highest fifth to lowest	9.1	7.1	6.9	5.5	5.9	4.8	3.1

*Total net income.
Source: Appendix, Table 4A.3

more of schooling) (D/S 13) or (as a second variant) with a post-primary education (9 years and more of schooling) (D/S 9), as an indicator of the demand-supply ratio of skilled manpower; 2) the unemployed as a percentage of the labor force (u); 3) the percentage of Jews aged 65 and more (A); 4) the percentage of married women in the labor force (LMW) 5) the percentage of one- and two-person families, in all families (SF).

Relatively significant results were received (Appendix, Table 4A.4) in spite of the small number of observations (14 and 13). During 1954-1975 the supply-demand ratio of skilled manpower was the most important explanatory variable. The coefficient of unemployment shows low significance and even a negative sign if other variables are added (regressions 1, 4 and 5). This stems from the low correlation of unemployment with the inequality index of employees for this period, the lack of correlation between unemployment and the inequality index of the total urban population (Table 4.11), and the considerable negative correlation between unemployment and the other variables (Appendix, Table 4A.5).

During 1957/58 — 1975, when 1954 is excluded (13 observations) unemployment had the greatest influence on inequality and was very significant especially for employees' families, because of the high correlation of the unemployment rate with the inequality index over that period.

Table 4.11 shows the correlation of the explanatory variables with the inequality index. The combined impact of the variables on the inequality index was, of course, influenced by the intercorrelation of the variables, which is reflected in the correlation matrix (Appendix, Table 4A.5).

Table 4.11
Correlation (R) of Demographic and Other Variables with Inequality Index (Gini)

Variables	*1954 – 1975* Inequality Index of Urban Families	*1954 – 1975* Inequality Index of Urban Employees' Families	*1957/58 – 1975* Inequality Index of Urban Families	*1957/58 – 1975* Inequality Index of Urban Employees' Families
% of unemployment (u)	−.052	0.319	0.591	0.897
Capital per employed/ % of labor force with 13+ years of schooling (D/S 13)	0.710	0.632	0.577	0.467
" with 9+ y. of schooling (D/S 9)	0.743	0.411	0.519	0.035
% aged 65+ (A)	0.523	0.113	0.176	−.349
Labor participation of married women (%) (LMW)	0.392	0.001	−.037	−.488
% of one and two person families (SF)	0.610	0.204	0.307	−.244

Regressions 1 and 5 (Appendix, Table 4A.4) show the impact of all five explanatory variables used for the period 1954-1975. Together they explain 82% of the changes in the inequality index of all urban families (regression 1) and 83% of those of employees' families (regression 5). The two variables with the highest explanatory power were the demand-supply ratio for skilled manpower (the 9 years of schooling variant) and the percentage of aged people. Both variables were highly significant in both regressions, but for all urban families the demand-supply ratio had the higher explanatory power (55% explanation) compared to 17% added explanation of the percentage of aged, while for urban employees, the percentage of aged had higher explanatory power (45%) than the 17% explanation of the demand-supply ratio (although the latter appeared first in the regression).

Interesting is the negative sign of the age factor in all regressions, which stems from its high correlation with the other variables — especially the demand-supply ratio (Appendix, Table 4A.5). Labor force participation of married women added 7% explanation for all urban families, but 13% in the case of employees' families, with higher significance (see the 3-steps variant, regression 5a).

The percentage of small families and the unemployment rate added little explanation with low significance, and — quite unexpectedly — with negative signs. The negative signs can be explained by the high correlations between these two variables and other variables (Table 4A.5), as well as by the relatively low correlation of the unemployment rate with the inequality index for the 1954-1975 period (Table 4.11).

The demand-supply variant with 13 years of schooling gave significant results only with one additional variable — labor force participation of married women (regression 2) or unemployment rate (regression 4 and regression 6). The demand-supply factor explained 50% of the changes in the inequality index of all urban families with high significance, and the labor force participation of married women added 8% explanation with low significance (regression 2). The demand-supply factor had lower explanatory power for the inequality index of employees' families (40% — regression 4), which is explained by the lower correlation of this variable with the index (Table 4.11).

The results of the regressions for the 1957/58 — 1975 period show high explanatory power and high significance of the unemployment rate, especially for the inequality index of employees' families (regressions 6, 7 and 8). In these regressions, the unemployment rate explains 80% of the changes in the inequality index, while the demand-supply factor and demographic variables add little explanation with low significance. The unemployment rate had lower explanatory power in the case of all urban families (35%, regression 3), but the percentage of small families added 33% explanation with high significance.

The beta coefficients[39] underline the importance of the supply-demand ratio of skilled manpower, when 1954 is included, and the importance of the unemployment rate, when 1954 is excluded (Appendix, Table 4A.6).

The intercorrelation of the explanatory variables, though connected with their interaction and counteraction, makes the interpretation of the results difficult. The demographic variables — percentage of the aged, percentage of small families and labor force participation of married women — show very high correlations among themselves, as all three variables were increasing over time (Appendix, Table 4A.5). The supply-demand variant for skilled labor with 9 years of schooling also had high correlations with the demographic variables, since its rising trend was interrupted only once — whereas the 13 years variant rose until 1967 and declined from then on, and therefore had low correlation with the other variables.

Since we believe that most of the rise in inequality occurred before 1954, and that the inequality index of 1954 represents an underestimate, we attribute more importance to the results for the period 1957/58 — 1975 than to the results, when 1954 is included. The low influence of the demographic factors in the regressions for 1957/58 — 1975 stems from their negative correlation with the unemployment rate (Appendix, Table 4A.5), and their negative or low correlation with the inequality index (Table 4.11). This indicates that there were other factors (among them full employment) which neutralized the influence of the aging of the population, of the rise of the percentage of small families, and of the rising labor force participation of married women. Since we had no variable expressing social benefits, and since the inequality index was that of gross incomes, the impact of the government's social policy was not caught in the regressions.

NOTES

1. Savings and income surveys were made from 1954 to 1976. But it is questionable whether 1954 can be included in the series, since the survey method and the definition of income were different from those in the later surveys. The 1954 survey seems not to have included the very poor and the wealthier inhabitants.
2. See Chapter 7.
3. They rose from IL940 million in 1972 to IL6,337 million in 1976 or IL2,067 million at 1972 prices. In 1977, their real increase was only 2%. (Annual Reports, Bank of Israel, 1975 and 1976).
4. We excluded 1975 and 1976 because social transfer payments were apparently influential in lowering the index in these years. The correlation coefficient was 0.897 for the period 1957/58-1975.
5. The equation is $Gp = 0.355 + 0.004\ u$. See also regressions in Appendix, Table 4A.3.
6. Soltow, L., *Towards Income Equality in Norway*, Madison, 1965.
7. Metcalf, L.E., "The Size Distribution of Personal Income during the Business Cycle", *American Economic Review*, Vol. 59, p.469.
8. The CBS publishes only the Gini index of the total urban population. It gives no details, because the income data of the self-employed do not seem sufficiently reliable.
9. For more details of the influence of age on income distribution, see Chapters 6 and 7.
10. See Introduction, which explains the method. The figures in Table 4.4 are based on an ordering of the population by income per S.E.A., and the inequality index was computed for income per S.E.A. The calculation of the inequality index for income per family (in the same ordering) gives a lower inequality index. In 1975/76 the inequality index for net income per S.E.A. was 0.297 when calculated for S.E.A. income, but only 0.225 when calculated for family income, because of the greater size of the families in the lower income brackets in such an ordering.
11. The inequality index of income per family declined 5.9% and that per S.E.A. 13.1%; the difference (7.2%) can be attributed to changes in the distribution of family size.
12. See Chapter 7 and Appendix, Table 7A.3, regression 1.
13. The inequality index by deciles for monetary family income without the wife's income from work was 0.346 compared to 0.371 for all monetary family income.
14. According to income surveys. In the family survey of 1968/69, the wife's contribution was 12% in employees' families and 11% in all urban families.
15. J. Baruch, "Educational Capital," *Bank of Israel Bulletin* No. 25, Jan. 1966.
16. Z. Hercovitz, *Educational Capital in Israel, 1961-1972*, Falk Institute, Jerusalem, 1976.
17. On the basis of tax data, R. Klinov — Malul, *Returns on Investment in Education in Israel*, Falk Institute, 1966, p. 41.
    See also wage differentials in industry, which rose substantially from 1947 to 1958, according to U. Baharal, *The Influence of Mass Immigration on Wages in Israel*, Falk Institute, Jerusalem, 1965, p. 79.

18. Jan Tinbergen, *Income Distribution*, Amsterdam, 1975.
19. The income differentials in Appendix Table 4A.2 relate only to employees' earnings. Table 6.2 shows that income inequality by educational groups was greater for family income than for earnings of family heads, and that it was greater for family income of all urban families than for that of employees.
20. L.C. Thurow explains the distribution of earnings by a job-competition model in which on-the-job training places are allocated to those with the lowest training costs. Education is the most important of the personal characteristics which affect training costs. The increase in more highly educated labor can lead to lower earnings of less-educated labor, since the latter will now be selected for training opportunities for lower income jobs. L.C. Thurow, *Generating Inequality*, Basic Books, Inc., London, 1976. According to this theory, the decline in educational inequality will not necessarily reduce earnings differentials.
21. Ch. Levi, *Wage Differentials of Employees in Israel, 1957-58 and 1963/64,* Bank of Israel, 1968. Based on the savings surveys.
22. The savings survey of 1954 also shows family income by occupations. The highest category's family income (professional and technical workers) was 141% of the average.
23. The educational level in 1948, 1954 and 1961 is for the total population; in 1965, 1970 and 1975, for the labor force. The change from 1961 to 1965 was calculated by comparing the educational level of the labor force and population in 1975.
24. Educational capital per head expresses the average educational level better than average years of schooling, since the different grades of schooling (primary, secondary, university) get different weights according to the amounts invested in them. The annual costs of secondary education were 3-5 times those of primary education, and costs of higher education on the average about three times those of secondary education.
25. Ch. Levi, op. cit., p. 27-28.
26. Since their occupations required higher education, this factor did not affect our conclusion.
27. S. Amir, *Incomes of Wage and Salary Earners in Israel 1968/69*, Falk Institute, Jerusalem, 1975, p. 34.
28. The survey of educational health and social services was based partly on "New Strategies for Social Development — The Role of Social Welfare", Israel Report to the International Conference on Social Welfare, 1970, prepared by Dr. Ruth Horovitz.
29. Direct taxes and compulsory loans, net indirect taxes on local production (after deduction of subsidies) and taxes on civilian imports (after deduction of the foreign exchange adjustment component).
30. J. Gabbai, "Changes in Public Finance and Fiscal Policy 1949-72" *Israel Economic Quarterly*, April 1973 (Hebrew).
31. J. Gabbai and J. Tawil, *The Incidence of Value Added Tax and the Compensation of Low Income Groups*. National Insurance Institute, Jerusalem, 1976.
32. J. Habib showed that social benefit payments reduced income inequality by 8½% in 1969. J. Habib, "Redistribution Through National Insurance", *Social Security*, Jerusalem, Dec. 1975 (Hebrew).
33. Moria Avnimelech, "Influence of Public Expenditure on Social Services on Redistribution of Incomes in 1968/69", Jerusalem, Hebrew University. Unpublished M.A. Thesis (Hebrew).
34. Social benefit payments reduced inequality of money income per SEA by 13.8%, direct taxes reduced it another 10%, and net indirect taxes by an additional 2½% (86.2 × 90 × 97.5), bringing it down to 75.6%. Public expenditure on social services brought a further reduction of 11% — i.e., to 67.3% (75.6 × 89).
35. Y. Menseli, "Price Developments of Consumption Baskets of Different Income Groups in Israel," *Bank of Israel Bulletin* No. 41, April 1973.
36. S. Maital, "The Impact of Inflation", Foerder Institute, Tel-Aviv, 1976, on the basis of J. Gabbai's data, op. cit.
37. Report 1966, p. 255.
38. See Chapter 6, note 9 for the technique of multiple regression analysis.
39. Regression coefficients in standard form; see Chapter 7, p. 137 and note 3 for the significance of the beta coefficients.

CHAPTER 5

A HISTORICAL ASPECT

An interesting question is the extent to which socio-economic disparities in present-day Israel stem from developments during the Mandatory period. The State's society and economy are continuations of developments in the Jewish sector during the Mandatory and pre-Mandatory periods, and even in the Arab sector during those periods.

Specifically:

(1) Was the pre-State Jewish society as egalitarian as people have been led to think by the socialist ideologies of politically influential people, the policies of the Histadrut and the impact of the kibbutz movement? The society was also influenced by the immigration of capital owners who built houses for rent, planted citrus groves, opened shops and established factories — and by the immigration of people owning human capital (doctors, lawyers, engineers, etc.). Furthermore, the competition of Arab laborers and Arab farmers depressed the wages of Jewish laborers and the incomes of Jewish farmers.

(2) Were socio-economic disparities different from those of the seventies? We are speaking of inequalities between communities, between occupations, between men and women, between the towns and villages.

(3) What was the influence of economic growth on socio-economic disparities? Does acceleration of economic growth necessarily result in higher inequality, or are other forces involved?

(4) The pre-State Arab sector had all the characteristics of a traditional society — low standard of living, high share of agriculture, extended family, etc. — while the Jewish sector showed features of a society developing along modern lines. How did these patterns of developments affect the socio-economic disparities in the two sectors?

(5) What was the influence of the business cycle before and after 1948?

(6) To what extent were the policies of the government, the national institutions and the Histadrut responsible for changes in inequality during the two periods?

When comparing post-1948 figures with our estimates for the Mandatory period, we have to be aware of the differences in the scales and methods used in compiling the data. Even during the relatively short period of 20 years, as we have seen, changes in the scopes and methods of the surveys have made comparisons difficult. The least-questionable pre-State data for comparison seem to be the 1930 census of Jewish wage and salary earners and the 1939 family expenditure survey of Jewish urban employees.

Income Distribution of Wage and Salary Earners

The 1930 census of Jewish employees seems to be comparable with the income data on Jewish employees from the 1972 census and from current income surveys.

The 1930 census was very comprehensive, and included agricultural workers. The data from the 1972 census and the income surveys relate only to urban employees — but those represented about 90% of all employees in Israel in the seventies.

Table 5.1
Income Distribution of Wage and Salary Earners
(in % by deciles)

Decile	*1930 Census of Jewish Employees* Monthly Income	*1972 Census of Jewish Urban Employees* Annual Income	*1972 Income Survey of Urban Employees* Annual Income	*Survey of Urban Employees* Monthly Income 1972	1975
1	2.6	1.4	1.3	2.6	3.0
2	4.3	3.2	2.9	4.8	4.6
3	5.6	5.1	6.0	6.3	6.3
4	6.7	6.8	6.8	7.5	7.3
5	7.6	8.1	7.5	8.7	8.6
6	8.8	9.5	9.2	9.7	9.8
7	10.2	10.9	12.0	10.8	11.2
8	12.1	13.3	13.3	12.5	12.8
9	14.8	16.6	16.4	15.1	14.8
10	27.3	25.1	24.6	22.0	21.6
Total	100.0	100.0	100.0	100.0	100.0
Gini Coefficient	0.340	0.362	0.358	0.289	0.284

Source: 1930 — Table 2.5; 1972 — Population Census, CBS Statistical Bulletin, Supplement No. 1, 1975; 1972, 1975 — Income Surveys, Special Publications No. 478 and 546.

There were no significant differences between the census and survey data, but the annual income distribution was more unequal than the monthly income distribution. This is contrary to the usual assumption that inequality is lower over a longer period[1] because it disregards short-term fluctuations. The assumption may hold when the income distribution of the longer period relates to the *same* population as the short-term income distribution. But in our case, the annual data and the monthly data come from different populations. The annual income distribution includes employees who worked any part of the year, while the monthly data include only those wage and salary earners who worked during the survey month.

The 1930 income distribution is based on earnings during the survey month; we compared it with the monthly income distributions of 1972 and 1975. Income dispersion was greater in 1930. If we take into account that agricultural workers were included in 1930 but not in 1972 and 1975, this reduces the difference. On the other hand, the 1972 and 1975 figures include Arabs — so it may be concluded that income inequality among Jewish wage and salary earners was somewhat greater in 1930 than in the seventies.

The figures also give some indication of income differences between men and women, and between the various occupations.

Table 5.2

Women's Earnings as a Percentage of Men's Earnings

	1930*	1972	1977
Monthly Earnings	49	65	61
Annual Earnings	. . .	60	58
Hourly Earnings	63**	75	79

*Monthly earnings of daily workers were calculated by multiplying daily earnings by 25; hourly earnings include only daily workers.

**In 1926, earnings of daily women workers were 66% of those of men.

Source: See Table 5.1.

There was less difference between men's and women's earnings in the seventies than in 1930 (Table 5.2). This may be explained by the greater educational and occupational progress of women over this period.

Wage differentials between blue and white collar workers were larger during the Mandatory period. In 1930, the monthly income of male daily wage earners was only about 65% of that of male monthly wage and salary earners; in 1975, the average monthly income of male workers in agriculture, industry, transport, construction and services was 72% of that of clerks, sales workers, administrators, managers, academic, scientific and other professional workers. However, these figures do not sufficiently indicate the decline in differentials. Z. Zussman[2] reported considerably higher wage differentials between skilled and unskilled workers in the Mandatory period compared with those after 1948, in spite of the Histadrut's explicit egalitarian policy; also, wage differentials among construction workers were larger at the beginning of the Mandatory period than in the years before the Second World War.

According to Zussman, three methods were used to realize the egalitarian ideology of the Histadrut: agricultural settlements on a strictly egalitarian basis (the kibbutzim); workers' communes; and equal wages (with family allowances) for those employed in Histadrut enterprises. Only the kibbutzim have remained as egalitarian cells (albeit with diminishing weight and considerable differences among themselves).

Workers' communes declined rapidly in importance during the Mandatory period. The various workers' and artisans' cooperatives now operating are far from the egalitarian concepts of those first days; they employ workers at market wages and salaries. As early as the thirties, the Histadrut had to pay professional salaries to attract physicians to the sick fund, higher wages and salaries to skilled workers and employees, and special allowances to some of the officials and elected officers.

The decline of wage differentials in the more advanced stages of development, is a generally observed phenomenon. In the early stages, the scarcity of skilled and professional workers and experts leads to a widening of wage differentials; in later stages, the rising supply of skilled and professional workers reduces wage differentials. The relative earnings of professional workers declined considerably in the United States and in Great Britain since the beginning of the century, as did the differentials between skilled and unskilled workers. The relative earnings of women factory workers also improved; their wages as a percentage of men's rose 2 to 11% in ten industrialized countries between 1963 and 1972.[3] In the latter year, the earnings of Israeli women workers in manufacturing (63% of men's wages) were higher than in Japan (48%), Ireland (57%) and the United Kingdom (59%); similar to those in Belgium (64%) and Switzerland (65%); but lower than in five European countries where they ranged from 71% to 83%.[4]

Inequality between Communities

C.O. Hirschman points out that tolerance of inequality is lower in a society composed of different ethnic groups than it is in an ethnically homogeneous society.[5] When most of the wealthy belong to a certain ethnic group, while most of the poor belong to other ethnic groups, social tensions are strengthened.

A society of immigrants from many countries — who bring with them the mentalities, the traditions, the customs and the cultural backgrounds of these countries — is more likely to develop social disparities. At the same time, it is less tolerant of differences in education, occupation and wealth, which lead to feelings of deprivation. The newcomer, who has to adapt himself and find his way in new surroundings, is easily convinced that discrimination of his ethnic group increases his difficulties. Such feelings of deprivation, when shared by veteran members of his group, may continue long after any objective basis has disappeared.

In Israel, two main groups of Jewish immigrants can be distinguished: those from European countries (Ashkenazi), and those from Asian and African countries (Orientals). Since most of the latter group lived in less-developed countries, their health, education and occupational structure were generally on lower levels than the European standards of the Ashkenazi groups. These differences were reflected in differences in the standard of living.

These differences were already apparent in the Mandatory period. The nutrition survey of 1930 shows that the average income of an Oriental family was about 70% of that of an Ashkenazi family, even though both belonged to the lower income groups and represented relatively large families (Appendix, Table 1A.5). The Oriental communities were overrepresented in this survey, in relation to their weight in the total Jewish population — but the survey seems to reflect their percentage within the population of large families in the lower income brackets. In the family survey of 1946, the average income of an Oriental family was 78% of that of an average Ashkenazi family. Because of the great difference in family size between the two groups, income per capita was only 54%.

Table 5.3 shows that income differences between these two main groups of Jews before and after the establishment of the State were quite similar, and that there was a considerable improvement in the seventies. This is even more striking when it is taken into account that the pre-State surveys investigated groups that were more economically homogeneous than those in the surveys of 1968/69, 1976 and 1975/76 (see Chapter 1), as reflected in the smaller differences in family size.

Table 5.3 also shows considerable differences in housing density. The substantial rise in the standard of living is reflected in the significant decline in housing density; however, the gap between the two communities did not change. The Orientals' housing density in the mid-seventies was similar to that of the Ashkenazim in the mid-sixties. Since crowded housing is an unfavorable situation for school children, the drastic decline in housing density should signify an important improvement in effective schooling. But a significant percentage of large families still lived in overcrowded conditions in 1976. Although only 3½% of Jewish families had three or more persons per room, 87% of these families consisted of six persons or more; 23% of families of six or more had three or more persons per room, compared with only one half percent of all other families.

The connection between income inequality and educational inequality has been shown by various studies in Israel[6] and elsewhere. Surveys made during

Table 5.3
Income and Housing Density in the Jewish Population by Communities

	Income per family	*Income per capita*	*Family Size*		*Housing density persons per room***	
	Oriental in % of Ashk.	Oriental in % of Ashk.	Ashk.	Orient.	Ashk.	Orient.
Nutrition Survey, 1930	70	65	5.0	5.4	2.5	3.5
Survey of Urban Families, 1946	78	54	4.3	6.3	2.7	4.5
Cons. Survey, Urban Employees' Families 1956/57*	73	47	3.4	5.3	2.1	3.2
Urban Family Survey 1968/69*	72	44	2.9	4.7	1.6	2.0
Income Survey, Urban Empl. Families, 1977*	81	55	3.2	4.8	1.0	1.6
Urban Family Survey 1975/76***	87	53	2.8	4.6		

*Community according to country of birth; in 1968/69, a family head who was born in Israel was classified according to his father's country of birth.
**1930 and 1946, from survey data; 1958, 1969 and 1976, for all Jewish families.
***Total income, including imputed income. For gross money income, family income of Oriental communities was 90% of that of Ashkenazis, and per capita income was 55%.

the Mandatory period lack information on the schooling of family heads, so occupation is their only indication of educational level. Z. Sussman[7] shows that the average salary of a secondary school teacher was about three times as high as the wages of an unskilled building worker during 1924-37, and a little more than twice as high in 1968. The salary of a university lecturer was five times as high as that of an unskilled building worker in 1937, and less than four times as high in 1965; the difference declined further in the seventies.

With the expansion of education and the growing supply of experts and skilled workers with high educational levels, the wage differentials between occupations requiring higher education and those that do not are declining. But educational differences were still one of the main causes of income differences in the seventies. Consequently, income differences between ethnic groups apparently stem to a great extent from educational differences. A general comparison shows that educational differences were even greater than income differences. In 1977, the average family income of an Asian or African-born family head who was an employee was 81% of that of a European-born family head, but his average years of schooling were only 75% of his counterpart's.[8]

Still, years of schooling explained only 26% of the income differences between family heads; number of weeks worked, occupation, age, sex and year of immigration added another 25% of explanation; country of origin added only about one per cent (see Chapter 6). This means that about half of the income differences stemmed from other factors such as personal talent, initiative, diligence, cultural and educational background, health and luck. It should also be noted that measurement of educational differences by number of years of schooling does not take into account the quality of education, and does not discern between those who graduated and those who did not.

The median primary school marks of pupils of Asian or African origin were 72% of those of European origin in 1957, and 82% in 1970.[9] This reflects considerable improvement, and shows that the number of years of schooling is only a partial indicator of the educational level.

G. Hanoch[10] found that country of origin explained only 3% of income differences between Ashkenazim and Orientals after education, age and year of immigration had been taken into account. Y. Peres[11] analyzed several studies to show that the income of an Oriental family was 80 to 98% of that of an Ashkenazi family after other factors were accounted for; the different results of the studies are explained by the different number of factors in each. S. Amir showed that average weekly earnings of male employees from Asian-African countries were in 1968/69 only 88% of those from European-American countries, after the influence of age, years of schooling, occupation and year of immigration had been taken into account.[12] It may be concluded that differences in the quality and effectiveness of education (which could not be taken into account in the above studies) may well account for remaining income differences.

The most important change in the structure of Israeli society after independence was the tremendous rise in the share of the Oriental communities in the Jewish population — from about 22% at the time of statehood to 53% in 1976. This increased the importance of the economic and social differences between the ethnic groups.

It is difficult to say whether the pre-State Jewish society was more unified in its mentality, its customs and its aspirations than it is today. Nevertheless, the political and quantitative weight of the Ashkenazim gave the pre-State society the appearance of greater homogeneity.

The mass immigration during the first three and a half years of statehood brought in people from every corner of the earth. They came with very different cultural backgrounds, and huge numbers of them had the customs and mentality of a traditional society. The process of modernization deeply affected great segments of these immigrants, especially the younger generation, during a relatively short period. Their health improved, their educational level rose, their way of life slowly changed, and their standard of living rose as they became more and more integrated into the economic and social life of the country. But, as we have seen, there remained considerable gaps in the standard of living, in housing and in education.

Because of the great influence of education on income, the standard of living and status, the educational gap is especially important. In 1976, the percentage of those with post-primary education was 71% among Ashkenazim, compared with 50% among Orientals. But the difference was much larger in regard to university education — 26% as against 7%. This relatively small percentage of Orientals with post-secondary schooling seems to be partly responsible for their relatively low share of important positions in the social, economic and political spheres. This may be partially due to the lower quality of some of the schools in the development towns and in some quarters of the towns with a high percentage of Orientals; however, the main cause appears to be mentality and aspirations of the home, in conjunction with the family's socio-economic situation.

The waiting period until the first substantial earnings after military service and a university education is quite long, and the difference in earnings is not strikingly large. Average annual earnings of male employees with 13 to 15 years of schooling were in 1976 only 14% higher than of those with 9 to 12 years, and the earnings of employees with 16 or more years were 37% higher. However, higher education is not only a condition for entry into certain occupations; increasingly, it is a stepping stone to important positions in all spheres of life. Though personal qualifications are decisive for any position of leadership or influence, the knowledge acquired through study and experience are becoming more and more necessary.

Educational capital per capita, which includes costs and foregone earnings, indicates educational differences between population groups better than do average years of schooling — since it reflects the different costs of the various grades of schooling. Hercovitz[13] shows that there was no substantial decline in educational differences between the communities in the Jewish population from 1961 to 1972 (Appendix, Table 5A.1).

Educational inequality between communities declined significantly in the lower age-groups from 1961 to 1972, by about one half in the 14-17 years group, and 13% in the 18-34 years group, but rose in the higher age groups. This indicates a future trend of declining inequality, since educational inequality was in 1971 already in the younger age groups lower than in the higher age groups. The decline in income inequality between the communities in 1975-1977 (Table 5.3) may be partly attributed to this trend.

Table 5A.2 (Appendix) compares the percentage of Oriental employees' family heads in various occupations in 1946 and 1974. Both years show a relatively low percentage in the highly paid occupations and a relatively high percentage in the less remunerative occupations. In spite of the more sophisticated classification in 1974, it is quite evident that the lower share of Oriental workers in the higher paid occupations was more conspicuous in 1946 than in 1974. Their percentage in the liberal professions was about half of their average share in 1974, but only about a quarter of their average share in 1946.

Regional Income Differences

Israel is a small country, and there are no substantial disparities in the standard of living among the regions. The various indicators (infant mortality rates, possession of durable goods, housing conditions) show small differences between urban and rural areas; there are, however, significant differences between the large towns and small veteran towns, on one hand, and the new towns on the other.

Income data reflect similar differences. The average income of Jewish families in 1968/69 and 1975/76 was lowest in the new towns. Interesting is the rise of the relative incomes of the inhabitants of Jerusalem over this period (Table 5.4).

Table 5.4
Urban Family Incomes by Type of Locality
(% of average)

	Average Monthly Gross Income of Jewish Families			
	1968/69		*1975/76*	
	Per family	Per person	Per family	Per person
Jerusalem	99	99	106	107
Tel Aviv	117	135	102	121
Haifa	109	122	104	120
Veteran Towns	102	104	104	106
New Towns	82	74	84	71
Average	100	100	100	100
Average IL	1,010	273	4,877	1,370

Source: Family Expenditure Surveys, 1968/69 and 1975/76.

Since reclamation of the soil and development of arid areas are major national objectives, the government directs new immigrants to rural and new development areas and discourages big urban agglomerations (which are undesirable for ecological reasons).

Small and middle-sized towns were established to serve as rural and regional centers, especially in new development areas. A considerable proportion of public housing has been erected in such towns, to provide people with an incentive for living there; priority has been given to constructing roads, schools, hospitals and other community facilities in these areas. Special conditions for investors — grants, loans on easy terms, and tax concessions — have helped to attract industries; similar inducements have been used to draw skilled manpower from among veteran residents.

The success of these towns depended on the development of industries and the quality of cultural facilities and social services. Other important factors were the extent to which they could attract veteran settlers able and willing to form part of the local community, and the evolvement of local leadership to promote social development and integration.

Because of the high share of new immigrants (especially from African and Asian countries) in new towns, the socio-economic differences between the development towns and other areas of the country parallel the differences between the two main Jewish ethnic groups. Thus, social and political tensions created by socio-economic differences between ethnic groups increased.

Since the development towns are a post-independence phenomenon, no such differences are found in the Mandatory period. However, the considerably lower income of Jewish families in Jerusalem than in other towns during the Mandate was partly due to the high percentage of Oriental Jews in Jerusalem (see Appendix, Table 1A.13).

Rural Urban Differences

In 1976, only 14% of the total Israeli population lived in rural localities. The Jewish population was preponderantly urban — only 9% lived in rural localities, compared to 25% during the Mandatory period. 39% of the Arabs lived in rural localities in 1976, compared to two-thirds during the Mandatory period.

The occupational structure of the rural population shows a high percentage of urban occupations — considerably higher than before the establishment of the State. Only 27% of the employed persons in the kibbutzim, 65% in the moshavim, 20% of the employed living in Jewish other villages and 27% in Arab villages were employed in agriculture in 1976. This reflects the gradual penetration of industrial and other branches into rural localities, and the increase in work outside the village, in nearby towns.

During the Mandatory period, rural incomes were 60-70% of urban incomes among Jews,[14] but about 25% among Arabs. This changed dramatically during World War II, as the prices of agricultural produce rose more than the general price level (see Chapter 1); rural incomes approached urban incomes among Jews and were about half of urban incomes among Arabs (Appendix, Table 1A.16).

Rural incomes were about 70% of urban incomes in most years after independence, and approached urban incomes in the mid-seventies. Differences between new immigrants and the veteran population were considerable in the rural areas, and persisted up to the present. For instance, in 1970 the average per-farm income in the new cooperative villages was only 62% of that of the veteran cooperative villages, and average income per standard adult was only 46% (since families were larger in the new settlements).[15]

With increased urbanization and the increase of urban occupations in the villages, differences between town and village became less important than the differences between the veteran towns and the new towns in development areas, and the differences between new and veteran agricultural settlements. These differences expressed themselves in all spheres of life: standard of living, consumption patterns, educational level, cultural and social activities and political involvement. The new towns, which were supposed to become the cultural and economic centers for the surrounding rural areas, could not compete with the old settlements or with the large cities a relatively short distance away. Thus, A. Berler came to the conclusion that "the classic urban-rural dichotomy loses most of its significance in Israel: the trend is toward an urban-rural continuum" and "the old-new dichotomy takes precedence over the urban-rural dichotomy."[16] In the new villages and towns, the majority of the population were new immigrants from African and Asian countries — so the old-new dichotomy was deepened by ethnic differences and feelings of deprivation.

A 1967 survey among 2000 families in three new towns and 40 new villages in the southern coastal plain examined urban-rural social relations, divergencies and common features.[17] No substantial economic or demographic differences between rural and urban populations were found, "both of which are typical of the new immigrant population in Israel". The proportion of European-born immigrants was somewhat higher in the towns (one-third as against 19% in the villages); the educational level was slightly higher; monthly family income was almost the same; but per capita income was 27% smaller in the villages, because of larger families. The main difference was in the occupational structure: two-thirds of the earners in the villages worked in agriculture, compared to 4% in the towns.

In 1977, persons employed in agriculture constituted only 6.8% of all employed,[18] compared to 9% in 1970 and 18% in 1955 (see Chapter 2). The share of agriculture in the net domestic product was 6.7% in 1977, so income per employed in agriculture was similar to the national average — while it had been only 73% of the national average in 1970, and 70% at the beginning of the sixties. This improvement stemmed mainly from the great improvement in production methods and the rise in efficiency. In spite of a decline in the relative prices of agricultural products and a deterioration in the terms of trade of agriculture[19] during 1965-1975, relative incomes in agriculture rose because of the great rise in productivity. In 1976 and 1977, output prices rose somewhat more than input prices, and relative prices of the net product in agriculture rose, raising product per employed to the national average.

However, average earnings of agricultural workers in 1976 were still considerably below the national average of wage and salary earners, though their relative earnings had risen. Net income per family farm in 1976 is estimated to have been higher than income per family of urban self-employed,[20] even if some under-reporting of the urban self-employed is taken into account.

Even though 1975/76 was especially profitable for farmers, the rise in their relative incomes seems to indicate a certain trend — since the income of the self-employed in agriculture in 1961/62 was only about 90% of that in other branches of the economy, according to income tax data. This trend is related to Israel's increasing agricultural exports to Europe, rising world agricultural prices, and the high efficiency of Israel's agriculture.

It is interesting that farm incomes have caught up with non-agricultural incomes in quite a few countries. In some agricultural exporting countries, income per employed in agriculture was above the national average in the sixties (Australia, Argentine, the Netherlands). West German farmers' incomes were above the national average in 1972, but were lower than that of the urban self-employed.[21]

As mentioned, there was no urban-rural division in the socio-economic sense in the seventies, but there was a significant difference between the veteran villages and the new villages founded by new immigrants. In agriculture, the age of a settlement is an important factor. In the Mandatory period, as well, incomes in newly founded cooperative and collective settlements were considerably lower than those in veteran settlements.

We should expect Jewish agriculture to involve relatively low income inequality, because of the cooperative system of the moshavim and the principle of equality in the kibbutzim.

There is income equality within each kibbutz, but there are income differences between the kibbutzim because of differences in location, age and structure (Appendix, Table 5A.3). Most settlements have undergone great changes in their economic structure, establishing various industries so that more than half of their incomes now come from manufacturing. But they are rural settlements, and agriculture still occupies an important position.

No trend appears in the income distribution data, but cyclical fluctuations had some influence. Inequality was higher in years of lower economic activity. Income inequality among the Kibbutzim in the seventies was similar to what it had been in the Mandatory period.

Income inequality was considerably greater among the moshavim than among the kibbutzim. There were differences between regions, and between veteran and new settlements, and there were great differences in efficiency and experience of the individual farmers (Appendix, Table 5A.4).

The income difference between new and veteran moshavim declined somewhat in the seventies. Average family income in the new moshavim was 62% of that in the veteran moshavim in 1969/70, and 65% in 1974/75. Income inequality in all moshavim appears to have changed very little over this period (according to the distribution of agricultural income).

The distribution of farmers by country of origin shows a preponderance from Asian and African countries in the new moshavim. 68% of the farmers in the veteran moshavim came from European countries, and only 15% from Asia and North Africa; 76% of the farmers in the new moshavim came from Asia and North Africa, and only 19% from Europe.

A comparison with the Mandatory period shows that income inequality rose considerably in the moshavim (Appendix, Table 1A.6). Also income inequality among the veteran farms was considerably greater in 1959 than in 1936. It seems that differences in efficiency increased with the passing of time. The employment of more hired labor and the addition of new immigrant villages were other important factors that increased the differences between individual farms and between moshavim.

We calculated income inequality in the Jewish rural population on the basis of the number of families in kibbutzim, moshavim and other villages in 1970, and the income distributions in moshavim and among kibbutzim. Income distribution in other villages was assumed to be similar to that in the urban population. The inequality index was 0.337 — i.e., 10% lower than in the urban population, but somewhat higher than our estimate for 1936, which was 0.317 (Table 1.4).

A family survey conducted in the southern coastal plain[21] gives income distribution in rural and urban families in 1967 for five income classes. The inequality was only about 2% lower among rural families (new moshavim) than among urban families (new towns). This corroborates our figures in which inequality in all moshavim was quite similar to that of the total urban population. The relatively low inequality of the kibbutzim caused the income inequality of the rural population to be lower than that of the urban population. However, income inequality of the total population was similar to that of the urban population, because of the income difference between town and village in 1969-1970.

The Changing Pattern of Income Distribution in the Arab Population

There was a dramatic change in the Arab population in Israel. Urbanization of the Arabs was quite rapid in the sixties and seventies. In 1961, about three-quarters of them still lived in rural localities; at the end of 1976, only 39% did so. Some of the larger villages lost their rural character, and there was continuing migration to the towns. The addition of East Jerusalem raised the share of the urban population considerably.

Urbanization was even more evident in the occupational structure. In 1955, almost half of employed Arabs were in agriculture; in 1976, only 16% were so employed. This reveals the high percentage of people living in rural localities and working in non-agricultural branches outside the village in factories, on construction sites and in service industries, or within the village in public and community services — which raised rural incomes. Half of all non-Jewish employed worked outside their locality of residence.

Thus, the large gap between urban and rural incomes which characterized the Mandatory period almost disappeared. In most rural families, members work in urban occupations and in nearby towns to complement family incomes and bring them up to the urban level. Furthermore, the Arab farmers adopted modern production methods which raised their incomes from agricultural work.

The only data available on income distribution are for urban families; the income distribution of rural families can only be estimated according to the data of the agricultural census. Table 5.5 shows the development of income distribution of urban Arab families.

Table 5.5
Income Distribution of Urban Arab Families
(% of Total Incomes)

Share in population	1944 *Estimate*	1968/69 *Family Expenditure Survey*	1972 *Employees' Families Census*
Lowest 40%	16.4	15.9	18.9
Middle 40%	35.9	41.8	38.5
Highest 20%	47.7	42.3	42.6
TOTAL	100.0	100.0	100.0
Gini Coefficient*	0.401	0.371	0.344

Source: 1944 — Table 1.6; 1968/69 Family Expenditure Survey; 1972 — based on data published in Supplement No. 1, Monthly Statistical Bulletin, 1975.
*Calculated by deciles.

A comparison of 1944 with 1968/69 shows a considerable decline in income inequality in the urban Arab population. The most important change is the rise in the income share of the middle 40%, which indicates the rise of the middle classes in Arab society — an important element in social and economic development. The income share of the highest 20% declined, while that of the lowest 40% remained quite similar to that of 1944. The 1972 figures show only income distribution of employees' families, which was more equal than that of the total urban population — since the self-employed and those not belonging to the labor force were not included. Net income data in 1975/76 indicate a further decline in inequality in the Arab population.

The degree of inequality was quite similar in the total urban population for both Arabs and Jews, but income distribution was more unequal among Arab employees' families than among Jewish employees' families.

We estimated income distribution of agricultural families on the basis of the 1970/71 census of agriculture, which gives data on persons employed outside the farm. The income distribution estimated on the basis of these figures shows that inequality in rural areas was somewhat lower than in the urban population, but that rural inequality was higher than in the Mandatory period. The level of rural incomes was almost equal to urban incomes, which greatly reduced income inequality in the total Arab population. According to our estimate, the income inequality index in the total Arab population in Israel was 0.37 (as compared to 0.52 in the Mandatory period), and declined further in 1975/76.

It has been maintained that a rising share of the urban population in developing countries raises income inequality, because such inequality is greater in urban areas due to the greater diversification of occupations and greater differentiation in educational levels.[23] But the main cause for the high income inequality among Arabs in the Mandatory period was the great gap between rural and urban incomes. The sharp reduction of this gap was the main factor in the decline of income inequality in the Arab sector (achieved by full employment in the Israeli economy and the full integration of the Arab sector into the economy). An important element in this development was the general rise in the Arabs' educational and health levels. The share of literate Arabs aged 14 and over rose from 25% at the end of the Mandatory period to 48% in 1961, 64% in 1972 and 77% in 1976 (90% among males); the average schooling of Arab employees was 7.2 years in 1974. The average life expectancy of Arabs, which had been about 50 at the end of the Mandatory period (Appendix, Table 1A.1), rose to about 70 in the seventies — approaching that of the Jews. The difference in the standard of living between the Arab and the Jewish population also declined substantially. In 1975/76, average family income of Arabs was 75% of that of Jews compared to 53% in 1936.

From the empirical evidence, we can conclude that urban employment opportunities are decisive in the development of income inequality during urbanization. When there is full employment, declining educational inequality and narrowing income differences between town and village, a decline in general income inequality may be expected. This happened in the Arab sector, in spite of the higher income inequality in the urban population compared to the rural population.

Income Distribution in the Total Population

The most comprehensive data on income distribution is to be found in the 1960/61 survey of taxpayers. This survey included the total population — urban and rural, Jewish and Arab. The problem is that the income unit was not the family or the household, but the family head and his wife; any additional earner in the family was counted as a separate income unit. The incomes of such "additional" earners constituted 6½% of total family incomes, and there were such additional earners (second earners who were not wives or third earners) in 15% of all families in 1968/69. Income distribution among a greater number of income units for the same population should show higher statistical inequality.[24]

The family surveys of 1968/69 and 1975/76 included only the urban population, but this accounted for 85% of the total population. We calculated income inequality in the total population by combining estimated income distribution in kibbutzim, moshavim and villages with the urban income distribution in 1968/69; the result was quite similar to the income distribution of the urban population. There was a considerable decline in inequality compared with the Mandatory period (Table 5.6).

The most important change is the rise in the income share of the lowest 40% of the population — especially when compared with income distribution after taxes, since there was no income tax in 1936. Of additional importance is the rise in the share of the middle classes, while the share of the highest income brackets declined considerably.

Of course, the great changes that happened have to be taken into account in any such comparison. One of the important changes was the transformation of the Jewish population from a minority into a majority within the bounds of Israel — a result of the large immigration waves of Jews after the establishment of the State, and of part of the Arabs leaving the area during the War of Liberation. The greater weight of the Jewish population determined the income distribution and the lower inequality of the total population in Israel to a decisive degree, compared to the Mandatory period. However, the decline in inequality in the Arab population also had some influence.

Table 5.6
Income Distribution of Total Population
(% of Total Incomes)

Share of Population	1936 *Estimate*	1960/61 *Tax Data* *Before Taxes*	*After Taxes*	1968/69 *Estimate* *Before Taxes*	*Urban Families* 1975/76 *Before Taxes*	*After Taxes*
Lowest 40%	11.0	16.2	17.9	16.3	18.0	20.0
Middle 40%	36.2	41.1	42.7	40.4	42.5	43.4
Highest 20%	52.8	42.7	39.4	43.3	39.5	36.6
Gini Coefficient	0.479	0.371	0.333	0.374	0.334	0.296

Source: Committee Report, 1966; Statistical Abstracts; Table 1.5; C.B.S.

The most important element was the integration of the Arab sector into the Israeli economy, which greatly furthered the modernization and urbanization of that sector. The improvement in education and health, and the changes in the occupational structure (and, consequently, in income inequality) were greatly influenced by developments in the Israeli economy and by its employment level.

The actual decline in inequality was greater than is reflected in Table 5.6; in addition to the changes in the tax system, the changes in the system of social benefits and services have to be taken into account. Inequality among Jews was about the same as in the Mandatory period (the inequality index was 0.324 in 1936), especially if income distribution net of taxes is compared — since income tax was not introduced until 1940. The decline in inequality in 1975/76 and the addition of the impact of social services point to an improvement in Israel for the Jews as well, compared to the Mandatory period.

NOTES

1. See A.B. Atkinson, *The Economics of Inequality*, p. 36.
2. Z. Zussman, *Wage Differentials and Equality Within the Histadrut*, Tel-Aviv, 1974 (Hebrew). According to his figures, the decline in the wage differentials between skilled and unskilled workers was very substantial — 28% in the building trade, and 70% in the metal industries.
3. See A. Atkinson, op. cit., p. 74/75.
4. "Equality of Opportunity and Treatment for Women Workers" I.L.O., Geneva 1974, p. 36.
5. C.O. Hirschman, op. cit. — see Introduction.
6. See Chapters 6 and 7.
7. Z. Zussman, op. cit., p. 23.
8. Income of Employees' Families, 1977, Statistical Monthly Bulletin No. 6, 1978. See also: Report of the Committee on Income Distribution and Social Inequality, p. 27. Median years of schooling of Asian or African-born family heads were 54% of those of European or American-born family heads in 1968/9, and gross family income was 71%. The difference in educational capital was even greater than that in years of schooling.
   In 1976, the relative income of the Asian or African born family head (employee) had improved and was 82%, and his relative educational level had risen.
9. Y. Peres, "Ethnic differences in Israel," *Megamot*, Jan. 1974.
10. G. Hanoch, *Income Differences in Israel*, Falk Institute, Report 5, Jerusalem, 1961.
11. Y. Peres, *Ethnic Relations in Israel*, Tel-Aviv, 1976 (Hebrew).
12. S. Amir, *Income from Work of Employees, 1968/69,* Falk Institute, Jerusalem, 1975.
13. Z. Hercovitz, op. cit.
14. Income per earner in agriculture was less than half that in other branches, but average family size was smaller in the villages than in the towns; furthermore, earners in other occupations have to be taken into account. Family income in villages was 69% of that in towns in the 1939 survey (Table 1.2).
15. *The Profitability of Family Farms in Israel, 1969/70.* Institute of Farm Income Research, Tel-Aviv, Jan. 1973.

16. A. Berler, "The Regional Structure" in: *Urban-Rural Relations in Israel.* Settlement Study Center, Rehovot, 1970.
17. Y. Ginsberg, "The Sample" in: *Urban-Rural Relations in Israel.* Rehovot, 1970.
18. Including workers from the administered territories, Annual Report 1977, Bank of Israel.
19. See Annual Report 1975, Bank of Israel, p. 256.
20. This estimate is based on the calculation of net income of farmers from agriculture (Annual Report 1976, Bank of Israel, p. 226) and the first results of the family survey 1975/76. The net income of farmers from agriculture in 1975/76 (Oct.-Sept.) was IL3,716 million — i.e., about IL66,000 per self-employed farmer. As 24% of the 56,000 self-employed farmers were women, net income per family farm is estimated at IL75,000-80,000. Gross money income of the urban self-employed family in 1975/76 (June-May) was IL61,750 or IL68,200 at the 10.5% higher prices of the agricultural year. In 1974/75, the average income of a Jewish farmer's family (moshavim and private farms) was IL58,500, or IL76,500 at 1975/76 prices, according to a study of the Institute of Farm Research (Nov. 1977). 42% of this income was from non-agricultural sources. It must be assumed that farmers' real incomes increased in 1975/76.
21. Deutsches Institut fuer Wirtschaftsforschung (DIW), *Economic Bulletin* No. 7, 1974.
22. Urban-Rural Relations, op. cit.
23. S. Kuznets, op. cit.
24. See the report of the Committee on Income Distribution, 1966, which distinguishes between statistical inequality when old parents and young sons and daughters are able to live in separate households due to the improvement in the level of living. This break-up of larger families into smaller household units may compensate, to some extent, for the different definition of income units.

PART II

INEQUALITY AND POVERTY IN ISRAEL — AN ANALYSIS

CHAPTER 6

FACTORS AFFECTING EARNINGS AND INCOME DIFFERENTIALS

We examined the data of the Survey of Family Expenditure 1968/69[1] for the major factors of income differentiation.

Factors of Inequality in Incomes

To measure inequality in the standard of living we should measure the dispersion of family income after its redistribution by taxes, subsidies, social payments and social services. The size of the families and the property owned by them should also be taken into consideration.[2]

Three types of income can be discerned: income from work, income from property, and income from transfer payments such as pensions and social welfare payments. The differences in income from transfer payments stem from the social and institutional system — arrangements for pensions, insurance companies, the social security system, social welfare services, and so forth. Income from property depends on differences in wealth. Wealth is derived from two sources; it may be inherited, and it may be accumulated during the family's lifetime. In the latter instance, differences are due to several factors: the age of the family's head, which expresses the length of time during which wealth has been accumulated; how much the family saves out of its income from work or property, which in turn is affected by the level of its income, family size, consumption habits, and so forth.

Income from work, and to a certain extent from pensions and property, is connected with the characteristics of the earners. Hence, the following factors are of importance in the creation of income differentials between families:

a. household size and composition;
b. the number of gainfully employed in the family;
c. the number of days they work during the year;
d. their personal characteristics:
    1. age (representing work experience);
    2. sex;
    3. state of health;

4. education;
5. occupation;
6. employment status;
7. natural capability (intelligence, talents, initiative, human relations);
8. social, cultural and educational background (parents' education and profession, living conditions in the parents' home);
9. country of origin;
10. length of stay in Israel;

e. family property;
f. the proportion of income saved.

Personal characteristics are interrelated. Different professions require different education and training, so that income differentials due to profession are also connected with differences in educational achievement. Differences in natural capability also appear partly as differences in education — but only partly, since the ability to study is not identical with that of utilizing knowledge for profit. Initiative and the ability to take reasonable risks again differ from the ability to learn. The educational level also expresses, to a certain extent, the cultural and educational background and social conditions in the parents' home.

Two methods were used in examining the data of the survey:

1. Incomes were compared for different population groups, such as age groups and educational categories, in order to demonstrate these factors' effects;

2. Stepwise multiple regression analysis was applied, in which one variable after another was included in the regression. Consequently, the contribution of all variables and the interaction between them could be examined; their order of appearance, together with the size of the coefficients and their significance, made it possible to make certain assumptions on the contribution of each individual variable.

Age

Income usually is relatively low when people are young — when they first begin to work — because they lack experience and practical knowhow. Sometimes the young man works only part-time, since he still devotes some of his time to vocational or academic studies. In the course of his employment he gains experience (on-the-job training), the rate and effectiveness of his work increase, and he may fill more responsible positions. Thus, income from work goes up.[3] There is also advancement in position and seniority due entirely to advancing age. Income increases with age to a varying degree in the different professions and places of work; this also differs if the individual is self-employed or becomes an entrepreneur who employs others. Income reaches a peak at a certain age, which again differs for the various professions and grades; after this, it declines while work effectiveness goes down because of various reasons.

Requirements also change with age. When the young man first establishes his family, he must provide lodging and furnishings — and then whatever his children need, including their education. At a later age, when the children have grown up and leave home to provide for themselves, his requirements contract. This constitutes a life cycle of income and requirements; the proportion of savings also changes with the ratio of needs to income. Total income throughout the entire life cycle can be computed by various methods in order to compare lifetime income in different professions and to figure how worthwhile investment in education is.[4]

It may be asked, to what extent age-income differences are part of social inequality, since each person experiences these income differences during his life cycle. M. Paglin[5] proposed an inequality index net of age-income differences, on the basis of life-time equality. However, the question arises, whether inequality between age groups at the same point in time can be disregarded.

Income differences between age groups may be of important social significance, when a considerable part of the old are poor, as this is the case in Israel. Each age group has its own life-cycle because of the rapidly changing conditions of modern societies: the rise of real incomes and of the educational level and the increase in occupational differentiation.

Hence, age-income differentials are one component of the general inequality in incomes. Though inequality due to age is relatively small, its part in total inequality is by no means negligible. Table 6A.1 (Appendix) shows income differentials by age groups. (See also Table 4.3.)

Income reaches a peak at ages 45 to 55, and then begins to decline. The lowest income is reported for the highest age group, 65+, when it is less than half of its peak. Income inequality due to age can be deducted from general inequality by computing the inequality index within each age group. Up to age 24, the index of income inequality for all families was 0.289; and in the age group 25-34, it was 0.288 (computed on the basis of ten income groups). These indices were 23% smaller than general inequality, for which the index was 0.373.

The Effects of Education

Income inequality by educational groups is greater than that by age groups (Appendix, Table 6A.2). However, income inequality within any educational group also was relatively high. For instance, among families whose head had between five and eight years of schooling, the inequality index was 0.311; in the group with 9 to 12 years of schooling the index stood at 0.329 (based on ten income groups) — only 12% and 17% less, respectively, than the general inequality index.

This classification by groups according to years of schooling indicates only superficially the differences in education. No distinction is made between those who merely attended school a certain number of years and those who graduated; the only fact is the number of years an individual visited school — 0-4, 5-8, and so forth.[6] There also are no data on the quality of the education or on actual achievement.

Education also varies with age. It may be assumed that among older people there are fewer graduates, while among younger ones more have completed at least elementary school — because compulsory education laws were enacted only during recent decades. Modern education usually constitutes more effective preparation for activity in a modern economy.

Classification of heads of families by both age and schooling shows that attendance at secondary schools and academic institutions was greater among the younger groups. In the 65+ age group, 37% attended school no more than four years — compared with 7% of the 25-34 age group. On the other hand, among those above the age of 65, only 21% had 9-12 years of schooling; for those aged 25-34, the corresponding percentage was 38%. These data reflect the expansion of education during the last twenty years (see chapter 2).

Graphs 1 and 2 in Figure 6.1 represent cash income per family in the entire population and among wage and salary earners, by age and years of schooling of the family head; Graph 3 represents the earnings from work of family heads among wage and salary earners. The graphs demonstrate that in the different educational groups, income rises from a fairly low level in youth to a peak for the 45-55 age group, and then declines. The correlation between the family head's years of schooling and income is very clear in these graphs. Family income rises with the amount of schooling within each age group. In the categories with more schooling, the income curve, by age, goes higher and is steeper, while in those with less schooling (0-4 years of schooling) it is lower and relatively flatter. In this educational group, family income also reaches its peak earlier (35-45), and income from the family head's work peaks at age 25-35. In other countries peak income from physical labor also is found in younger age groups, since work experience starts at an earlier age, while income from more sophisticated work (where experience gained in the course of work is more important) peaks at a higher age.[7]

The rise of income with age reflects on-the-job training, which enhances speed and efficiency. The value of experience varies with the individual's personal characteristics, and with his profession and the amount of formal education.

The fact that income increases more rapidly with age for the groups with more schooling (9-12 and 13+ years) probably reflects the higher value of work experience. To a certain extent this rapid rise in the highest educational group (13+ years of schooling) also reflects the relatively small income at an earlier age, because of part-time and non-professional employment while

GRAPH 1

Average monthly cash income for all families

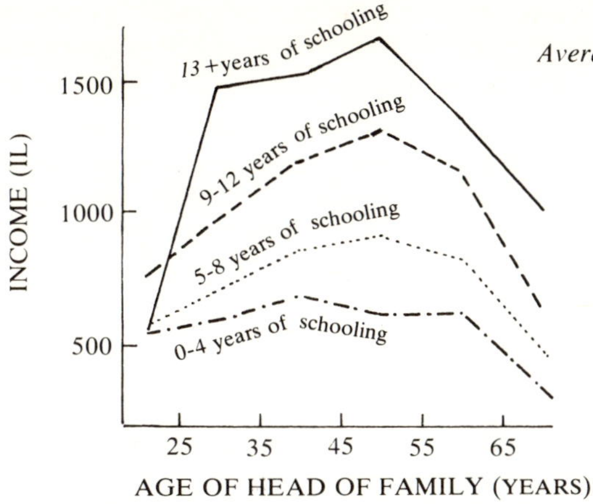

GRAPH 2

Average monthly cash income for families of wage and salary earners

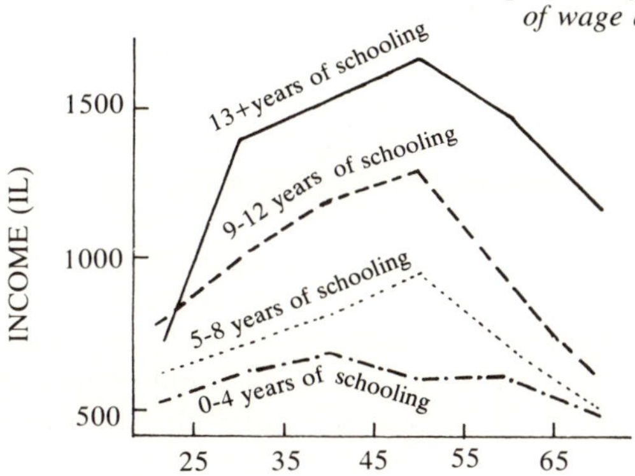

GRAPH 3

Average monthly cash income from work of wage and salary earner head of family

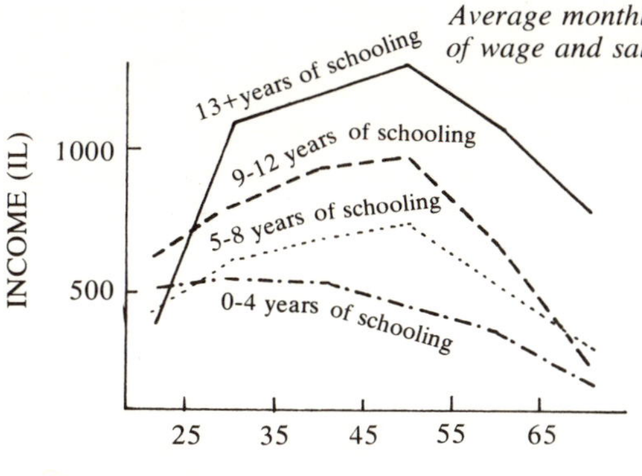

Figure 6.1

studying.[8] In this educational group the family head's income from work in the youngest age group (up to 25) is the lowest of all educational groups (see Graph 3), and even in terms of family income it is below that of the next educational group.

Marginal income derived from greater work experience gradually declines, as shown in Graph 3, where the curve for every educational group gradually flattens out until the rise stops. At times, experience becomes a disadvantage if it prevents people from learning new methods; this is more likely to happen in the higher age groups, where people are set in their ways. Of course, the point at which income peaks should not be considered identical with that at which experience ceases to confer benefits, since other factors also affect the rise (and later the decline) of income, especially hours and weeks of work.

The economic value of education as brought out by earnings differentials by educational level has been calculated as rate of return to investment in education — in Israel and elsewhere (see also chapters 3 and 4). Blaug[9] tries to summarize the various explanations of this phenomenon — the economic, the sociological and the psychological explanation, by emphasizing that education teaches not only specific skills, but "imparts also certain social and communication skills" which make people more productive. Primary education inculcates punctuality, and respect for authority as well as the ability to work to standards, and secondary and higher education enables people to shoulder responsibilities, to make decisions, and to develop initiatives.[9]

Factors which cause income to go up with advancing age are the following: 1. seniority pay, which gives higher income as experience increases, and which is also paid when additional experience no longer confers any benefit (or even impedes progress); 2. overtime or additional work, which often is related to the greater needs at a relatively young age, when families are established; at a certain age, these requirements decrease, as does also the physical ability to work very many hours; 3. income from additional earners in the family. Apparently, the wife's work increases family income mostly between the ages of 35 and 55; after that, the income of children may modify the decline, as demonstrated in Figure 6.1 by a comparison of Graph 2 (wage and salary earner families' income) with Graph 3 (income from work of the heads of wage and salary earner families); 4. professional progress, such as advances in grade, a move to more profitable work or the opening of an independent business. These fundamental changes often lead to substantially increased income; they usually occur at ages 24-45, reflecting experience gained, better utilization of personal qualifications, and occasionally additional education. In such instances, the family head may move from one educational category to another.

Graphs 1 to 3 represent gross income before tax deductions. Because of the progressiveness of income tax, any representation of net income would be flatter, and the differences between the educational groups would also be smaller.

The comparison of data on the family income of the entire population, as shown in Graph 1, with those of the wage earning population (Graph 2) shows that income rises more steeply at an early age and declines more rapidly at an advanced age in the group with the most schooling (13+ years) in the total population, than is the case among the same group of wage and salary earners alone. On the other hand, in the next educational category (9-12 years of schooling) the decline is slower among the entire population.

Extremely interesting are the differences between the income from work of family heads and the total family income among wage and salary earners (Graphs 2 and 3). The distances between the curves (educational groups) are smaller and the decline after age 65 is steeper in regard to income from the head of family's work than in regard to total family income. From this one may conclude that the earnings of additional members of the family and income from property increase the differentials between educational categories, but reduce somewhat the differentials connected with age. This conclusion holds not only for wage and salary earners, but for the entire population. Thus, it was found that a greater percentage of wives work in the higher income brackets than in the lower ones. Among all families, 23% of wives were gainfully employed, but only 2½% of those in the lowest income decile; on the other hand, in the highest decile 57% of all wives were employed.

Lifetime Income

Does an income curve, by age, represent the curve of family income — or of that by the family head — throughout his lifetime? A curve of this kind represents the income of all family heads of a certain educational category, by age groups, at a certain point in time; in other words, it represents lifetime income only if we assume that the general income level does not change during the lifetime of such a family head. Naturally, such an assumption is unacceptable in a dynamic economy, where the per capita product constantly increases.

Table 6.1 presents the computation of a family's income, assuming that it is headed by a person with 9 to 12 years of schooling, and that certain other assumptions apply. Column 2 of this table shows the family's monthly income when its head belongs to the different age groups, on the basis of the 1968/69 Survey data, which also are represented by the third curve from the bottom in Graph 1. Column 3 indicates in which years the family's head — who was between 35 and 44 years old in 1968/69 — belongs to the different age groups. The index in Column 4 represents the development of the per capita product, in real terms, between 1948/49 and 1968/69, and its expected development until 1998/99, on the basis of a 4% annual rise.

On the assumption that incomes increase in line with the rise in per capita product, family income on the basis of the Survey's data for age and educational brackets will rise very sharply — by a factor of 10 — between 1948/49 and 1988/89; of this rise, an increase by a factor of 5.7 is due to the increase in real per capita product, and the remainder to the rise in income over time (work experience, etc.) as revealed in income by age groups. In 1988/89, the family's head will be in age group 55-64. During the following ten years, income will go down to a relatively small degree (Column 5).

However, in such a calculation one must also take into consideration that part of the increase in the national product was due to the general rise in educational levels during the last twenty years; in other words, the same educational level, say 9-12 years of schooling, assured a family a higher rung on the income scale twenty years ago than now, because at that time there was a smaller supply of people with such educational background. The change in the population's composition, by educational categories, must also be taken into consideration for the future, together with expected changes in demand for people with various degrees of education and training. Because of this, Column 7 computes family income on the assumption that the supply of any

Table 6.1
Estimated Cash Income over Fifty Years, of Families Headed by Persons with 9-12 Years of Schooling

Age of family head	Average monthly cash income per family 1968/69	Year	Estimated monthly cash income, per family in terms of 1968/69 prices: Income based on development of per capita product		Assuming changes in supply and demand of education	
			Index	IL	Coefficient of change	IL
(1)	(2)	(3)	(4)	(2)x(4)=(5)	(6)	(5)x(6)=(7)
up to 24	753	1948/49	38	268	1.2	330
25-34	968	58/59	61	592	1.1	670
35-44	1,185	68/69	100	1,185	1.0	1,185
45-54	1,297	78/79	148	1,920	0.9	1,730
55-64	1,148	88/89	219	2,514	0.8	2,010
65+	618	98/99	324	2,002	0.8	1,600

Source:see Appendix, Table 6A.1.
Per capita product: *Statistical Yearbook*, 1971.

given standard of schooling increases more than demand, reducing family income by some 10% every decade, except for the last one.

On these assumptions, lifetime income is likely to yield a curve radically different from that which describes the income of different age groups in any one year. It will show a much more rapid increase from youth until the age when income is at a peak; and this peak comes later, followed by a relatively modest decline, thanks to the expectation of constantly rising incomes in general.

Income Inequality in Homogeneous Groups

The great influence exerted by age and education on income inequality also becomes clear from an examination of groups more or less homogeneous in these two factors. Within groups of families whose heads are members of the same age category and who have had similar years of schooling, income differentials are considerably smaller than among all families. The heads of 9% of all families were aged 35-44 and had attended school between 5 and 8 years. The inequality index for the income of these families was 0.236, or 37% smaller than for all families (0.373). Among the wage and salary earners in this homogeneous group, the index was only 0.204, or 35% below that for all wage and salary earner families. The index for the head of wage and salary earner families' income from work was only 0.157 for this homogeneous group. It is reduced even further, to 0.147, if inequalities due to differences in the number of days worked during the year are eliminated: this is 38% less than the inequality index for all wage and salary earners who worked at least 43 weeks a year. Similar comparisons for another educational category (9-12 years of schooling) yielded similar results. Appendix, Table 6A.3 presents the inequality indices for homogeneous groups.

The greatest degree of inequality is to be found in the lowest educational category. For the other educational groups, a certain similarity of inequality indices is observed, although its variation for the different age groups within each educational bracket shows some differences.

These indices reflect a situation which includes still some inequality due to differences in education. As was pointed out above, these categories by the number of years of schooling do not allow for differentiation between those who graduated from an institution and those who merely visited it, and it does not make any allowance for differences in the quality of teaching and the marks gained. It can be assumed that the availability of such data would make it possible to create homogeneous groups with smaller differentiation in the family heads' income from work.

The argument may be advanced that educational differences are connected with other differences, such as the cultural and educational background of the family head's parents' home, and his inborn abilities. Aside from that, whatever inequality remains in family income is due to the number of its members who are gainfully employed, its property, and the family head's personal characteristics such as IQ, industriousness, health, talents, personal relations and luck — a factor which must not be ignored in its effect on the choice of profession and other decisions.

The effects of age and education on income distribution have been represented by the curves that show incomes by age and educational categories of family heads (Figure 6.1). Reduced inequality in homogeneous groups makes it possible to make certain quantitative estimates of the effect of these factors. In groups homogeneous in terms of age and education, the index of inequality of family income was 20% to 37% below that of the entire population. This method enabled us to take into consideration only these two factors, and — as has been explained — available data did not make it possible to allow for differences in educational achievement due to graduation, specialization, and so forth.

The technique of multiple regression makes it possible to examine additional factors such as occupation, land of origin, length of stay in Israel, and so forth, in addition to the family head's age and length of schooling. However, this method, primarily measures differences in income linked with different factors in regard to all families (not only of those belonging to certain groups). The final result yields a formula which makes it possible to compute family income on the basis of the variables included in the formula; however, the determination of income by the variables is given in conclusion for all the variables together, as a general explanation.[10]

Multiple Regression Analysis

The first analysis was prepared in order to explain the dependent variable in this instance, the earnings of the wage earner head of family; this was followed with analyses of total family income, and of net and gross cash family income of the total population, wage earners and self-employed.[11] The independent (explanatory) variables were the following characteristics of the head of the family: age; number of years of schooling; sex; profession; the year he immigrated to Israel and continent of origin; number of weeks employed during the year; interaction of profession and years of schooling; interaction of profession and age; interaction of age and years of schooling.

The Family Head's Earnings

Earnings of the family head constituted 78% of the cash income of wage and salary earner families, so that it is important to investigate the determining factors. This income, more than any other, depends to a great extent on the family head's personal characteristics.

Table 6A.4 (Appendix) presents the results of regressions in which the dependent variable is income from work of the wage earning family head (or his income per week of work), and the explanatory variables are his personal characteristics. In all four regressions in this table, the strong influence of the family head's education on his income from work is outstanding. If one adds on-the-job training, as reflected in age and in interaction between the number of years of schooling and profession, and between age and profession, it will be found that formal education and on-the-job training together explain about 40% of the earnings differentials.

In the first regression, years of schooling of the family head as primary factor can explain 26½% of income from work. Its regression coefficient is significant and considerable; each year of schooling adds IL 49 (or 6%) to monthly income. The second factor is the number of weeks worked by the family head, which adds 9% to the explanation; this is followed by the interaction of years of schooling and profession,[12] which adds 7%, and with age, which adds 5% more. Age in parabolic form with a negative coefficient clarifies the influence of this factor: income goes up until age 45, and then declines. The sex of the family head adds 2% of explanation, with a considerable positive coefficient for the male family head; continent of origin, combined with length of residence in Israel, adds another 1% of explanation, showing this factor to be of relatively small importance.[13] The explanation provided by these variables adds up to 51%, so that about one half of the income differentials of wage earners must be ascribed to other factors which are not included in the above statistical information — such as personal ability, initiative, industriousness, health and luck.

Regression 2 takes for its dependent variable the wage earning family head's income per week of work, so that the number of weeks worked during the year becomes unimportant. The explanatory power of all other variables becomes slightly greater than in Regression 1. Education again is the most important factor, with an explanatory power of 28.5%, and age adds 5.5%, so that age and education together explain 34%.

These results parallel the data in Appendix, Table 6A.3, which show that inequality is smaller in groups homogeneous in terms of age and education. The wage earning family head's income per week of work yielded an inequality index between 14 and 40% smaller in homogeneous age and educational groups than among all wage earners. In our regression, age and the number of years of schooling appear not as groups but in a continuous manner, making it possible to measure more accurately the effect of these two factors on the income of all wage earning family heads per week of work. The stepwise regression also emphasizes the fact that education is a more important factor than age and all other factors. Age appears only seventh or eighth, after the interaction of years of schooling and profession, and after the family head's sex.

Regressions 3 and 4 take for their dependent variables the logarithm of income from work, and of the wage earning family head's income from a week's work; its independent variables are the same as before. The results show a higher degree of explanation for the logarithm than for income itself; in other words, the explanatory variables in the regressions exerted greater influence on the *relative* differences between incomes than on the absolute differences. In Regression 3, where the dependent variable is the logarithm of income from work, the most important factor is the amount of time worked by the head of the family, which explains one-fourth of the relative differences; education is the second factor, which adds 19% of explanation, out of a total of 63%. Regression 4, in which the dependent variable is the logarithm of income per week of work, shows education to be the first factor, with 25% of explanation, and the total explanation adds up to 52%.[14]

The great weight of the length of time worked in income differentials from work (Regressions 1 and 3) points to the importance of a full employment policy in this context. Practical experience leads to the same conclusion: income inequality increased during recession and declined during the subsequent period of full employment (see Chapter 2).

Among the explanations of relative differentials appears the combination of occupation and age (and not occupation and education, as was the case in regard to the absolute differentials). Sex offers a greater degree of explanation for relative differences (4 and 6%, respectively). Again, the effects of country of origin and length of stay in Israel are extremely small.

It appears that this is due to the fact that the income differentials between the various categories according to continent of origin and length of residence in Israel parallel those connected with the amount of education of the family head.[15] Because of this, an examination is in order as to what extent there is a positive correlation between the family head's education and his continent of origin and length of residence in Israel.

Table 6A.5 (Appendix) shows that differences between incomes of persons of Asian and African origin and of those born in Israel are smaller than the differences in their education. This can be seen very well when comparing veterans from Asian and African countries with native-born Israelis: They have a slightly higher income though they have a lower level of education. Veterans from Europe and America also exceed native Israelis to a greater extent in terms of income than of education; on the other hand, new arrivals from European and American countries have more education than those born in Israel, but their income is lower as brought out by the correlations. The comparison of the two origin groups — Asia-Africa and Europe-America — also shows that the differences between them are greater in terms of education than of income.

This helps to explain the small importance of origin and length of residence in Israel as explanatory factors of income differentials, since these factors already found their expression in the differences in education.

In various regression analyses prepared in the United States and Great Britain concerning income from work of wage earning males, the percentage of explanation arrived at was similar to that found above.

In his exhaustive study, Mincer[16] reports that Adams[17] found a coefficient of determination of 43% when he analyzed the 1949 income from work of white males, on the basis of a Michigan survey. Explanatory factors included, in addition to education and the parabolic age variable, geographic area, size of town, work status and profession. Mincer quotes a smilar result obtained by Hill in his analysis of wages earned by men employed full time in Great Britain in 1953. Hill's variables included age, profession, area and branch of industry. Morgan explains 34% of wage differentials of heads of families in the 1959 Michigan survey in regressions using as variables age, education, profession, size of town, geographic mobility, and work status. Morgan also used an index of motivation and ability.[18]

Mincer reports that Giora Hanoch, using data of that same survey, obtained similar percentages of explanation of men's annual income in the United States in 1959 with the variables of education, age, race, place of residence, number of weeks worked, family size and branch of industry.

NOTES

1. Conducted by the Central Bureau of Statistics. Survey data were collected from 2,400 urban families, each of which was investigated during an entire month between September 1968 and August 1969, and each of which reported annual income.
2. See Introduction.
3. On the effect of on-the-job training, see Gary S. Becker, *Human Capital*, Columbia University Press, New York, 1964. Mincer Jacob, *Schooling, Experience and Earnings*, NBER, New York, 1974.
4. See H.P. Miller, *Rich Man, Poor Man*, New York, 1971. For a study on investment in education in Israel see R. Klinov-Malul, *Profitability of Investment in Education*, Falk Institute, 1966.
5. M. Paglin, "The Measurement and Trend of Inequality: A Basic Revision", *American Economic Review*, Sept. 1975.
6. In regression analysis we used years of schooling in a continuous manner, so that these computations represent the effect of schooling in a more complete manner.
7. J. Mincer maintains that experience rather than age is the dominant factor in earnings. He measured years of work experience by subtracting the age of completion of schooling from reported age. Mincer Jacob, op. cit.
8. This loss of income is considered part of the investment in education, in addition to tuition, the cost of books, and so forth.
9. M. Blaug, *Education and the Employment Problem in Developing Countries*, I.L.O., Geneva, 1973.
10. In the attempt to measure the influence on income of each variable by itself, stepwise regression was employed. In step one, the independent variable appears which offers the greatest degree of explanation concerning the variable to be explained, that is, family income. The second step adds the variable which is second in importance as an explanation, and which offers additional explanation after the first factor has been taken into consideration, and so forth. In this manner, an overall explanation is obtained for all available variables which can significantly explain income differentials.
    The order in which variables are introduced depends on the size of their correlation with the dependent variable (which is to be explained). Naturally, in most cases the variable with the greatest influence should not be thought to offer by itself the entire explanation as revealed in the first step of the regression, since it also includes correlations with other variables.
11. For results of these analyses see Chapter 7.

12. In the method of dummy variables, the free professions were chosen as reference group. Regression 1 shows four other professions with a negative coefficient in regard to their interaction with the number of years of schooling; in other words, in these professions the income of family heads from work was smaller, compared with members of the free professions with the same amount of schooling. The size of this negative coefficient shows the difference between each of these professions and the "free professions", to be multiplied by the number of years of schooling of the family head. This negative coefficient is greater for industrial employees than for managerial and clerical workers, and even greater for those engaged in commerce; greatest of all is that for agricultural and common laborers.
13. In this regression of ten steps those family heads who had come to Israel from Europe and America before 1948, appeared with a positive coefficient of 130, compared with Jewish native-born Israelis as reference group. In other words, monthly income from work of old time residents born in Europe and America was IL130 above that of native-born Israelis, after taking into consideration six variables that appeared earlier in the regression. However, this difference explains only 1% of all the differentials in income from work of family heads. Regression coefficients in standard form (beta coefficients) show the relatively low influence of country of origin and years of immigration on income (see Chapter 7).
14. A precise comparison of R^2 (explanatory power) according to both methods would necessitate the transformation of the values computed in the logarithmic regression to antilogs, and the computation of R^2 for these antilogs; this was not done in this case.
15. For income differences and educational differences see also Tables 5.3 and 5.4 and Appendix, Table 5A.1.
16. Jacob Mincer, *The Distribution of Labor Incomes: A Survey with Special Reference to the Human Capital Approach*, Journal of Economic Literature, Vol. 8, March 1970.
17. This should be compared with Regression 2 (income from a week's work of wage earning heads of family), which explains a total of 46%. If the factor of sex is eliminated — Adams only analyzed the income of males — then Regression 2 also is found to explain 43%.
18. J.N. Morgan, "The Anatomy of Income Distributions", *Review of Economics and Statistics*, Aug. 1962.

CHAPTER 7

DETERMINANTS OF FAMILY INCOME

Introduction

It was evident from the analysis of family income that one of the most important factors accounting for income differences was the different character, composition and size of families; consequently, the main purpose of this chapter is to analyze determinants of family income by different family groups. The families were divided into two major groups: (1) regular families — i.e., husband and wife, with and without children and other dependents, and (2) one-parent families and independent individuals. The husband-wife families were divided into families with and without working wives (because of the importance of the wife's work to family income) and by the employment status of the husband (who was considered to be the family head). One-parent families and independent individuals were divided into male-headed and female-headed families.

Composition of Family Income

The composition of family income is shown in Appendix, Table 7A.1.

The family head's income from work made the largest contribution; it represented 64% of total family income, and 70% of the income of employees' and self-employed families. Families whose heads did not belong to the labor force had no such income; their income was less than half the average family income, and about two-fifths of the income of families whose heads were economically active. Hence, families whose heads did not belong to the labor force were concentrated largely in the lower income brackets. Major sources of income of these families were pensions, allowances and supports, which represented about half their income and 60% of their cash income — whereas these sources contributed only 8% of average total family income.

The family head's wife's income from work contributed 10% of average family income, similar to the share of imputed income from the use of owned dwellings and cars. Since the family head's wife worked in only part of the families, her income from work made a much larger contribution to the income of these families — approximately 30%. The fact that the wife worked was therefore an important element in income differentials. Income from the work of the other family members contributed only 7% of family income — but as much as 17% in families whose heads did not belong to the labor force.

Income from work constituted 80% of total family income and 90% of family cash income.[1] It may therefore be expected that family income is largely determined by the characteristics of the family's working members — their capabilities, education, training and occupational specialization — and, first and foremost, whether the family head or other family members are economically active. The income of families whose heads did not belong to the labor force (constituting 19% of all families) was about 48% of average income; but in families without any earner (about 14% of all families), income was only about one-third of the average.

Examination of Incomes in All Families

In an examination of family incomes by stepwise multiple regression, the influence of the following variables on family income was investigated: number of earners in the family; family size and number of children; dwelling locality; characteristics of the family head and his wife: age, years of schooling, occupation, interactions of these three variables, weeks worked during the year, country of origin and year of immigration.

In regressions on incomes of all families (including individuals and one-parent families), the main explanatory variables were educational level, number of earners in the family and interactions of age and education with occupation. The surprising result was the high explanatory power of the wife's educational level, explaining 21% out of a total explanation of 41% for total family income[2] (Appendix, Table 7A.3, regression 1).

The family head's education appeared only at the sixth step, and at the fourth step in interaction with occupation, adding 2% of explanation. Each year of schooling of the family head added IL 21 or 2% to monthly total family income, but that of the wife added IL 29 or 3% in the regression presented (11 steps). For relative income differentials (logarithm of total family income), similar results were obtained (regression 2), with an explanation of 62%.

Since income from work was the main component of family income, labor force participation and duration of work were expected to have an important impact on income differences. The number of earners in the family appeared at the second step with an additional explanatory power of 8% (regression 1).

One of the problems of multiple regression analysis is evaluating the separate effects of each explanatory variable. Because of the intercorrelations between the explanatory variables, their order of appearance in the stepwise regression and the additional explanatory power of each gives only a superficial indication of the importance of each variable in influencing income. The regression coefficient of each explanatory variable expresses the extent of its influence on income. Because the size of the regression coefficients varies with the units in which each variable is stated, it lacks a basis of comparison. These coefficients can be made comparable by using the beta coefficient, which expresses the coefficients in terms of the standard deviation of each variable.[3]

Table 7.1 shows the beta coefficients and the explanatory power of the variables. The beta coefficients indicate that labor force participation and duration of work were more important than the other variables.

Table 7.1

Beta Coefficients and Percentage Explained – All Families

Dependent Variable:	*Total Family Income*		*Log Total Family Income*	
Regression No.	1		2	
Independent Variables	*beta coeff.*	*% explained*	*beta coeff.*	*% explained*
Weeks worked, family head	0.314	0.45	0.489	3.78
Age x head not in labor force	0.270	1.10	0.405	1.02
No. of earners	0.218	7.82	0.318	16.73
Schooling of wife	0.183	21.45	0.210	30.34
Age x liberal professions, head	0.178	3.94	...	...
Schooling of head	0.122	0.52	0.272	4.74
Eur.-Am., Veteran, head	0.107	1.09	0.154	1.37
Family size	0.079	0.36	0.126	1.59
R^2 (total explanation for 11 steps)		0.392		0.622

Remark: x denotes interaction of two variables.
Reference groups: Occupation: traders, agents, salesmen.
Country of origin: Israel, Jews.
Source: Appendix, Table 7A.3.

The low explanatory power of the family head's education compared with that of his wife stems from the high correlation between the two (Table 7.3).

Thus, the wife's educational level stands also for that of her husband in the explanation of family income. The wife's educational level had a higher correlation with family income than did that of the family head, and one additional year of her schooling had a greater influence on family income than that of the family head, as also shown by the greater beta coefficient. Relative income differentials were influenced more by the family head's schooling than by that of his wife (Table 7.1, regression 2). The great weight of the wife's educational level seems to reflect two kinds of income differences: those between families with and without wives (regular families as against individuals and one-parent families), and those between families in which the wife worked and those in which she did not.

In order to investigate in greater depth the significance of the influence of the various variables on family income, it appeared useful to examine families with a regular pattern of husband-wife (with or without children and with or without other family members) separately from independent individuals and one-parent families.

Income of Husband-Wife Families

After independent individuals and one-parent families were omitted from the sample of all families, there remained some 2000 husband-wife families (1988); in one quarter of these families, the wife worked outside her home.

Table 7A.2 (Appendix) shows that average family income was higher by 57% in "husband-wife" families in which the wife was working, compared with those in which she did not work. Even without the wife's earnings, the average income of the families with working wives was higher by some 10%; this seems to be the result of the husband's longer working time (6% more working weeks) than that of husbands with non-working wives, and his better educational background (33% more years of schooling).

In the families in which the wife worked, both husband and wife were younger and their education was higher than in families in which the wife did not work. The difference in the wife's education was especially large — the average working wife had almost 50% more years of schooling than the wife not working outside her home. As might be expected, the number of young children was smaller in the families with working wives. Only about a quarter of the families in which the wife worked came from Asian-African countries (as against 37% in all husband-wife families); another quarter was Israeli-born (compared with 13% in all husband-wife families); and about half of the families with working wives came from European or American countries (similar to their share in all husband-wife families). This seems to be partly the result of the differences in educational level connected with the country of origin.

Women's labor force participation was determined mainly by their educational level; labor force surveys show a high correlation of labor force participation with years of schooling for women. The percentage of women in the labor force rose dramatically from 10% for women without any schooling to 60-70% for women with university education, while no such correlation exists for men (Appendix, Table 7A.17).

The high correlation of women's labor force participation with educational level explains the much higher educational level of working wives than that of non-working wives. The high correlation of the husband's educational level with that of his wife was responsible for the higher educational level of husbands of working wives compared with those of non-working wives — but here the difference was smaller. The relatively low percentage of working wives born in Asian or African countries stems from the general low labor force participation of women who immigrated from these countries. According to the labor survey, labor participation of women born in Asia/Africa was 28%; for those born in Europe/America, 40%; and for those born in Israel, 48%. Though labor force participation of women born in Asia/Africa was somewhat lower in all categories of education compared with women born in Europe/America and in Israel, the main reason for their lower labor force participation was their lower educational level.

The relatively low earnings of wives compared with those of their husbands (about half) is to a certain extent explained by their working part-time. Some 41% of married working women worked only part-time in 1969, as against 10% of working men. Furthermore, they also had lower-paid jobs, partly because of their somewhat lower education than that of their husbands (and presumably less training).[4] But, on the average, women earned less than men with the same education. Although women belonging to the labor force averaged more years of schooling than did men belonging to the labor force because of the women's high correlation of labor force participation with schooling, earnings per hour for female employees were 27% lower than for male employees (in 1970).

Husband-Wife Families by Employment Status

Incomes of husband-wife families differed by employment status of the family head. Average family income was somewhat higher among the self-employed than among employees, and essentially lower among those not belonging to the labor force. But in all categories, total family income was considerably higher in families with working wives. This difference was largest among employees, who also had the highest percentage of working wives — 29% — and smallest among the families whose heads did not belong to the labor force. In all three categories, we find the same differences, though in different degrees: husbands and wives were younger and more educated in the families with working wives, and the percentage of Israeli-born Jewish husbands and wives was significantly higher. Among the employees, a much larger percentage came from European-American countries in the families with working wives, compared with families in which the wife was not working; among the self-employed, almost no such difference was found; among those not belonging to the labor force, a considerably higher percentage came from European-American countries in the families in which the wife was not working.

The husband's income from work among employees with working wives was considerably higher (by 22%) than that of those whose wives were not working, whereas in the other categories this difference was negligible. This income difference has to be attributed mainly to educational differences of the family head, and the much greater correlation of educational and income level among employees compared to self employed.

Only about 11% of the heads of husband-wife families in the sample did not belong to the labor force (compared with 19% in all families), since a considerable percentage of those not belonging to the labor force were heads of one-parent families, or singles (mostly women). Heads of husband-wife families did not belong to the labor force mainly because of their age (65 years on the average); a few were physically or mentally handicapped. Their relatively low educational level (and that of their wives) was also connected with their relatively high age. In only a small number of these families did the wife work. Age and educational differences between working wives and non-working wives were much greater in this category than in the other categories.

When the incomes of families with working wives are compared with those of the other families, some facts have to be taken into account which reduce the significance of the income differences. In order to get a valid comparison, expenses caused by the wife's work should be deducted from her income — such as wages paid to household help or a nursemaid, expenses for day-long nursery schools, etc.

Furthermore, expenses for meals of the various family members outside the home, and laundry outside the home, etc., have to be taken into account. Purchases (especially of food) are often made at higher prices in neighborhood shops or by telephone order, in order to save time; also, food is often bought in prepared form. Significant comparison could also be made by adding to family income the value of the wife's work in her home, which would of course be considerably smaller in the case of the wife working outside her home. Since the husband and children are helping in such cases, their leisure time would be affected.

R. Gronau found that the value of time of housewives in Israel was "within a range of −20 to +5 per cent of the average wage of working women." [5] The wife's decision not to enter the labor force is regarded to indicate "that the wage offer facing the woman falls short of the value that she places on her time." The reason may be a high valuation of her time (in which case her average value of time exceeds the average wage rate of working women by 5%) or a low wage offer (when her value of time is 80% of women's wage rates).

A comparison of family incomes evaluating the housewives' work on such a basis would greatly reduce the differences caused by the earnings of working women. Any consideration of the greater leisure time of housewives would reduce the differences further. But in such a comparison of total family welfare we would also have to take into account such unmeasurable psychic factors as satisfaction from work outside the home and from the changes in human and physical environment connected with such work.

Examination of Husband-Wife Families' Incomes by Regression Analysis

We examined the influence of the fact that the wife was working (or that there were other earners in the family besides the family head) by regression analysis, and in most regressions we added the wife's data to those of her husband in order to examine their influence on family income.

The use of the following explanatory variables: the husband's characteristics (age, schooling, occupation, country of origin, year of immigration, employment status), number of earners in the family, wife works, dwelling locality, gave the following results: The number of earners in the family was the first factor in the explanation of net cash family income (with an explanatory power of 18% out of a total explanation of 45%). The husband's education appeared second, adding 15% explanation. The husband's other characteristics together added 11%. The variable "family head's wife works" had little influence, since this fact had already found expression in the number of earners in the family. Beta coefficients showed the following order of importance: husbands' weeks worked, number of earners, his occupation, his education, his employment status. The husband's duration of work and labor force participation of family members ranked before the husband's educational level. When the variable "wife works" was added and the number of earners was omitted from the regression, this added 6% explanation as the third factor (after years of schooling and weeks of work of the husband). According to beta coefficients, the fact that the wife worked was second in importance after weeks worked by the husband.

The influence of the wife's characteristics in addition to those of her husband (age, years of schooling, occupation, country of origin, year of immigration, and employment status) on family income, as well as the influence of family size, number of earners and dwelling locality, was examined for all husband-wife families.

In the Appendix, Table 7A.4, the results of the multiple regression on net cash income of husband-wife families are presented (regression 3).

The most conspicuous feature was the high explanatory power of the wife's educational level, which corroborated the results of the regression on incomes of all families (including individuals and one-parent families). The wife's education appeared first, with an explanatory power of 19% out of a total explanation of 50%.[6] The number of earners in the family appeared second, adding 15% explanation. The husband's education appeared only at the eleventh step, with a very low additional explanatory power.

Two main influences on family income can be discerned in the regression: labor force participation and duration of work of the family members (number of earners, weeks worked by husband and wife, employment status of husband and wife), and the educational and occupational level of husband and wife. These two main factors contributed 46% explanation out of a total 50%. (Labor force participation and duration of work explained 21%, and educational and occupational level explained 25%). Country of origin and year of immigration, mainly of the husband, and family size added the remaining 4%.

The beta coefficients indicate that the variables expressing labor force participation and duration of work of the family members were more important for income differences than were the educational and occupational levels of husband and wife. Weeks worked[7] by husband and wife, their employment status (working or not working) and the number of earners in the family had higher beta coefficients than the educational level of the wife. The husband's age and education in interaction with his occupation had a smaller influence on income differentials, according to the beta coefficients (regression 3).

Table 7.2 shows beta coefficients for husband-wife families, with working

Table 7.2
Results of Regressions on Net Family Cash Income of Husband-Wife Families
Beta Coefficients

	All H.-W. families	*With working wives*	*With non-working wives*
No. of observations	1,988	488	1,500
No. of regression	3	5	7
Explanatory Variables			
Weeks worked, husband	.399	.360	.434
Weeks worked, wife	.394	.254	—
Age × not working, husband	.337	.157	.383
Wife not in labor force	.311	—	. . .
No. of earners in family	.301	. . .	.318
Years of schooling, wife	.293	.329	.190
Age × liberal professions, husband	.226	.111*	.203
Family size	.141	.163	.157
Eur.-Am., Veteran, husband	.130	.188	.141
Coefficient of determination (R^2)	.476	.580	.363

*Lib. prof. × schooling

Source: Appendix, Tables 7A.4, 7A.5, 7A.6.

Remark: Beta coefficients from 10-step regressions.

and non-working wives. As may be seen, the labor force participation of the family head and his duration of work were more important for family income than his wife's duration of work or her schooling in families in which the wife was working. But in *all* husband-wife families, weeks worked by the wife and her labor force participation were almost as important as those of her husband, because of the considerable income difference between families with working wives and those with non-working wives.

The high explanatory power of the wife's education for family income in all husband-wife families as the first factor, is the result of two effects — the high correlation between the wife's education and that of her husband, and the higher correlation of the wife's education with family income than that of her husband. Table 7.3 reveals that this higher correlation in all husband-wife families is caused by the higher correlation of the working wife's education with family income, whereas the non-working wife's education shows a somewhat lower correlation with family income than that of her husband. The higher correlation of the working wife's education with family income appears to be connected with the fact that the participation of women in the labor force (especially of married women) increases with educational level (Appendix, Table 7A.17).

The high correlation of the wife's education with that of her husband explains the low explanatory power of the husband's education for family income in our regression, as it is already expressed by that of his wife. As may be remembered, in the regression in which the wife's characteristics were not used as explanatory variables, the husband's education had considerable explanatory power.

The correlation of the husband's education with that of his wife was similar in the total population and among employees, but the correlation of the educational level with income was considerably higher among employees.

It must be stressed that the relatively high correlation between education and family income found in the total population and in all husband-wife families seems to be influenced by the great weight of the employees (about two-thirds of all husband-wife families). The correlation coefficient of the family head's education with total family income was much higher among employees than among the self-employed (about double). According to these findings, education pays more to employees than to the self-employed — or else, other factors (including native talent, luck and property) influence incomes to a greater extent among the self-employed.

Table 7.3 also reflects a much higher correlation of the husband's and wife's education with income in all families with working wives, compared with those in which the wife was not working. This correlation was 42% greater in the husband's case, and 66% greater in the wife's case. This difference was also influenced by the especially large weight of employees in the families in which the wife was working (80%).

Table 7.3
Correlation Coefficients (r) of Years of Schooling of Husband and Wife with Total Family Income

		Correlation Coefficients		
	No. of families	*Husband's schooling with wife's schooling*	*Years of schooling with total family income*	
			Husband	*Wife*
All husband-wife families	1,988	0.707	0.407	0.423
H-W families with working wives	488	0.695	0.467	0.520
H-W families with non-working wives	1,500	0.680	0.328	0.314
Employees				
All husband-wife families	1,365	0.706	0.524	0.532
H-W families with working wives*	377	0.683	0.523	0.563
H-W families with non-working wives	972	0.672	0.450	0.394
All families	2.412	...	0.418**	0.463

* The families in which the wife was self-employed and the husband was an employee were not included.

** Family head.

Source: Data of Family Expenditure Survey 1968/69.

The importance of the wife's educational level to the socio-economic situation of the family has been stressed by others. An investigation into deprived families in Jerusalem showed the influence of the parents' (especially the mother's) educational level on the social situation of the family.[8] Morgan[9] cites the findings of investigations in the U.S. and Sweden which reflect the importance of the wife's education. These investigations showed that "the wife's education has a higher correlation with the family's standard of living than the husband's",[10] and that "there is sociological evidence that the wife determines the standard of the family".[11]

The influence of the wife's educational level on the standard of living of the family finds expression not only in her earnings, which increase family income — but also in the efficient use of the family budget, in the organization of work in the home, in the atmosphere of the home and its cleanliness, and in her children's educational achievements.

The results of the regressions on the incomes of employees' families were quite similar to those obtained for all husband-wife families as to the explanatory power of the variables, but with a higher total explanation (60% for net cash income) (Appendix, Table 7A.4, regression 4). This has to be attributed to the high percentage of employees' families in all husband-wife families(69%).

The beta coefficients, however, indicate that in this group in which all husbands were employees (and therefore belonged to the labor force), the husband's duration of work had much less influence on income differences than in all husband-wife families, but that his educational and occupational level carried more weight. The importance of the wife's labor force participation and duration of work was more pronounced among the employees.

Income of husband-wife families whose heads were self-employed was determined to only a modest extent by the variables used, and for net family cash income only a total explanation of 27% was obtained.

The low explanation obtained shows that family income of the self-employed was to a considerable extent determined by factors not included among our explanatory variables (property, personal talent and initiative, luck and opportunity, business connections, etc.).

In the regression on net cash income of husband-wife families whose heads did not belong to the labor force, the most important influence was exercised by the numbers of earners in the family. There were on the average only 0.46 earners in these families; hence, the existence of an earner (wife or other) was the most important determinant.

Incomes of Husband-Wife Families with Working Wives

Table 7A.2 (Appendix), shows that the average income of families with working wives was 57% higher than that of families in which the wife was not working. The most striking difference between working and non-working wives in husband-wife families was the 47% higher educational level of the working wives. The relatively high correlation between the working wife's years of schooling and family income (Table 7.3) makes this variable the first factor in explaining incomes of these families.

The regressions are presented in Appendix, Table 7A.5 (regressions 5 and 6). The wife's education contributed about two-fifths of the total explanation of 60% for net cash income of all husband-wife families with working wives (regression 5). Additional factors of importance were the number of weeks worked by husband and wife, the country of origin of the husband, the year of his immigration, and family size. The husband's occupation in interaction with age and education also had some influence. A comparison with the regressions on incomes of all husband-wife families shows that the explanation obtained for incomes of families with working wives was much higher.

The beta coefficients indicate that the husband's labor force participation and duration of work (weeks worked) were more important than the wife's educational level. The husband's educational level (also in interaction with age) had a very high beta coefficient, but to some extent these coefficients neutralized each other (two being negative and one positive).

In most of the husband-wife families with working wives, the husband was an employee (80%). For employees' family income, a relatively high explanation was obtained — 62%. The wife's education in interaction with age appeared as the first factor, with an explanatory power of 31%; the interaction of education with age in parabolic form was the third factor. Weeks worked by husband and wife added 10% explanation, and the husband's education in interaction with age and with occupation added 4-6% (regression 6). The husband's country of origin and family size had also some influence on family income. Beta coefficients showed a similar order of importance.

We saw that the earnings of married women increased income inequality by 7% and we concluded that the increase in the percentage of married women working outside their homes raised the inequality index (see Chapter 4, especially *Analysis of Combined Impact*). We expected, therefore, a higher inequality index among *all* husband-wife families than among husband-wife families with non-working wives. However, the inequality index (coefficient of variation) of *all* husband-wife families was lower (0.760)[12] than that of the husband-wife families with non-working wives (0.833). Further investigation revealed that the reason for this was the low coefficient of variation of husband-wife families with working wives (0.524) because of the great weight of employees' families (80%) among them.[13] Among *all* husband-wife families who were employees, inequality was higher (0.577) than among husband-wife families with non-working wives who were employees (0.562), reflecting the negative influence of working wives' incomes on statistical income inequality.

Incomes of Families with Non-Working Wives

The regressions on the income of husband-wife families in which the wife was not working are presented in Appendix, Table 7A.6 (regressions 7 and 8).

In all husband-wife families with non-working wives, labor force participation and duration of work of family members and the husband's characteristics carried much more weight than did those of his wife. His education explained (as second factor) 13% out of a total explanation of 38% for net cash income (regression 7).

Even the non-working wife's education had some influence. The husband's age in interaction with occupation and with employment status, his education in interaction with occupation, and his weeks worked had influence. This reveals the importance of the extent of his labor force participation for family income, which is accentuated by the great influence of the number of earners on income, which as first factor had an explanatory power of 12%. This variable indicates the difference between families in which there was no earner (about 8%) and those with earners, as well as the difference between families with one earner and those with more than one. The influence of weeks worked by the husband expresses the difference between families in which the husband did not belong to the labor force (12% of husband-wife families with non-working wives) and other families, as well as income differences resulting from fewer or more weeks worked. Beta coefficients underline the importance of the husband's labor force participation and duration of work (weeks worked), and of other family members (number of earners) (Table 7.2).

Among employees (65% of the families with non-working wives), the explanation obtained was higher (46%) but was along similar lines. The most striking difference was the greater weight of the husband's education, which appeared first with an explanatory power of 14% (regression 8); according to the beta coefficients, however, labor force participation of family members and the husband's duration of work were more important. His other characteristics also carried greater weight compared with all families.

The Wife's Earnings

Though the wife's income from work averaged only about 10% of total family income of all husband-wife families (Appendix, Table 7A.2), its influence on income differentials was considerable. About 80% of the income difference between families with working wives and families with non-working wives can be attributed to whether the wife was working.

In one-fourth of the husband-wife families, the wife worked and earned an average income of IL 451 per month in 1968/69. We examined the influence of the following variables on the wife's earnings: years of schooling, age, weeks worked, status of employment, occupation, country of origin, year of immigration, dwelling area, number of children up to the age of 17, and number of children up to the age of 5 (Appendix, Table 7A.7).

As in the case of the family head's income from work (Chapter 6), the wife's education had the main explanatory power with 25% out of a total explanation of 45% for income from her work. The second factor was the number of weeks worked, with an additional explanatory power of 17% (regression 9). Profession, country of origin, year of immigration and dwelling area had little influence, and the number of children had no influence at all.

According to the beta coefficients, the number of weeks worked was more important than the educational level; the other variables had the same order of importance as by explanatory power.

The fact that many women work in part-time jobs (half or three-quarters of a work-day) no doubt influences income differentials. However, the data at our disposal shed no light on this factor.

In regression 10 we sought to discover the factors motivating the wife to work outside her home. We received a total explanation of only 15%. But in such a regression where the variable to be explained is a dummy variable of yes or no, the beta coefficients are decisive. They reflect the great importance of education and age (the latter with negative influence, used in parabolic form). A further important negative influence was that of small children (up to age 5), while children aged 13-17 had some positive influence. Weeks worked by the husband had some small negative influence, as did family income exclusive of the wife's income from work. The smaller percentage of working wives from African-Asian countries is indicated by a small negative beta coefficient (Table 7.4)

Table 7.4
Regression on "Wife Worked Outside Home"
(Regression 10)

Explanatory Variables	*Beta Coefficients*
Years of schooling, wife	.306
$(\text{Age})^2$ of wife	−.250
Children up to 5 years	−.128
Weeks worked by husband	−.067
Wife from Asia-Africa, new imm.	−.060
Family income less wife's earnings	−.060
Children aged 13-17	.048
R^2 (% of explanation)	0.152

One must differentiate here between the wife's motivation to work and the objective situation which might indicate such motives. We have seen that the income of families in which the wife worked (exclusive of the wife's income from work) was higher than in those in which the wife did not work. It is, of course, possible that a relatively high family income seems low in relation to the demands of the family or the wife, and she therefore goes to work.

Morgan et al.,[14] in their analysis of family income, contend that the difference between the husband's education and that of his wife is an important factor in her decision to look for a job. If her educational level is higher than that of her husband, she will work in order to raise the family's income to the level desired by her; if her education is lower, she will more easily adapt herself to the income provided by her husband and will refrain from working outside of her home (especially as it may be difficult for her to obtain a job compatible with his position in society).

We attempted to find out whether similar motivations were effective in Israel. The husband's education was higher than that of his wife in 40% of the families with working wives and in 43% of the families in which the wife did not work. The wife's education was higher than that of her husband in 32% of the families with working wives and in only 21% of the families in which the wife did not work. Thus, among working wives, the percentage of those with a lower education than their husbands was greater than the percentage of those with a higher education; among non-working wives as well, a considerable percentage had a higher education than their husbands, though this percentage was much lower than among working wives. We may, therefore, conclude that in Israel the educational differences between husband and wife were not important. The more important factor was the educational level of the wife as such, as it promised adequate remuneration for her work.

The relative unimportance of the educational difference for the wife's decision to work in Israel was also shown in a regression. The difference in the educational level between husband and wife was used as an explanatory variable, instead of their educational level. Total explanation was even smaller (11.7%) than in the previous regression. The higher educational level of the wife compared with that of her husband had a relatively low positive beta coefficient (.077). Age was the most important factor according to beta coefficients (−.295), and children up to the age of 5 and country of origin ranked before the educational difference (regression 10a). Since the educational level of husband and wife were omitted from this regression, the wife's age proved most important; country of origin was more influential than in the previous regression because of its considerable correlation with educational level.

A comparison of the two regressions reveals the importance of the wife's educational level for her decision to work. The wife's educational level carried much more explanatory power than did educational differences between husband and wife, and more influence as expressed in the beta coefficient.

In Israel, a wife's educational level is an important factor in her decision to look for paid work, since this (usually in connection with occupational training) assures an attractive remuneration. Hence, we find a high correlation of married women's educational level with labor force participation. However, the question of why the wife works outside her home requires further investigation — preferably by interview methods, since motivations are concerned.

Incomes of Independent Individuals and One-Parent Families

Individuals not living in a family, and one-parent families, constituted about 17% of all families in the 1968/69 survey — but only 8% of all persons. 70% of all individuals and 73% of all heads of one-parent families were women.

The average age of the independent individuals, especially of the women (a large percentage of whom were widows) was quite high. Single men were, on the average, only 12% older than the heads of husband-wife families; but single women were 51% older than the wives in husband-wife families. Male heads of one-parent families differed little in their age from heads of husband-wife families — but female heads of one-parent families were quite older (on the average, by 18%), than wives in husband-wife families (Appendix, Table 7A.18).

The average educational level of the men was similar to that of heads of husband-wife families; however, that of the women was considerably lower than that of the wives in husband-wife families — even than that of non-working wives. This lower educational level is connected with the high age of these women; the steady expansion of the educational network has made the younger generation more educated than the older one.

The lower average income level of this group, in comparison with the average income of all families, is to some extent explained by the smaller size of these families (singles, or three persons in one-parent families). When family size is taken into account and income per person and per standard equivalent adult is compared, the average income of single men is higher than the average, and that of one-parent families with male heads is slightly lower than the average but higher than that of husband-wife families in which the wife did not work. The income of single women and that of one-parent families with female heads was considerably below the average, though only to a small extent lower than that of husband-wife families in which the wife did not work. (Table 7.5).

Table 7.5 shows the great difference in income per standard equivalent adult between husband-wife families with working wives and those in which

Table 7.5
Average Monthly Total Family Income
(% of average in all families)

	per family	*per person*	*per standard equivalent adult*
All families	100	100	100
All husband-wife families	109	83	102
with working wives	150	127	145
with non-working wives	96	71	89
Individuals, men	60	185	132
women	35	108	77
One-parent families, men	91	83	92
women	73	71	81

Source: Survey-data 1968/69.

the wife did not work. As already pointed out, it has to be taken into account that part of this difference is illusory and that real income differences were smaller.

The low income of single women and of one-parent families with female heads was a consequence of the high percentage of those not belonging to the labor force. 71% of single women and 52% of female heads of one-parent families did not belong to the labor force.

Regressions on the incomes of individuals and one-parent families are presented in Appendix, Table 7A.8. Remarkably high explanations were obtained. The variables used had an explanatory power of 72% and 74% for income from work for men and women respectively, and an explanatory power of 54% for net cash family income of women and of 75% for that of men. For relative income differentials, even higher explanations were obtained.

Weeks worked, as the first factor, explained 51-53% out of a total explanation of 72-74% for income from work (regressions 11 and 13). Education alone and in interaction with age or occupation added 10% explanation for men, but almost none for women (for whom age in interaction with occupation — with a negative coefficient — was of greater importance). Additional determinants were employment status, country of origin in combination with year of immigration, and occupation alone and in interaction with age. The high explanatory power of weeks worked and of not belonging to the labor force[15] for income from work reflects mainly the decisive difference between those working and those not working (and therefore having no income from work). The other variables mainly explain differences in income from work among those who work.

Beta coefficients not only indicate the great importance of labor force participation and duration of work for this category, but also underline the importance of age in interaction with occupation (for women) and in interaction with education (for men).

In the explanation of family income (which includes other income in addition to that from work, such as pensions, social assistance, etc.) it was still important, whether the individual or family head worked, but less decisive than for income from work. The most important determinant of family income was the number of earners, with an explanatory power of 34% for men out of a total explanation of 75% (regression 14) and 33% for women out of a total explanation of 54% (regression 12).

It is interesting that the educational level proved more important for family income than for income from work. Education was second in importance after the number of earners for net cash family income (women), and third, after the number of earners and children aged 6-13 (for men) according to beta coefficients. This may be due to the high percentage of pensioners in this group; the size of old-age pensions is, to a considerable extent, determined by previous occupations — which were greatly dependent on educational level.

Occupation (also in interaction with age and education) had considerable influence on family income in this category. 63% of all women (individuals and heads of one-parent families) and 25% of all men in this category did not belong to the labor force.

Determinants of Income per Standard Adult

We have seen that income per standard adult is a better measure of income differences between families than is income per family because it adjusts for the variations in family size and composition. We examined differences in family income so extensively because most statistics on inequality relate to distribution of income per family or household. Family size was one of the determinants of family income, and so was the number of children. However, we also examined the differences in family incomes by income per standard adult.

Regression analysis shows the following main determinants of income per standard adult: the degree of labor force participation of the family head and his wife; the number of children (with a negative sign); the educational level, age and occupation of the family head; and his country of origin and year of immigration. The main difference compared with determinants of family income is the greater influence of the number of children on income per S.E.A.[16] and the greater importance of country of origin.

Table 7.6 shows the regression coefficients in standard form (beta coefficients) after the first six steps of the regression for all families on net cash income per standard adult. The full results of the regression (10 steps) are presented in Appendix, Table 7A.9, regression 15.

Table 7.6
Regression on Net Cash Income per Standard Equivalent Adult
All Families (2,412 observations)

Explanatory Variables	*Beta Coefficients*
Number of children	−.220
Years of schooling, family head	.217
Weeks worked, family head	.217
Weeks worked, wife of family head	.216
Family head from Europe-America, veteran citizen	.180
Age × liberal profession, family head	.152
Coefficient of determination (R^2)	.386

Source: Appendix, Table 7A.9, regression 15.

The beta coefficients have been chosen for presentation here, since they best indicate the net effect of each individual variable. The number of children is the most important negative determinant of income per standard adult. The family head's duration of work, his educational level, and the wife's duration of work, are the most important positive determinants. The age of the family head, his country of origin and his occupation are further determinants of importance. The explanation obtained by these variables is 39%. The full results of the regression (25 steps) show a relatively smaller influence of children, and a greater influence of age, with a total explanation of 45%.

Family size had a two-fold impact on income per standard adult. Regression analysis had shown that family size had a certain positive influence on family income. The beta coefficient of family size on net cash family income was 0.141 for all husband-wife families (Table 7.2, regression 3). This influence seems to work both ways. Dependents may cause the family head to make greater efforts to increase his earnings, and a well-paid job may encourage the beginning of a family and its enlargement. Tax exemptions and child allowances are further factors. But family size had a negative influence, when income was calculated per standard adult, since family income was divided by the number of persons according to the chosen equivalence scales. The negative influence appearing in regression 15 (Table 7.6) is net of the positive influence.

The above families include independent individuals and one-parent families. In additional regressions, regular husband-wife families and individuals and one-parent families were examined separately.

Among husband-wife families, the wife's educational level has highest explanatory power, and is second in importance as a determinant of income per S.E.A. according to beta coefficients (Appendix, Table 7A.10, regression 16). (But among *all* families, the husband's educational level had highest explanatory power and was second in importance (regression 15)). As in the regressions on family incomes, the husband's educational level is also expressed by his wife's educational level — because of the high correlation between the wife's and the husband's years of schooling — and therefore appears only late or not at all in the regressions for husband-wife families. After the families were separated into those in which the wife worked and those in which she did not work, the husband's schooling in interaction with occupation appears earlier (Appendix, Tables 7A.10, 11, 12,regressions 16-18).

Among all husband-wife families, the number of weeks worked by the wife had more influence on income per standard adult than did those worked by the husband; whereas among the families in which the wife worked, weeks worked by the husband were much more important than weeks worked by his wife. The reason for this is that in the regression for all husband-wife families, weeks worked by the wife indicated the difference between non-working wives (with zero weeks worked) and working wives, in addition to showing the difference in weeks worked among working wives. Income per standard adult was 63% higher in families in which the wife worked.

The main determinants of incomes per standard adult for individuals and one-parent families were educational level, labor force participation (or volume of employment), age, occupational level, and country of origin (Appendix, Table 7A.13).

Results of regressions on net cash income per standard equivalent adult by employment status of the family head reveal the causes of different income levels *within* each group. Income per standard adult among families whose heads did not belong to the labor force was determined mainly by educational level[17] and number of earners in the family (Appendix, Table 7A.14). Country of origin was an additional factor, as well as whether the family head was a woman or whether the male family head had a wife. But the main cause of low income per standard adult in this category was its characteristic — the fact that the family head did not belong to the labor force. Hence, average net cash income per standard adult was only 60% of that of employee families, and 55% of that of self-employed families.

Income differences among employee families were caused mainly by the labor force participation of the wife, the number of children (with a negative sign), the family head's educational level, and the extent of his employment (weeks worked). His country of origin, age and occupation were additional factors (Appendix, Table 7A.15). Income differences among self-employed families were caused by age and occupation, the number of children, educational level of the family head and his wife, country of origin and the extent of employment. But it has to be taken into account that the explanatory power of the regression was relatively low for this category (Appendix, Table 7A.16).

Main Determinants of Family Income

The following is an examination of the influence of each of the main factors on family income.

Labor Force Participation of Family Members[18]

Since 80% of total family income and 90% of family cash income came from work, the labor force participation of the family head, his wife and other family members was decisive for the level of family income.

In families without any earner, average gross cash income was 29% of the average of all other families. While there were no earners in 14% of the families (including independent individuals), about two-thirds of the families in the lowest decile and only 1% in the two highest deciles had no earners (Table 7.7).

A calculation of the inequality index, after families without earners were omitted from the sample, showed a reduction of 15%. Labor force participation of the various family members was expressed in the regressions by the

Table 7.7
Urban Families by Deciles of Gross Money Income by No. of Earners
(in %)

Earners per family	*Lowest decile*	*Second lowest decile*	*Ninth decile*	*Highest decile*	*Total*	*Average income per family* (% of average)
No earner	67.4	36.7	1.0	1.2	13.7	33
One earner	31.4	54.6	35.9	28.1	51.6	91
Two or more earners	1.2	8.7	63.1	70.7	34.7	140
Total	100.0	100.0	100.0	100.0	100.0	100

Source: Family Survey 1968/69.

following variables: employment status and weeks worked of the family head and of his wife, and number of earners in the family.

In the regressions on income of all families (including individuals), the family head's weeks worked, his employment status, and the number of earners in the family explained 9% of absolute income differences out of a total explanation of 41% — but as much as 22% of relative income differentials out of a total explanation of 66% (regressions 1 and 2).

Since intercorrelation between the explanatory variables blurs their order of importance as expressed by explanatory power, their beta coefficients were used as indicators of their importance in influencing family income. The beta coefficients of the variables expressing labor force participation of family members indicated their greater importance in influencing family income than the educational and occupational level of the family head and his wife.

The separate examination of husband-wife families and of individuals and one-parent families revealed the great importance of labor force participation for income differences in these more homogeneous groups.

Because of the decisive influence of labor force participation of family members, and especially the family head, on family income, the causes of no or low labor force participation are important. Old age and disability are the main causes of lack of labor force participation in a situation of full employment.[19] Family heads left the labor force because of old age and total disability, or worked only part of the year because of sickness and temporary disability. Some very young family heads worked only part of the year because they entered the labor force during the year. The labor force participation of wives was influenced by their educational level, the number of children, the labor force participation of the husband and his income (regression 10).

The great influence of the employment volume of family members on family income explains the great impact of the unemployment rate on income inequality (see chapter 4).

Education

The great influence of the educational level on income is well known, and an entire literature has sprung up dealing with the returns on investment in education.[20]

The data of the 1968/69 family survey reflected the high explanatory power of education, especially of the family head's wife, for family income; in some cases it even had pride of place over the labor force partipation of family members. Relatively high correlations of education with family income were found in all families, in husband-wife families, and for individuals and heads of one-parent families.

The higher correlation of the wife's education with family income than that of her husband in all husband-wife families was caused by that of working wives. The high correlation of the working wife's education with family income had its impact on income differentials of all families, as reflected in the correlation of education of the family head's wife with income in all families (including individuals and one-parent families), which was higher than that of the family head (Table 7.3). This was the main reason that the wife's education appeared in the regressions on income of all families (regressions 1 and 2), and of all husband-wife families (regression 3), with a high explanatory power. Beta coefficients indicated that the educational level of the wife ranked immediately after labor force participation of family members.

The labor force participation of married women was considerably correlated with their educational level. Hence, the educational level of the wife expresses two kinds of income differences: (a) between families which had additional income from the wife's work and those which had no such income, and (b) income differences stemming directly from the educational differences of husband and wife who worked. (The wife's educational level also stands for that of her husband because of the high correlation between the educational levels of husband and wife).

Family income of individuals and one-parent families was determined first and foremost by labor force participation of the individual or family head; education was second in importance, by explanatory power and by beta coefficients.

The influence of education on family income is reflected in the high percentage of family heads with a low educational level in the lower income brackets. Family heads without any schooling or less than 5 years of schooling represented 54% of the lowest decile, but only about 5% of the two highest deciles — whereas family heads with higher education (13 years or more of schooling) constituted less than 5% of the lowest decile but 47% of the highest decile. Average family income of those with 13 years and more of schooling was two and a half times as high as that of family heads who had less than 5 years of schooling.[21]

Hourly earnings of employees by years of schooling show somewhat smaller differences than the above income differences of families, since income of all families included income from other sources than work, as well as that of self-employed and of those not belonging to the labor force. Hourly earnings of employees with a university education (16 years of schooling or more) were 2.5 times higher than those of employees with no schooling at all. (See Appendix, Table 4A.4). The differences in earnings stem to a great extent from differences in skills and occupations, and the educational level appears to reflect these differences.

Education appeared in the various regressions in interaction with occupation or employment status, revealing the kind of income difference expressed by education. Part of this combined influence has to be attributed to occupation or labor force participation.

Age

Age had its main influence on family income in the lowest (18-24) and highest (65 and more) age groups of family heads. Total family income in the highest age group was about half of that in the middle age groups (35-54). The highest age group was therefore concentrated in the lower income brackets.

Family income rose with the age of the family head — rather quickly in the beginning, and more slowly later — until it peaked in the 45-54 age group. This is to a great extent the result of increasing experience and on-the-job-training. After the family head reached age 55, family income declined slowly until the pension age of 65, after which it decreased rapidly. (See also Chapter 6).

Income from work therefore shows greater inverse correlation with age than does family income. The inverse correlation of the age of the family head with the logarithm of his income from work was −0.526, but only −0.311 with the logarithm of total family income, since old-age pensions replaced income from work for those over 65.

Thus, age carried relatively little weight in the explanation of family income by regression analysis, and was more important in the explanation of income from work. Beta coefficients underlined the importance of age in interaction with employment status (not belonging to the labor force). The relatively low explanatory power of age in the regressions on family income stems from the high correlation of age with the variables reflecting labor force participation.

The interaction of age with employment status appeared in various regressions. Age in interaction with occupation also had some influence on family income.

Occupation

Social status is greatly determined by the occupation of the family head, and there is no doubt that occupation decisively influences the level of family income. The classification available to us showed only 9 occupational groups, and most groups contained different grades of skills and different levels of responsibility. For instance, the category of "administrative, executive, managerial and clerical workers" brings together the manager of a factory, his bookkeeper and his typist — whose wages are very different from one another. Wages of employees by occupation and years of schooling showed great differences for the same occupational group by educational level. Family income by occupation of family head shows that income of professional and scientific workers was three times as high as that of unskilled workers (Appendix, Table 7A.19).

In the above regressions, occupation had a relatively modest influence on family income, appearing mostly in interaction with age or education. After this had been taken into account, occupation of the family head and of the wife (if she was working) explained 3.4% out of a total explanation of 41% for income of all families (regression 1).

Beta coefficients indicated the relative importance of occupation in interaction with age, ranking immediately after labor force participation and education. The relatively low explanatory power of occupation in our regressions stems from the importance of education for occupation, and from the classification into broad groups including different levels of occupational skill. The differences of educational level in relation to income already express part of the occupational differences.

Sex

Average monthly total income of families in 1968/69 with a male head was IL 1,080, while that of families with a female head was only about half — IL 517. But this comparison is somewhat misleading, since families with a female head were individuals or one-parent families, while those with a male head (87.4% of all families) consisted mainly of husband-wife families. The following comparison is therefore more relevant (Table 7.8).

The differences reflected in Table 7.8 are due only partly to sex; to a great extent differences in labor force participation and education were responsible. Thus, among individuals and one-parent families, the educational level of the men was 43% (individuals) and 46% (one-parent families) higher than that of the women — and they worked, on the average, 136% and 77% more weeks, respectively.

Table 7.8
Total Monthly Income by Sex of Family Head (IL)

	Male		Female	
	Family income	*Income from work*	*Family income*	*Income from work*
Individuals	609	429	355 (58%)	103 (24%)
One-parent families	917	513	741 (51%)	234 (46%)
Husband-wife families with working wives		854		451 (53%)
Families with one earner	974		602 (62%)	

Source: Family Survey 1968/69.
Remark: In parentheses % of male.

Therefore, the low income of families with a female head is, to a great extent, the outcome of advanced age, low labor force participation, low education and low-paid occupation. Though females may get lower pay for the same job, mostly they get the lower-paid jobs because of their education, training and experience, and often because they work part-time, but sometimes because they are women. Of greatest importance was the fact that a high percentage of these women did not work at all (71% of the individuals and 52% of the heads of one-parent families) because of advanced age or other reasons.

However, on the average, women earned less than men with the same educational and occupational level.[22] Hourly earnings of males were 20-60% higher than those of females in the same educational groups. Weekly earnings of employees, too, show considerable differences between males and females for the same occupational groups (Appendix, Table 7A.19). There were also considerable differences in hourly earnings by occupational groups. In some occupations, hourly earnings of males were almost double those of females. On the average, hourly earnings of females were 25% lower than those of males, while weekly earnings were 38% lower because of more women working part-time.

In our regressions, the sex of the family head had very little influence on family income. This was because of the relatively high correlation of the male family head with weeks worked (0.425) and his considerable negative correlation with his not being in the labor force (−0.428); both variables had a high correlation with family income.

Country of Origin

Country of origin and year of immigration of the family head had only a modest influence on family income, explaining 2.5% of income differences of all families out of a total explanation of 41%. Beta coefficients rank it after labor force participation, education of family head and of wife, and age, in interaction with occupation of the family head (regression 1). Family income by country of origin and year of immigration shows a greater concentration of family heads born in Asian-African countries in the lower income brackets, and of those born in European countries and in Israel in the higher income brackets (Appendix, Table 7A.20).

There were considerable income differences between veteran residents and new immigrants, and between families whose heads were born in Africa-Asia and those born in Europe-America and Israel. The income of families whose heads were born in Asia-Africa and who had immigrated after 1955 was 43% lower than that of Jewish families whose heads were born in Israel, and only slightly different from that of non-Jewish families. Veteran families whose heads were born in Asia-Africa had a slightly lower income than those of new immigrants who came from Europe-America.

However, these characteristics carried relatively little weight in our regressions. This appears to be connected to the stronger correlation of country of origin with education than with family income (see Appendix, Table 6A.3). Hence, after the influence of education on family income had been taken into account, country of origin and year of immigration had little influence.

Differences in education by country of origin were more pronounced than differences in family income by country of origin. A high percentage of families whose heads came from Asian-African countries had a low educational level, while those from European countries and born in Israel had a higher educational level.

From Table 7.9 it can be concluded that income differences between ethnic groups stem almost entirely from educational differences. For instance, average total income of families from Asian-African countries calculated according to the educational level of their heads in 1968/69 would amount to IL874; it was actually IL802. The small remaining difference (8%) finds its explanation in the difference in the quality of education and many other factors influencing income in different directions such as labor force participation, year of immigration, age, work experience, etc. The table also shows a decline in income differentials between ethnic groups in the mid-seventies connected with the decline in their educational differences (see also Chapter 5).

Family Size

Family size and the number of children influenced family income. In "all families", family size expressed to some extent the difference between independent individuals and families. In husband-wife families, this seems to stem from the fact that working wives had fewer children. For individuals and one-parent families, family size indicates the difference between the two heterogeneous groups within this category.

Table 7.9
Family Heads by Country of Origin and Years of Schooling (in %) (1968/69)

Country of birth	*Total*	*Years of schooling* 0-4	5-8	9-12	13+	*Monthly family income* (% of average) *1968/69*	*1975/76*
Asia-Africa	35.9	60.7	41.4	26.1	14.8	79	88
Europe-America	49.5	32.1	45.5	58.0	61.5	111	102
Israel: Jews	12.6	3.8	9.6	15.4	23.7	122	120
non-Jews	2.0	3.4	3.5	0.5	—	60	76
Total	100.0	100.0	100.0	100.0	100.0	100	100
All family heads	100.0	19.6	32.5	30.6	17.3		
Monthly total family income (% of average)							
1968/69	100	57	81	119	150		
1975/76	100	63	82	104	130		

Source: Family Surveys 1968/69 and 1975/76.

Income from work of the family head was considerably higher in families with dependents (see Appendix, Tables 7A.2 and 7A.18). This may indicate that dependents caused the family head to work more (overtime) and better; on the other hand, the obtaining of a well-paid job encouraged the founding of a family.

Family size becomes important in an evaluation of social differentiation.[23] Since old people are concentrated in the lowest income brackets, these are mainly composed of independent individuals and small families. Large families are found in all income brackets, but are concentrated more in the third to fifth deciles. Thus, one and two-person families constitute 87% of the lowest decile, but only 17% of the highest decile and 34% of all families. Families with 7 persons or more constitute only 1% of the lowest decile, but 13% of the third, fourth and fifth deciles, and 9% of all families. Average family size was 1.8 in the lowest decile, 4.2 in the fifth decile and 3.8 in the highest decile — compared with 3.7 in all families.

In an ordering of families by income per person, large families are concentrated in the lower income brackets. In this case, average family size was 6.0 in the lowest decile, and 2.1 in the highest decile.

Income per standard equivalent adult takes into account economies of scale in large families in addition to family size, and therefore reflects the standard of living of families better than does income per family or income per person (see Introduction). In an ordering of families by net income per standard equivalent adult in 1975/76, large families were concentrated in the two lowest deciles, and small families in the higher deciles. Average family size was 4.7 in the lowest decile, 4.6 in the second decile and only 2.5 in the highest decile.

The population in poverty consisted mainly of independent individuals and small families, on one hand, and large families, on the other (Chapter 8). Hence, almost half the population in poverty were children, while these constituted only 37% of the population above the poverty band.

Dwelling Locality

Family income was higher in the large towns, and lower in smaller towns — especially the new development towns.[24]

The most important difference is found between the immigrant towns and the large towns. Some 19% of all families lived in new towns, and their average income was about 20% lower than that of the families in the large towns. When the difference in family size is taken into account, income differences widen. Any such comparison also has to consider the higher cost of living in the large towns, which reduces real income differences between larger and smaller localities.

In our regressions, dwelling locality had a very small influence on income differentials, since it was expressed in differences in educational level and labor force participation.

NOTES

1. In 1975/76 — 73% and 83% respectively.
2. For 19 steps, 11 steps yielded an explanation of 39% (Table 7.1).
3. The beta coefficient or regression coefficient in standard form shows the average number of units of the standard deviations' increase or decrease in the dependent variable (income) which occur with each increase of one unit of the standard deviation in the independent variable. For the use of the beta coefficient to measure the separate effect of individual variables in multiple regression, see M. Ezekiel and K.A. Fox, *Methods of Correlation and Regression Analysis*, New York: Wiley & Sons, 1959, p. 196.
4. The working life of women is usually shorter than that of men; so is work experience at the same age, as many women leave their jobs for a period when their children are small. L. Thurow explains the discrimination of women in his job competition model by the higher probability of women leaving their jobs after short periods — i.e., training costs may not pay.
5. Gronau Reuben, *The Measurement of Output of the Nonmarket Sector: The Evaluation of housewives' Time*. Falk Institute, Jerusalem, 1974, p. 184 and p. 168.
6. This analysis refers to the 19-step regression, whereas in the Appendix the regression has been presented after 10 steps.

7. Weeks worked expressed labor force participation as well as duration of work, since not belonging to the labor force meant no weeks were worked.
8. Y. Rosenfeld, lecture in the Demographic Center, Jerusalem, 1971.
9. I.N. Morgan, M.H. David, W.I. Cohen and H.E. Brazer, *Income and Welfare in the United States*, McGraw Hill, New York, 1962.
10. R.A. Dauley and Ch. E. Ramsey, *Standardization and Application of a Level of Living Scale for Farm and non-Farm Families*, Cornell University, 1959.
11. C.A. Anderson, *Employment, Occupation and Socio-economic Status of Swedish Wives in Relation to Occupation and Status of Husbands*, Statistics Tidskrift, 6, 1957.
12. Standard deviation divided by the average.
13. Inequality among employees' families was considerably lower than that among all families (see Chapter 4).
14. Morgan et al., op. cit.
15. Whether the family head belonged to the labor force explained 45-50% as the first factor out of a total explanation of 70% for income from work per week.
16. The greater importance of the number of children stems from the definition (income per standard adult), and the greater importance of country of origin seems to be connected with this, due to the great difference in family size between the communities (see Chapter 5).
17. Schooling appeared in this regression in interaction with age. In this category, the average age of family heads was 64 years (standard deviation 13.8); thus, most family heads did not belong to the labor force because of old age, and the main variations in this variable stemmed from the variations in educational levels. Average years of schooling were 6 (standard deviation 5.13).
18. Duration of work during the year (weeks worked) is included under the heading "labor force participation" since it indicates whether labor force participation was full or only part of the year.
19. See the findings of Morgan et al., *op. cit.*
20. Jacob Mincer, "The Distribution of Labor Incomes: A Survey with Special Reference to the Human Capital Approach", *Journal of Economic Literature*, March 1970. Mark Blaug, "Human Capital Theory: A Slightly Jaundiced Survey", *Journal of Economic Literature*, Sept. 1976.
21. Family Expenditure Survey 1968/69, CBS Special Series No. 388.
22. But it must be assumed that work experience of women was generally smaller.
23. See Chapter 8 for an analysis of low income groups by income per standard adult.
24. See also Chapter 5, especially Table 5.5

CHAPTER 8

POVERTY IN ISRAEL

Introduction

This analysis of poverty in Israel combines the two approaches to poverty outlined in the Introduction — the "absolute" approach and the "relative" approach. The data of the family expenditure survey 1968/69 have been grouped according to income and consumption per standard equivalent adult in order to take into account differences in family size and economies of scale. (For the equivalence scale used see Appendix, Table 8A.1).

The lowest income group (in poverty) was defined as having a monthly gross cash income per standard adult below IL100 in 1968/69; this poverty line was approximately one-third of the average and about 38% of the median. If imputed income from an owned dwelling is added and direct taxes are deducted, this line was equivalent to a total net income of IL118 per standard adult — 40% of the average, and almost half the median — since imputed income constituted a higher percentage of total net income in the low income groups than in the average and median groups.

An additional group bordering on poverty (near-poverty) was defined as having a gross cash income per standard equivalent adult above IL100, but below IL125 — i.e., about 40% of the average, and almost half of the median.[1]

A cash income of IL100 per S.E.A. was equivalent to a total net income (included imputed income) of about IL390 for a standard family of four (husband, wife and two children). This is estimated to have covered the minimum needs in 1968/69, as calculated in 1963 by a committee appointed by the Minister of Welfare and adjusted for the rise in the general standard of living.[2]

Characteristics of Poverty Groups: Statistical Analysis

Regression analysis showed that the main causes of low income per standard equivalent adult were lack of earning power of the family head due to advanced age or disability; or the low earning power of the head of a large family because of low educational level and lack of occupational skills; or some combination of these causes.[3]

The low-income groups (according to an ordering by income per standard equivalent adult) therefore consist of the old and disabled, on one hand, and of large families whose heads had low earning power because of low educational level and low occupational skills or some disabilities, on the other hand.

Families with a cash income per S.E.A. below IL100 in 1968/69 (poverty group) accounted for 12.3% of all families and 13% of all persons (Appendix, Table 8A.2). An additional 6.2% of the families and 7% of all persons had cash incomes per S.E.A. of between IL100 and IL125 (near-poverty group). The poverty group included 16% of all children (another 9% of all children were in the near-poverty group) and 29% of all family heads aged 65 and over. One-third of all family heads with less than five years of schooling were in the poverty group, as were 35% of all family heads who did not belong to the labor force.

Food consumption constituted more than 40% of total consumption expenditure in the poverty and near-poverty group, compared with only one-fourth in the remainder of the population.

As Table 8A.2 (Appendix) shows, the poverty population consisted of a relatively high percentage of individuals living alone, two-person families, and many large families. Hence, almost half of the poverty and near-poverty population were children below the age of 17, compared with only 37% in the remainder of the population. This high percentage of children was the most disturbing aspect of poverty in Israel in 1968/69. About one-fourth of all children lived in poverty and near-poverty, seriously impairing their prospects in society because of the great influence of the home environment on aspirations and educational achievements.

58% of the family heads in the poverty group and 46% in the near-poverty group were over 55 years old, compared with only one-third in the remainder of the population. 54% of the family heads in the poverty group and 32% in the near-poverty group did not belong to the labor force, compared with only 12% in the remainder of the population. This shows the preponderance of family heads who did not work because of old age, especially in the poverty group. In the near-poverty group, working family heads with low earning power and large families were more numerous.

A high percentage of family heads in poverty had less than five years of schooling: 53% in the poverty group and 41% in the near-poverty group, compared with 13% in the remainder of the population. The low educational level, combined with low occupational skills, explains the low earnings of the working family heads; however, these factors also caused the low incomes of the old and retired, since pensions are determined by previous income from work — which was greatly influenced by educational and occupational levels.

Low-income groups show a relatively high percentage of family heads born in Asian-African countries, and relatively low percentages of those born in Europe, America and Israel. Among the old and retired, the share of those born in Europe and America was considerable; among the working heads of large families, the percentage of those born in Asia and Africa was relatively large.

A relatively high percentage of new immigrants and women living alone were in poverty. 22% of all families in the poverty and near-poverty groups had immigrated after 1958, compared with only 11% in the remainder of the population. 27% of all family heads in the poverty group and 21% in the near-poverty group were women, compared with only 11% in the remainder of the population. Two-thirds of these women lived alone. Most of these single women in the lowest income groups were old and did not work. Some 30% of all one-parent families with women heads also lived in poverty and near-poverty.

A large percentage of the low-income population lived in the smaller towns, mostly in new development towns. Less than one-quarter of the families in the poverty group and only 35% in the near-poverty group lived in the three large cities, compared with 42% of the remaining population.

An ordering of families by deciles according to consumption per standard equivalent adult shows a similar picture (Appendix, Table 8A.3). The low consumption groups had a preponderance of aged family heads not belonging to the labor force, as well as a relatively high percentage of large families.

The consumption data allow a comparison with the highest deciles, as well as with the average. Table 8A.3 shows that 48% of all family heads in the lowest decile and 27% in the second-lowest decile did not belong to the labor force, compared with only 10% in the two highest deciles. 29% of all families in the lowest decile and 50% of those in the second lowest were families of five or more persons, compared with only 4% in the highest decile.

The low income categories consisted of two distinct groups: families whose heads did not belong to the labor force because of old age or some disability, and families whose heads worked but had low incomes. In the first group, the family heads were much older and had a lower education, and the families were small. Most of the individuals and two-person families were in this group. Among those working, a considerable percentage worked only part of the year; the families were relatively large; and the family heads had low educational levels (although higher than those not belonging to the labor force).

46% of all families with heads not in the labor force were in poverty and near-poverty, and only 12% of the families whose heads worked.

54% of all family heads in the poverty group did not belong to the labor force, but their families constituted only 32% of all persons in that group, i.e. 68% of all persons in poverty belonged to families whose heads worked. In the near-poverty group, family heads who worked had a greater weight than those not in the labor force and their families were 84% of all persons in the near-poverty group.

The causes of low income were different in these two categories.

Non-participation in the labor force, due mostly to old age, combined with low educational level were the main causes of low income of families whose heads were not in the labor force; in the second category, the low earnings of the family head, combined with large family size, were the main causes of low income per standard equivalent adult. Almost three-quarters of all persons in the poverty and near-poverty groups belonged to families whose heads worked, but their earnings were too low to guarantee their families (which were mostly large) an income above the poverty band. Hence, the high percentage of children living in poverty and near-poverty.

Non-Participation in the Labor Force

More than half the families in the poverty group and one third of those in the near-poverty group had heads who were not in the labor force (Appendix, Table 8A.2). Their incomes were low primarily because the main earner in the family did not work due to old age or some disability, and income from other sources was very small.

Table 8.1 shows the composition of families whose heads were not in the labor force.

Table 8.1
Composition of Families

	Head not in Labor Force %	*Head Self-Employed or Employee* %
Husband-Wife Families, wife working	8	23
Husband-Wife Families, wife not working	41	67
Independent Individuals, men	5	2.5
Independent Individuals, women	29	2.5
One-Parent Families, men heads	2	2
One-Parent Families, women heads	15	3
TOTAL	100	100

Only about half of the families whose heads were not in the labor force were husband-wife families, compared with 90% among all other families. Women living alone constituted 29% of those not in the labor force, compared with 2½% of those working; one-parent families with women-heads constituted 15% of those not in the labor force, compared with only 3% in the remainder of the population.

35% of the families whose heads were not in the labor force were in the poverty group, and 11% were in the near-poverty group. The composition of the families of this category in the poverty band was quite similar to that shown above — with some preponderance of individuals, and with fewer husband-wife families with working wives. Most of these families had no earner at all.

Non-participation of the family head in the labor force was caused by old age or disability. But a substantial percentage of those who retired because of advanced age lived in quite comfortable circumstances, since they received considerable pensions on the basis of previous earnings or had incomes from other sources. Hence, even the highest income groups had families whose heads were not in the labor force. Low educational level of the aged (indicating low earnings before retirement and lack of pension rights stemming from previous work) was, therefore, an additional cause of low income; 71% of all family heads more than 65 years old who were not in the labor force and were in the poverty group had less than five years of schooling. This combination of non-participation in the labor force with low educational level caused low income in most cases.

Most family heads not in the labor force were more than 55 years old in all income ranges (about 80% or more); but in the poverty and near-poverty groups the percentage of those with a low educational level was much higher than in the rest of the population. 65% of family heads not in the labor force in the poverty group, and 48% of those in the near-poverty group, had less than five years of schooling — compared with 26% in the other income groups (Appendix, Table 8A.4). This, too, is a relatively high percentage connected with the higher age groups in this category. Only 13% of all family heads above the poverty band had less than five years of schooling (Appendix, Table 8A.2). This is connected with a certain inverse correlation between age and educational level due to the rapid expansion of education during the last 25 years.

Because of the large percentage of independent individuals, old couples and one-parent families among families whose heads were not in the labor force, average family size in this category was small. Though 47% of all families in poverty and near-poverty belonged to this category, they constituted only 26% of all persons. The great majority (about three-quarters of all persons in poverty and near-poverty) belonged to families whose heads were working, but their income per standard equivalent adult was low.

Low Income of Families with Working Family Heads

Low income per standard equivalent adult in families in which the main earner was working had the following main causes:

1. Partial employment due to age or poor health;
2. Low income due to low educational level and low occupational skills;
3. Low income per standard equivalent adult due to large family size.

In most cases, we find a combination of these causes.

Partial Employment, Education and Age

46% of all family heads in the poverty group and 68% of those in the near-poverty group were working. A considerable part of these were only partially employed during the year. 27% of the working family heads in the poverty group and 18% of those in the near-poverty group worked less than 43 weeks per year compared to only 5% in the rest of the population.

A small percentage of those who were partially employed entered the labor force during the year, after military service or after completion of their studies; they were in the lowest income ranges only temporarily. Some additional cases were temporarily in distress due to a work or traffic accident or ill health. But the majority of those partially employed were workers who changed jobs frequently because of low work capacity, lack of skills, mental or physical disability, or chronic illness.

While we had data on partial employment during the year (weeks worked), we did not have data on part-time work — which was more frequent in the lower income brackets than in the higher ones.

The most important cause of low income per standard equivalent adult in families whose heads were working was their lack of occupational skills and their low educational level.[4] Table 8A.5 (Appendix) shows that 41% of the employees in the poverty group and 36% in the near-poverty group had less than five years of schooling, compared with 11% in all other income ranges. Only about one-fifth in the poverty and near-poverty groups had more than eight years of schooling, compared with 58% in the other income brackets. Among the self-employed, too, the educational level of those in poverty and near-poverty was decidedly lower than that of the others.

Family heads in the poverty and near-poverty groups who were employees were somewhat older than those in the other income brackets — but among the self-employed, age was no cause of low income. Self-employed family heads in general were older than employees.

Occupation

The data available to us allow a classification of occupations only in very broad groups.

The data show that working family heads in poverty and near-poverty groups were concentrated in the lower-paid occupations. There were no professional and scientific workers, and very few managerial and clerical workers, in the poverty group; these two occupational groups were also very sparsely represented in the near-poverty group. Against this, there was a considerably higher percentage of traders, agents, salesmen and service workers in the poverty and near-poverty groups (compared with the rest of the population), comprising numerous small peddlers, hawkers and occasional service workers. But the relative share of blue-collar workers (industrial, agricultural, construction and transport workers) was only somewhat higher in the lowest income brackets. It has to be assumed (according to the earnings of these family heads) that they belonged to the least skilled and were among those with the lowest earnings in each occupational group. Each occupational group had a broad range of earnings. Thus, for instance, average earnings per hour of an employee among the clerical workers were IL. 5.26 in 1973, but 10% of them earned less than IL. 2.50 per hour, and 14% earned more than IL. 8.

Family Size

There was a preponderance of large families in the lowest income ranges (by income per S.E.A.). Almost 30% of all families in the poverty and near-poverty groups had six persons or more, compared with about 11% in the other income brackets. Most of the heads of the large families in the two lowest income brackets worked.[5] The combination of low earning power of the family head and large family size caused the low income per standard equivalent adult in these families. Large family size can cause low income per S.E.A. even in families with middling incomes. Thus, a family of nine would be in the poverty group, even if family income was 55% of the average — as would a family of six if family income was 45% of the average.

The causes of large family size have not been investigated in this study. Educational level, age, degree of religious observance, country of origin, environment (dwelling locality), housing facilities and (to some degree) earnings are factors influencing family size. Since low educational level of the family head (and his wife) causes low earnings and influences family size, this was the most conspicuous feature of large families in the lowest income ranges.

This, of course, had a negative influence on the socio-economic prospects of the many children in the poverty band (about one fourth of all children), as the low educational level of their parents was the most important cause for low aspirations and low educational achievements, seriously impairing equality of opportunity.

Country of Origin

There was a preponderance of families who had immigrated from Asian-African countries in the poverty and near-poverty groups. 60% of Jewish family heads in the lowest brackets (income per standard equivalent adult) were born in Asian-African countries, compared with 32% in the other income brackets.

Regression analysis showed that income per S.E.A. was influenced by country of origin to a certain degree.[6] In the main, the fact that the family head had immigrated from Europe or America before 1958 had a considerable positive influence on income per standard equivalent adult, compared with Jewish Israeli-born family heads. The fact that the family head was born in Asia or Africa had a smaller negative influence compared with Jewish Israeli-born heads. An investigation into the determinants of family income showed that after the influence of the family head's education on family income had been taken into account, country of origin and year of immigration had little influence — because of the stronger correlation of country of origin with education than with family income. (Chapter 7).

The lower educational level of family heads who had immigrated from Asian and African countries was also the main cause of the relatively large percentage of these families in the lowest brackets by income per standard equivalent adult.

Table 8A.6 (Appendix) shows that the educational level of family heads who had immigrated from Asia or Africa was considerably lower than that of the other family heads in the poverty and near-poverty groups. It was also lower in the other income brackets. The higher percentage of families whose heads had immigrated from Asia or Africa in poverty and near-poverty is well accounted for by their lower educational level.

Income per S.E.A. was, as we have seen, decisively influenced by family size in addition to the other determinants of family income. Large family size as an additional cause of low income per S.E.A. was found mainly among families whose heads had immigrated from Asian or African countries (Appendix, Table 8A.7). Though there was a greater percentage of one- and two-person families in the poverty group than of families with seven or more persons, the latter had much more weight among the number of persons. In the near-poverty group, the percentage of large families was greater than that of small families.

The majority of families of European-American origin in poverty and near-poverty were among those not in the labor force — mostly widows, widowers or old couples — and average family size was therefore small. The majority among those of Asian-African origin were large families whose heads worked.

Families whose heads had immigrated from European-American countries were, on the average, older in all income categories, compared with the other segments of the population. The relatively high percentage of young family heads born in Israel in poverty groups stems from the very low percentage of Israeli-born family heads in the poverty groups. It includes students with low part-time incomes and persons who started work only during the year — i.e. whose low incomes were only temporary and who did not really belong to the poverty groups.

Dwelling Locality

A considerable part of the families in poverty and near-poverty groups lived in smaller localities, mostly in the development towns. The three largest cities accounted for only 26% of the families in poverty and 35% of those in near-poverty compared with 42% in all other income ranges. Jerusalem was exceptional among the three cities; the percentage of families in near-poverty living in Jerusalem was higher than that in the other income groups.

The greater concentration of low-income groups in the new towns is a well-known phenomenon, connected with the lower educational and occupational level of the population and the less-prosperous employment opportunities in these towns compared with the other towns. An additional factor is the fact that some of the people in the well-paid occupations (engineers, doctors, teachers) do not live in these towns, but commute from a nearby town or suburb.

Housing

An important dimension of poverty is overcrowded housing of low quality. In 1968, 9% of all Jewish families lived in a housing density of three persons or more per room (this share declined to 3½% in 1976), and we have to assume that almost all of them belonged to the lowest income ranges. The large families in the lowest income brackets usually lived in crowded conditions. 90% of the families who lived in a density of more than three persons per room were families of six persons or more. One-third of the families in the poverty group and 39% of those in the near-poverty group owned their dwellings and one-half had paid key-money for their rented dwellings.

The relatively high percentage of owner-occupiers even in the lowest income categories stems from the special conditions in Israel. The law on rented dwellings, which was imposed in World War II and is still valid for old buildings, made construction of rented dwellings unprofitable. Thus, it was necessary to buy a dwelling or to buy the right to occupy it; public financing of housing through mortgages and loans made this possible even for low-income groups.

Crowded, low-quality housing, together with the low educational level of the parents and low income, are mainly responsible for the vicious circle of poverty for children from large families in the lowest income groups. The crowded living conditions, and the lack of encouragement by parents and the environment, make it difficult for a child to persevere in his studies and to achieve the school marks necessary for the continuation of his education. Hence, there are many school dropouts among these children, and only a small percentage continues to secondary schools and the university. But only education and vocational training can enable these children to obtain an occupation which will assure them and their families an income above the poverty band.

The above analysis shows the great importance of the educational level to income per standard equivalent adult. The effect of education on the reduction of poverty (and the ills connected with it) has been recognized by the government; many measures have been introduced to encourage educational achievements of the children of poor and uneducated parents. The fact that only 7% of the family heads of Jewish families in poverty and near-poverty were born in Israel, compared with 14% in the other income groups, is an indicator of some success of these measures. Our figures pertain to 1968/69; in 1975/76 the figures were 10% and 22% respectively.

The causes of poverty and near-poverty are summarized in Table 8.2.

Table 8.2
Causes of Poverty, 1968/69

Causes of Poverty	*Characteristics of Family Heads*	*% in poverty group* (1)	*% in near-poverty group* (2)	*% in remainder of population* (3)	*ratio (1) : (3)* (4)
1. Non-participation in labor force	not belonging to labor force	54	32	12	4.5
2. No or low education	0-4 years of schooling	53	41	13	4.1
3. Large families	7 members or more	19	23	7	2.7
4. Women heads of families	women	27	21	11	2.5
5. Old age	aged 55+	58	46	33	1.8

Estimated Situation in the Mid-Seventies

Since 1968/69, the absolute and the relative positions of the low income groups have improved notably. Unemployment declined, and there was a considerable rise in the standard of living of all strata of the population, including those in the lowest income brackets. Social transfer payments rose dramatically in the mid-seventies, raising relative incomes of the lowest income groups.

The percentage of unemployed declined from 5.3% in 1968/69 to 3-3½%. GNP per capita at constant prices rose 27% from 1969 to 1976. The average income of employees' families at constant prices rose 30% from the beginning of 1969 to the beginning of 1976.

Inequality declined little from 1968/69 to 1974, but decreased remarkably in 1975 and 1976. According to the data of the family survey, the inequality index for gross cash family income declined from 0.371 in 1968/69 to 0.334 in 1975/76 — i.e., about 10% during the seven years from 1968/69. The income share of the two lowest deciles rose by one fifth from 4.7% in 1968/69 to 5.6% in 1975/76.

In 1975/76, the median net income (including income in kind and imputed income) per standard equivalent adult was IL.1,370.[7] The lowest decile of families in an ordering of net income per S.E.A. was in the net income range of IL 132-636 per S.E.A. Only 6½% of all families (comprising 8½% of the population) were in the poverty group — i.e., had a net income per S.E.A. below 40% of the median (IL.538). 11.3% of the families and 15% of the population had a net income per S.E.A. below half of the median (IL.660), i.e. were below the near-poverty line.

The share of families in poverty and near-poverty declined from 18% in 1968/69 to 11% in 1975/76, and the share of the population in poverty and near-poverty from 20% to 15%. In 1977, the proportion of those in poverty and near-poverty appears to have declined further.

The characteristics of the poverty and near-poverty groups also changed. The rise in the percentage of large families and in the percentage of working family heads indicates that the decline of the extent of poverty and near-poverty in 1975/76 was more pronounced in the group of aged family heads who were singles or had small families than in the group of working family heads with large families.

Table 8.3 presents a comparison of the characteristics of poverty and near-poverty groups in 1968/69 and 1975/76.

Heads of families living in poverty and near-poverty in 1975/76 were younger and more educated than those in 1968/69. Only 35% were above 55 years of age, compared to 54% in 1968/69; 25% had post-primary education, compared to 17% in 1968/69. However, a comparison with the total population shows that the educational level of those living in poverty and near-poverty was much lower. 61% of all urban family heads had post-primary education in 1975/76 (compared with 25% in the poverty and near-poverty population). The percentage of family heads aged more than 55 years was similar in the total population (34%), but the percentage of those aged 65 and more was higher in the poverty and near-poverty group — 22% compared to 17% in the total population.

An important change was the rise in the percentage of families from Asia-Africa in the poverty and near-poverty group from 60% of Jewish families in 1968/69 to 67% in 1975/76 and that of Jewish Israel-born family heads (part of whose fathers had immigrated from Asia-Africa) from 7% to 10%. This was connected with the rise in the percentage of large families (5 persons and more) in the poverty and near-poverty group from 35% in 1968/69 to 50% in 1975/76, and the increase in the percentage of children from 48% in 1968/69 to 55% in 1975/76.

The absolute number of large families with working heads whose country of origin was in Asia-Africa and who were in poverty and near-poverty declined, though their weight in the poverty and near-poverty population increased. The absolute number of children in poverty and near-poverty also declined.

This estimate of the poverty and near-poverty population is based on the relative concept of poverty. The absolute poverty line of 1968/69 in 1975/76

Table 8.3
Characteristics of Poverty and Near-Poverty Groups
1968/69 and 1975/76

	1968/69	*1975/76**	*Change (%)*
% of families	18.5	11.3	−39
% of persons	20.0	14.7	−27
Family size (%)			
1 — 2	48.4	35.2	−29
3 — 4	16.5	14.6	−11
5+	35.1	50.2	+43
Age of Family Head (%)			
18 — 34	14.6	24.5	+68
35 — 54	31.2	40.5	+30
55+	54.2	35.0	−35
Education of Family Head (%)			
0 — 4	48.6	33.5	−31
5 — 8	34.6	41.5	+20
9 — 12	10.4	17.3	+66
13+	6.4	7.7	+20
Country of Origin of Jewish Family Head (%)			
Asia-Africa	59.9	67.3	+12
Europe-America	33.2	22.2	−33
Israel	6.9	10.5	+52

Source: Table 8A.2 (Appendix); Statistical Abstract 1977, p. 266.
*Characteristics of lowest decile of net income per standard adult.

was a total net income of IL.415 per S.E.A. and the near-poverty line IL.490 per S.E.A.[8] According to this definition of the poverty line, only 5% of the families lived in poverty and an additional 2% in near-poverty. The proportion of the population living in poverty and near-poverty according to the 1968/69 definition was about 9%.

The additional real income was used as follows: 37% for the additional population, 13% increased the income of the families crossing the near-poverty line (to the lower income brackets above that line), 2% raised the income of those remaining below the near-poverty line, and 48% increased the income of the non-poverty population.

Most of the families in poverty and a great part of those in near-poverty lived in crowded conditions. 3.6% of all Jewish families had 3 persons or more per room in 1976, and 84% of these were large families (six persons or more) which had on the average 4-5 children below the age of 17. Hence, about 11% of all children lived in crowded conditions in 1976.

This is a great improvement in comparison with the situation in 1968/69, when about 9% of all Jewish families still had a housing density of 3 and more persons per room, and about 30% of all Jewish children lived in crowded conditions.

One of the most important consequences of the improvement in 1975/76 was the decline in the number of children in poverty and near-poverty. Even for the latter, equality of opportunities was greatly improved by better housing conditions and special educational arrangements for children from deprived homes, such as a prolonged schoolday, supervised homework, and individual coaching.

The various measures of income maintenance were instrumental in achieving the decline in the proportion of the population in poverty and near-poverty in the mid-seventies. However, there exists a hard core of multi-problem families for which an increase in incomes can solve only part of their problems. Long-term measures and patient work are necessary to better their situation and to improve the equality of opportunities for their children, as well as for all children in the lower income brackets.

NOTES

1. This is equivalent to a total net income (including imputed income) of about IL140 per S.E.A. — i.e., about 58% of median income.
2. Minimum needs of a standard family of four were calculated at IL260 in 1963. The cost of living index rose by 26% from 1963 to September 1968 (center of the income period of the 1968/69 survey); the cost of the same consumption basket in September 1968 was IL328 for a family of four, and IL100 per standard adult — but real consumption per head rose by approximately 17% over this period. If it is agreed that the minimum requirements rose in line with consumption per head at current prices (46%), they were in September 1968 about IL380 for a family of four or IL115 per standard adult.
3. See Chapter 7.
4. See Chapter 7: Determinants of income per S.E.A.
5. Regression analysis showed that income per standard adult was negatively influenced to a considerable degree by the number of children in all families, all husband-wife families, and in the families of employees. In the families whose heads were not in the labor force, no such influence was found (Chapter 7, Appendix — Regressions 15-18, 22, 23).
6. See Chapter 7 on Determinants of Income per Standard Equivalent Adult, and Appendix, Table 7A.9, regression no. 15.
7. Data of family survey 1975/76.
8. The poverty line in 1968/69 was IL. 118 total net income per S.E.A. and the near-poverty line was IL. 140 total net income per S.E.A. Consumption prices rose three and a half times between the two surveys (see Statistical Abstract 1977, p. 259).

PART III

ECONOMIC DEVELOPMENT AND INEQUALITY

CHAPTER 9

ISRAEL IN THE WORLD

International comparisons of income distribution involve even more difficulties than do intertemporal comparisons within a single country. There are different definitions of income-receiving units and incomes, different coverage of the population, different sampling methods and different degrees of underreporting.

J. Jain of the World Bank[1] assembled data on 81 countries, denoting the income-receiving unit and coverage. M. Sawyer[2] gives "reasonably comparable" data on income distribution in 10-12 OECD countries. We used these sources to compare income distribution in Israel with that in other countries.

Income Inequality in Less-Developed and Developed Countries

55 countries for which data gave the household as the income-receiving unit were arranged in six groups by per-capita income. Income inequality was considerably higher in countries with low per-capita incomes. Income inequality rose with per-capita income up to about \$1000, fell slightly in the \$1000—\$2000 group, and declined considerably in the \$2000—\$4000 group; above \$4000, no trend can be discerned. The rise in the standard of living from group to group is also indicated by the rise in life expectancy and the decline in the share of agriculturists among the employed. (Table 9.1). The rise in income inequality during the first stages of development and its decline in the later stages was early recognized by S. Kuznets and later demonstrated by others (see Trends over Time).

We included some data on urban populations only when they were assumed to be representative of the total population, such as in Israel, Japan and Ireland.

The data on Japan show some of the difficulties we encountered. Jain gives two sets of figures for Japan; both are for households covering the total population, and both are for 1971. The first set, an estimate based on survey figures by Wada, has a Gini coefficient of 0.422; for the second set the Gini coefficient is 0.287. Sawyer uses 1969 figures with a Gini coefficient of 0.333;

Table 9.1
Income Distribution in 55 Countries
(Grouped by GDP per capita in 1973)
(% of income)

GDP per capita in 1973	*up to* $*200*	$*200-* $*500*	$*500-* $*1,000*	$*1,000-* $*2,000*	$*2,000-* $*4,000*	$*4,000+*
Lowest 40%	14.5	13.5	13.4	14.6	17.3	16.3
Middle 40%	34.9	33.8	33.1	34.4	39.0	40.3
Highest 20%	50.6	52.7	53.5	51.0	43.7	43.4
Gini Coefficient	0.449	0.473	0.481	0.444	0.376	0.374
Ratio of highest to lowest decile	21.3	23.1	25.7	18.3	13.8	16.2
Expectation of life, years	46.3	54.2	61.8	67.9	71.6	72.6
% of agriculture in economically active population	62	53	38.5	23.7	13.4	8.7
No. of countries	10	10	14	6	6	9

Source: J. Jain, op. cit., M. Sawyer, op. cit., Statistical Yearbook, U.N., 1975.
Yearbook of Labour Statistics, ILO, 1975.
Yearbook of National Accounts, U.N., 1975.

since he found these to be "reasonably comparable" to his other figures, we used his data — though they are only for the urban population. It may well be that the Wada estimate represents income distribution in Japan more accurately — but which set of figures is comparable to the data for other countries? Income distribution data based on surveys seem in general to suffer from underreporting, especially in the highest income brackets; estimates adjusted for such underreporting may make income distribution appear to be more unequal than that in other countries, although in reality there is no such difference.

Some data about which we have some doubt are included. For instance, the data for Bangladesh and Pakistan show very low inequality — similar to previous data on India. But recent data on India which are more comprehensive and more representative reveal much higher inequality.[3] We are inclined to assume that income inequality in Pakistan and Bangladesh is not very different from that in India; nevertheless, we used the available data.

Household surveys apparently include more strata of the population and become more representative of the total population as the standard of living rises. In some countries, adjustments were made to compensate for deficiencies in the data; in other countries, such adjustments are lacking. We hope that the group averages compensate for some of these differences. Nevertheless, it seems to us that there is a certain bias in the group figures as well, since income inequality seems to be reflected in the data more accurately for the high-income countries. Hence, the differences in income inequality between the various groups are estimated to be larger than those appearing in Table 9.1, especially between countries above and below the $2000 line.

Israel's per-capita income in 1973 was $2883. Since there is almost no difference in income inequality between the $2000—4000 group and the $4000 plus group, we compared the Israel data with those of the OECD countries in both groups.

Comparison with OECD Countries

In a distribution of pre-tax incomes in ten OECD countries, Israel ranked sixth in 1968/69 after Australia, Japan, United Kingdom, Sweden and Norway — but it had the second lowest inequality index in 1975/76, although it had the

Table 9.2
Inequality of Family Incomes in OECD Countries (Gini Coefficient)

Country	*Year*	*Pre-Tax*	*After-Tax*	*GDP per capita 1973 ($)*
Australia	1966/67	0.313	0.312	5,448
Japan	1969	0.335	0.316	3,782
United Kingdom	1973	0.344	0.318	3,088
Sweden	1972	0.346	0.302	6,185
Norway	1970	0.354	0.307	4,842
Canada	1969	0.382	0.354	5,412
Netherlands	1967	0.385	0.354	4,435
West-Germany	1973	0.396	0.383	5,671
United States	1972	0.404	0.381	6,167
France	1970	0.416	0.414	4,797
Spain	1973/74	. . .	0.355	1,751
Italy	1969	. . .	0.398	2,515
Israel,				
total income	1968/69	0.357	. . .	2,883
money income	1968/69	0.371	0.327	
total income	1975/76	0.314	0.282	
money income	1975/76	0.334	0.296	

Source: Appendix, Tables 9A.1 and 9A.2.

lowest GDP per capita. In a distribution of after-tax incomes among twelve OECD countries, Israel again ranked sixth after the same five countries (although in different order) in 1968/69, and had the lowest inequality in 1975/76, while it had the third lowest GDP per capita after Spain and Italy (Table 9.2).

Sawyer emphasizes that the greatest differences between countries are in the two lowest deciles and the top decile. The income share of the two lowest deciles was relatively low in Israel (ranking sixth) in pre-tax incomes; but in post-tax incomes their income share compared better, and Israel ranked second to fourth with Sweden and Australia. Its top decile had the lowest pre-tax and post-tax income share. This shows that the economic gap between the low and high income brackets was relatively small in Israel in 1975/76. The net income of the highest quintile was only 5.5 times higher than that of the lowest quintile. If underreporting was more extensive in Israel than in other countries, this would impair our comparison. Sawyer shows that there was considerable underreporting for entrepreneurial income and less for wages and salaries. In Israel, too, underreporting appears to be greater among the self-employed than among wage and salary earners, but it is difficult to estimate the extent of underreporting.

Sawyer sees underreporting as the most important statistical difficulty. Differences in income-receiving units — tax unit, household, family — were avoided in his comparisons as far as possible; the income-receiving unit was the household.

The differences in age structure and in the distribution of family size should be taken into account in intercountry comparisons. Sawyer shows that the income distribution of households with heads aged 25-54 years is more equal than that of all households, because the very young and the old household heads are concentrated in the lowest income brackets. The proportions of old persons in the six countries for which data are available are not very different, so the difference in inequality between the two categories (25-54 years old and all family heads) moves in a narrow range between 17% and 22%. The difference is 17% in Israel, Australia and Canada (Appendix, Table 9A.3).

Per capita distribution of income compensates for differences in household size (Appendix, Table 9A.4). Inequality of household incomes was generally smaller per capita than per household. In particular, the income shares of the two lowest deciles were higher in the per capita distribution — even for Australia, where per-family distribution shows smaller general inequality. In Israel, the difference between the per capita and per family distributions was especially large — because of the great variation in family size, and the concentration of small families in the lowest income brackets in the per family distribution. The average family sizes in the two bottom deciles were 1.8 and 2.8 in the per family distribution, compared with 5.7 and 4.1 in the per capita distribution. Sawyer cites the case of Sweden, with household sizes of 1.1 and 1.2 in the two lowest deciles of the per household income distribution and 3.0

and 3.2 in the per capita income distribution. The share of the two bottom deciles was two-thirds higher in the per-capita distributions in Israel and Norway, and 54% in the United Kingdom. In the other countries, the difference ranged between 26% and 45%.

The one-person and two-person households cluster in the two bottom deciles to a greater extent in Israel than in the OECD countries. But the large families (five or more persons) are concentrated in the higher income brackets in the OECD countries, while they tend to be in the middle and lower income brackets in Israel (Appendix, Table 9A.5). As we have seen, a considerable part of the poverty population in Israel consisted of large families (Chapter 8) including a considerable number of children.

The best way to avoid the difficulties of different intra-country variations in household size is to compare income distribution by adult equivalent units. Sawyer has data only on the after-tax distribution in Yugoslavia in 1963; these show a somewhat higher inequality index (0.331) than do comparable Israeli figures for 1968/69 (0.328) — and a somewhat higher income share of the two lowest deciles as well as of the highest decile. In 1975/76 the inequality index for net income per standard adult in Israel was much lower — 0.297.[4]

In Israel, 59% of the family heads aged 65 years and over were in the two bottom deciles in 1968/69, compared with 47% in six OECD countries, but the proportion of old persons in the total population was somewhat higher in the OECD countries. A high percentage of old persons is the result of the relatively high life expectancy and the relatively low birth rate in the developed countries. In Israel, life expectancy is relatively high, and a large part of the population has a relatively low birth rate. Family heads over 65 constituted 17% of all family heads in Israel, and about 20% of the arithmetic mean of the six OECD countries. Though the percentage of old people in Israel was somewhat smaller than in the OECD countries, they were concentrated more heavily in the lowest income brackets, and they constituted a large portion of those in poverty (Chapter 8).

The high percentage of social transfers (pensions, allowances and supports) in the lowest income brackets is another feature, which Israel has in common with the OECD countries. Social transfers accounted for 69% of gross money income of the bottom decile in Israel in 1968/69 and for 75% in 1975/76, and for 77% in six OECD countries. The six OECD countries are Canada, France, Germany, Norway, the United Kingdom and the United States, whose average per capita income was three-fourths higher than that of Israel.

The share of wages and salaries in family income by deciles is quite similar in Israel and the OECD countries.

Educational inequality is one of the most important factors in income inequality. Table 9.3 shows earnings differentials between educational levels for Israel and six OECD countries.

Israel had the lowest earnings differentials between primary, secondary and higher education. But in Israel, 9% of the labor force had had no schooling (this percentage had declined to 4% in 1976), while in the six OECD countries there were none. This introduces additional earnings differentials between those with no schooling and the other educational levels in Israel, and earnings inequality by educational groups in Israel, was therefore, similar to that in Great Britain and only lower than that in the United States.

The low correlation between the earnings inequality by educational level and inequality of family income stems from the other sources of family income apart from wages and salaries (profits, interest, dividends, rent, pensions and social transfers) and other factors influencing earnings.

Table 9.3
Earnings Differences between Educational Levels

Ratio of	*United Kingdom*	*Norway*	*Israel*	*Canada*	*Nether-lands*	*United States*	*France*
Primary to None	—	—	1.60	—	—	—	—
Secondary to primary	1.45	1.40	1.36	1.44	1.29	1.48	1.50
Higher to secondary	1.61	1.50	1.51	1.83	1.74	1.65	1.73
Higher to primary	2.33	2.13	2.05	2.63	2.24	2.44	2.59
Inequality Index by Educational groups*	.150	.102	.153	.147	.133	.174	...
Gini Coefficient of Family Income	0.344	0.354	0.357	0.382	0.385	0.404	0.416

*Calculated on the basis of G. Psacharopoulos' data, p. 183-185.
Source: G. Psacharopoulos, *Returns to Education*, N.Y. 1973, p. 132.

Earnings differentials by educational level were much greater in less developed countries. In Hong Kong, the mean income of families whose heads were university graduates was seven times higher than that of families whose heads had no formal education, and 5.5 times higher if the family head had some university education (13 years of schooling or more).[5] In West Malaysia, the income of a university graduate was fifteen times that of an employed without formal education, and nine times that of an employed with primary education.[6] Even differences in household expenditure by educational level in less-developed countries were higher than earnings differentials in developed countries by educational level. Thus, consumption expenditure of a household whose head had 13 years or more schooling was 4.6 times higher in Mexico than that of a household whose head had no formal schooling.[7] (See also Psacharopoulos for the larger income differences by educational level in less-developed countries).

Trends Over Time

Kuznets analyzed long-term trends by using historical data on income distribution in nine countries, which he calls "crude approximations" due to difficulties in measurement and comparability.[8] The data show "some narrowing in income inequality" between the beginning of the century and the post-World War II years, and especially from the twenties and thirties to the fifties.

Data available for the nineteenth century show some rise in inequality in Prussia from 1854 to 1913 (and from then on, a decline), and in Saxony from 1880 to 1896. On the other hand, it started declining in the United Kingdom as early as 1880, and in Denmark from 1870 on. This might hold some support for the theory that inequality is widening in the first stages of development.

But Soltow's figures[9] for eight Norwegian cities show a steady decline in inequality from the middle of the nineteenth century, and the changes in inequality had to be attributed to cyclical fluctuations. F. Paukert in his excellent "survey of evidence"[10] cites a study on Great Britain by Soltow which indicates that there was no increase in inequality over a very long period — from the fifteenth century.

Thus, the historical data (which are very scarce for the early stages of today's mature economies) do not unequivocally support the theory that income inequality rises at first. Cross-sectional data, however, show a more pronounced trend of rising inequality with rising per-capita income up to a certain level. Table 9.1 showed some rise in inequality from the group with the lowest per-capita income(below $200) to the second group ($200—$500) and to the third group ($500—$1000); above $1000, inequality declined as per-capita income rose (1973 values).

Kuznets was the first to show the difference in income inequality between developed and developing countries in a number of pathbreaking articles based on cross-section data.[11] Paukert [10] uses grouped cross-sectional data to show that inequality increases with rising per-capita income up to the $300-500 group (1965 values); from then, it declines.

Adelman and Morris[12] analyzed data from 41 countries and concluded that inequality widens in the first stages of development. They saw as the main reason the dual character of developing countries — where a small modern sector develops without having much influence on the large traditional sector in which absolute poverty perpetuates and relative poverty grows.

Ahluwalia investigated short-term changes in the income share of the lowest 40 percent of the population during economic growth in eighteen countries. "In both high-growth and low-growth countries there are some which have experienced improvements and others that have experienced deteriorations in relative equality."[13] However, on the basis of multiple regression analysis of cross-sectional data, he concludes that income inequality first increases and then decreases with development. The income share of the lowest 40 percent first declined with rising per capita income, then rose. High economic growth rates and school enrolment rates had a positive influence on the income shares of the lowest 40%, but high population growth had a negative influence. A large share of agriculture in the GDP had some negative influence.[14]

Since we believe that underestimates of inequality are generally greater in developing countries, the actual difference in inequality between developed and developing countries may be greater than indicated. The cross-sectional evidence is stronger than the historical evidence. Kuznets denotes urbanization as the most important factor in increasing inequality, which is higher in urban areas (where occupational differentiation is greater) than in rural areas. Our data on the Mandatory period showed that the most important cause of high inequality was the income difference between town and village — which is quite large in less-developed countries, and considerably smaller or non-existent in developed countries.

The Impact of Urbanization

Simulation shows that the change in relative incomes of rural areas is decisive for overall inequality during urbanization. In Phase I of our model (Table 9.4), the rural area has 70% of the population and rural incomes average 30% of urban incomes. In Phase II, the rural population is 50% of the total; if relative rural incomes remain the same, and income inequality in each sector does not change, income inequality will rise (Phase IIA). If income inequality in the urban sector rises, total income inequality will increase more (Phase IIB). In Phase III, the rural population declines to 25% of the total. If rural incomes rise from 30% of urban incomes to 60%, while income inequality in each sector remains the same, total income inequality will somewhat decline (Phase IIIA). If there is a decline in inequality in the urban sector and rural incomes rise to 80% of urban incomes this will reduce total inequality considerably (Phase IIIB).

Phase IIA, with the same relative incomes as in Phase I shows a rise of 5% in total inequality. The income share of the lowest 40% declined 11%, although their absolute incomes rose 14% due to urbanization. Phase IIB shows a greater rise in inequality (10%) due to the increase in urban inequality. The relative incomes of the lowest 40% declined 17%, and their absolute incomes rose only 6% due to urbanization. In Phase II average incomes rose 27% due to urbanization, which represents an annual rise of 3% in per capita income during eight years.

Phase III with an urban population of 75% shows a reduction in inequality because of the rise of the relative incomes of the rural population. In Phase IIIA total inequality declined 7% (from Phase I), although income inequality in each sector remained the same. In Phase IIIB total inequality declined much more (24%), since the relative incomes of the rural population rose more than in Phase IIIA and urban income inequality declined. The relative

Table 9.4
Changing Income Inequality During Urbanization

	Phase I (30% Urban, 70% Rural)			*Phase II* (50% Urban, 50% Rural)		*Phase III* (75% Urban, 25% Rural)	
	Rural incomes 30% of urban incomes			*Rural incomes 30% of urban incomes*		A *Rural incomes 60% of urban incomes; same inequalities*	B *Rural incomes 80% of urban incomes; decline in urban inequality*
				A *same inequalities*	B *rise in urban inequality*		
Population Shares (%)	*Urban*	*Rural*	*Total*	*Total*	*Total*	*Total*	*Total*
Lowest 40	13	18	12.6	11.2	10.5	13.7	16.4
Middle 40	34	44	33.0	31.8	31.1	34.9	41.4
Highest 20	53	38	54.4	57.0	58.4	51.4	42.2
Gini Coeff.	.463	.322	.476	.503	.523	.445	.364
Incomes as % of urban incomes	100	30	51	65	65	90	95

incomes of the lowest 40% rose 9% in Phase IIIA and 30% in Phase IIIB, and their absolute incomes jumped 92% and 142% respectively. Average incomes rose 38% in Phase IIIA (annual growth of 3% in per capita income during 11 years) and 46% in Phase IIIB (annual growth of 4% in per capita income during 10 years). The period from phase to phase can be assumed to be longer. In that case economic growth would be larger than that connected with urbanization, and absolute incomes would have been greater.

The main factors influencing inequality during urbanization and development are:

1) The amount of migration from rural to urban areas, and the degree of social and economic integration of the migrants. This depends on the level of employment in urban areas, investment in labor-intensive industries, expansion of social services, and construction of housing.

2) The difference between urban and rural incomes. This difference declines when agricultural productivity rises. Industrial development increases the demand for agricultural products, but the farmers have to adapt their output to the changing demand (more vegetables, fruit, eggs, meat and

milk; less rice and bread cereals) and to modernize their production. If agriculture is export-oriented, the rise in productivity may be quicker. In some countries, drastic measures such as agrarian reforms are required to achieve this; in all countries, credits to small farmers and agricultural extension services are essential.

3) The differentiation among urban incomes, which may grow in the first phase of development due to the scarcity of skills and the growing concentration of wealth. The supply of skills depends on education and vocational training; the demand for skills depends on the degree and structure of investments. The concentration of wealth depends on the tax system (inheritance taxes, capital gains taxes, income taxes) and on the special privileges granted to investors in order to promote private investment. Measures to increase the savings rate may increase the concentration of wealth and income inequality.

4) The extent of poverty. A full-employment policy and a minimum wage can assure that those able to work will not live in absolute poverty. Social transfers to the old, the disabled and the unemployed are another means for combating absolute poverty. The maintenance of social transfers and social services on an appropriate level depends on the efficiency of the tax system along with investment in the country's infrastructure and on the level of development. In the first stages of development, when incomes are still very low, taxes and savings cannot supply the necessary means for investments, social services and a social security system, and deficit spending of the government will create inflationary pressures which increase income inequality. On higher stages of development, the efficiency of the tax system becomes important.

As in the first stages of development income inequality in urban areas usually rises due to growing occupational differentiation, scarcity of skills, and unemployment, while income differences between town and village may even increase, a rise in total inequality has to be expected. The rise in productivity in agriculture which reduces income differentials between towns and rural areas, can arrest the rise in total inequality, and a decline in urban inequality — usually in later stages of urbanization — due to full employment and higher educational levels, will reduce inequality.

The trend of income distribution in developed countries was towards greater equality, as shown by Sawyer for a relatively short period (from the fifties to the beginning of the seventies). The decline in the weight of agriculture (the poorest sector) is cited as one factor in reducing inequality; another was the decline in the percentage of self-employed (among whom inequality is especially high). Sawyer also claims that the reduction in inequality would have been larger but for the aging of the population, and the formation of smaller households (which raised statistical inequality without influencing the distribution of economic welfare).

All of these factors were present in Israel, too, but with different degrees of effectiveness. The decline in the percentage of self-employed was very small. The decline in the weight of the agricultural sector does not affect our results over time in Israel, since our comparison was only within the urban sector; however, this factor was very important for our comparison between the Mandatory period and Israel. We found that the most important cause of the decline in inequality was the dramatic reduction of the income difference between the rural and urban sectors.

The formation of smaller households was influential in Israel. Income inequality per family declined less than inequality measured by income per standard equivalent adult. The aging of the population contributed considerably to inequality; changes in the age composition of family heads raised income inequality about 6% (Chapter 4), but other factors compensated for this rise, especially the decline in educational inequality.

The effect of the employment level on income inequality was shown to be very strong in Israel, and is evident in the historical data of Kuznets and Soltow. Changes in the demand/supply situation of skilled manpower were also very influential in Israel. Some changes in income distribution in the OECD countries may well be attributed to cyclical fluctuations and to changes in demand and supply of skills, but no such analysis was made in the Sawyer study.

Optimal Income Distribution

Measures of income inequality usually move between total equality and total inequality, and measured inequality is thus compared with total equality. An optimal income distribution which maximizes social welfare and represents the aim of a society could be a more useful basis of comparison.

A.P. Lerner[15] sees in an equal distribution of a given income the maximization of social welfare, but recognizes the necessity of providing incentives to achieve an increase in total income. We would maintain that incentives and hence some degree of inequality seem to be essential also for the proper functioning of the economy and society (see Introduction). A. Sen[16] emphasizes in his analysis the contrast between the principle of distribution according to needs and that of distribution according to desert. According to Sen "it appears that egalitarianism may be optimal under ignorance about relative needs", but there remains the necessity of work rewards and incentives. Sen comments on the Chinese experiment with "non-material incentives" in the "Leap Forward" which had to be abandoned, but achieved some change. Sen sees the achievement of work motivation as part of a moral value system.

R.C. Fair[17] attempted to calculate an optimal distribution of lifetime incomes based on individual earnings functions and on the assumption that individuals are given equal opportunity to achieve their potential (everyone receives a high school education) and to maximize lifetime utility. Inequalities stem from the distribution of innate ability (assumed to be normal), the different valuation of income and leisure and the different valuation of education after high school. His results are 27 different before and after-tax income distributions, when the Gini Coefficient ranges from 0.099 to 0.366 for after-tax income. For an average standard deviation (16) of innate ability, the Gini coefficient is 0.261 for after-tax income (0.303 for before-tax income).

This reflects a somewhat higher inequality than the optimal (normative) distribution suggested by us in Table 9.5.

An optimal income distribution[18] may be different for each society according to its social and economic structure and its prevailing views of social justice (connected with its moral value system). Nevertheless, we can delineate some very general features which may be more or less common to an optimal income distribution in most societies, in which rewards and sanctions are assumed to be necessary.

The normative features are: first that there should be no poverty — i.e., the lowest income brackets should not be too much below the median or mean income. Second, there should be no stratum of very rich people — i.e., the highest income bracket should not be too far above the median income. Third, middle incomes should be spread quite evenly — i.e., the median income should be quite close to the mean income.

Table 9.5
Income Distributions Compared to Optimal Income Distribution
(Income Shares in %)

Population Shares (%)	*Optimal income distribution*	*Israel after-tax income 1975/76*	*Average of twelve OECD countries after-tax*	*40 countries under $2000 p.c. income (pre-tax)*	*15 countries over $2000 p.c. income (pre-tax)*	*Average of 55 countries*
Lowest 40	24-26	20.2	17.7	13.9	16.7	14.6
Middle 40	42-44	43.2	40.5	33.9	39.8	35.5
Highest 20	34-30	36.6	41.8	52.2	43.5	49.9
Lowest 20	11-11	6.6	5.9	5.0	5.5	5.2
Middle 70	71-73	72.3	67.8	58.8	66.9	61.0
Highest 10	18-16	21.1	26.3	36.2	27.6	33.8
Median	9.4-10	9.3	8.6	6.6	8.2	7.0
Ratio of highest to lowest decile	3.6-3.2	9.2	12.5	22.8	15.2	20.7
Gini Coeff.	0.230-0.194	0.296	0.350	0.466	0.375	0.441

Table 9.5 shows how income distributions in Israel, in the 12 OECD countries, in 40 less-developed countries and in 15 developed countries compare wich such an optimal distribution.

Israel compares more favorably with the proposed optimal income distribution than does the average of twelve OECD countries. Still, there is a considerable difference between Israel's after-tax distribution and the optimal distribution — especially in the income shares of the lowest 20% and the highest 10%, as well as the ratio of the highest to the lowest decile. The income share of the middle income brackets was similar to that in the optimal distribution.

The relatively high income share of Israel's middle stratum (compared to the OECD countries and to all other countries) apparently stems from a very progressive system of social security and social services in an economy which is still in an intermediary stage of industrial development. The middle classes, which occupy the positions of political and economic power to a considerable degree, benefit extensively from social benefits (social security, pensions, educational and health services, children's allowances, etc.) and subsidies. They also maintain relatively high incomes on the basis of educational advantages and their strong bargaining power as skilled and professional workers.

The Israeli system of universal eligibility for many of the social benefits was designed to spare the feelings of the needy and to assure coverage of everyone in need. This constitutes a heavy burden on the national budget, and contributes to the relatively high income share of the middle classes.

The above data show only after-tax income distributions, without taking all social services into account. The inclusion of these services (health, education) would raise the share of the lower income brackets and lower the share of the highest income groups — thus narrowing the differences between each country's actual distribution and the optimal income distribution.

NOTES

1. J. Jain, *Size Distribution of Incomes*, World Bank, 1975.
2. M. Sawyer, *Income Distribution in OECD countries*, OECD Economic Outlook, July 1976.
3. The Gini coefficient was 0.33 for India (1956/57) in F. Paukert, "Income Distribution at Different Levels of Development: A Survey of Evidence". *International Labour Review*, Aug.-Sept. 1973; and 0.48 for India (1967/68) in J. Jain, op. cit., (i.e., 43% higher). The Gini coefficient for Bangladesh (1966/67) is 0.34 and for Pakistan (1970/71) 0.33 in J. Jain.
4. In a calculation for inequality of family income by net income per standard adult, the inequality index was only 0.224.
5. R. Hsia and L.S. Chan, *Income Distribution in Hong-Kong*, 1971. ILO, WEP 2-23, WP 15, 1975.
6. Lim Lin Lean, *Pattern of Income Distribution in West-Malaysia*, ILO, WEP 2-23, WP-6, 1974.
7. W. van Ginneken, *Mexican Income Distribution*, ILO, WEP 2-23, WP-5, 1974.

8. S. Kuznets, *Modern Economic Growth*, London 1966, p. 206. The analysis and data appeared first in S. Kuznets, "Quantitative Aspects of the Economic Growth of Nations: VIII, Distribution of Income by Size". *Economic Development and Cultural Change*, Chicago, 1963.
9. L. Soltow, *op. cit.*
10. F. Paukert, *op. cit.*
11. S. Kuznets, "Economic Growth and Income Inequality" and "Inequalities in the Size Distribution of Incomes", *Economic Growth and Structure*, New York, 1965.
12. I. Adelman and C. Morris, *Economic Growth and Social Equity in Developing Countries,* Stanford, 1973.
13. M.S. Ahluwalia, "Income Inequality", *Redistribution with Growth*, World Bank, 1974.
14. See also M.S. Ahluwalia, "Inequality, Poverty and Development", *Journal of Development Economics*, December 1976.
15. Lerner, A.P., *The Economics of Control*. London, 1944.
16. Sen Amartya, *On Economic Inequality*, Oxford, 1973.
17. R.C. Fair, "The Optimal Distribution of Income", *Quarterly Journal of Economics*, 85, 1971.
18. We are not dealing here with the problems connected with the definition and calculation of an optimal income distribution. For these see K.J. Arrow, *Social Choice and Individual Values*, Yale U. Press, 1963, and A. Sen, *On Economic Inequality*, Oxford, 1973.

CHAPTER 10

INCOME DISTRIBUTION IN THE WORLD

Since the Second World War, world attention has focused increasingly on the enormous differences in the standard of living between countries. Before then, awareness of such differences was vague; most attention was devoted to class distinctions and to differences within the mature countries. Still, the theory of imperialism (the economic exploitation of backward countries by more developed ones) had already dealt with the disparity of wealth between countries and regions; Marxism regarded the colonies as a class of proletarian nations being exploited by the capitalist countries.

The Gap Between Countries

The workers' class has been well able to organize itself and stand on its rights in the industrial countries — so that, with the growth of wealth in these countries, the standard of living of wage and salary earners rose. The development of technology has created a favored group of scientists and experts whose salaries are as high as the incomes of many capitalists and who accumulate wealth. Moreover, this class has become powerful through its central influence on the allocation of resources — which, in turn, has increased its political influence.

With the rise in the general standard of living in wealthy countries income inequalities have been reduced — even though their proportions are still considerable; poor regions still exist, and there is still poverty in the great cities. However, the modern welfare state has improved the conditions of the poor through income redistribution, social services and social insurance. Some of the wealthy countries have set minimum annual incomes and try to maintain incomes above those lines. In contrast, the gap between rich and poor nations has increased.[1] Furthermore, inequality within the less-developed countries is considerable, and seems to be increasing in the least-developed countries.

A less-developed or developing country is in transition from a subsistence or traditional economy to a modern economy; this entails revolutionary changes in the form of its society, its customs, its approach to life and its values. A developed country has already undergone this development (which may also be described as industrialization accompanied by urbanization); as a result, it has reached a relatively high standard of living. It is, therefore, necessary to distinguish between economic growth (i.e., the economic expansion which all countries, even the economically most developed ones, go through) and economic development.

Many indicators illustrate the essential differences between less-developed and developed countries. There is a tendency to see per capita national income as a general indicator, and some economists speak in terms of poor and rich countries; the idea is that economic development transforms a poor country into a less poor one — and, after a continuous period of development, it reaches the stage of a comfortable or even wealthy country. However, the terms "developing country" and "poor country" are not synonymous (nor are "developed country" and "wealthy country"). For example, the United States does not have the highest per capita income; Kuweit is the wealthiest country in this respect. But can Kuweit be called a developed country? It is very small, its entire income is derived from oil, its economy does not reflect the structure of a developed economy, and its wealth may dry up as soon as the demand for oil declines sharply or its oil resources are used up.

Hence, some countries cannot be classified as developing countries, because of high per capita incomes or other reasons — but neither do they belong in the category of developed countries. Israel can be included in this intermediate category. Per capita income in Israel is relatively high — but the Israeli economy depends on capital imports and, in its present structure, is unable to balance its international accounts. Leontieff believes that Israel's economic structure at the end of the fifties was that of an underdeveloped country.[2] Development with the help of capital imports results in a structural dependence on funds from abroad; this problem is far more common than is generally thought, and it is especially conspicuous in Israel.[3] Our point here is that a country so dependent on capital imports cannot be considered a developed country, notwithstanding its relatively high standard of living.

Estimated Income Distribution in the World

The per capita product is apparently the best single indicator of a country's standard of living; therefore, with the exception of the special cases pointed out above, it indicates the level of development of a country. However, calculation of the national product is especially difficult in developing countries because of severe problems in collecting data, determining their reliability and analyzing them.[4] It is also difficult to compare such data collected in a variety of ways from diverse sources. Another problem is how to make calculations in a uniform currency unit — that is, to determine an exchange rate which reflects the purchasing power of the various currencies.

Several factors distort the exchange rate — such as inflation, high taxes, export subsidies, and capital imports (which expand the supply of foreign currency and thus influence the exchange rate). Even in a country that balances its international accounts, the exchange rate is but an expression of the local currency's purchasing power in internationally tradable products and services. Studies by Gilbert and Kravis[5] and later by Gilbert et al.[6] found that in non-tradable services and goods (education, medicine, management, interior communications, personal services, etc.) the purchasing power of local European currencies was higher than their exchange rates — since the level of wages was markedly lower than in the United States, while the difference in labor productivity was relatively small. Hence, the gap between the real per capita products in Europe and the U.S. was smaller than the difference calculated at exchange rates.

In a country with a low level of technology, an important share of the economic activity occurs in households — and therefore is not included in national product calculations. An attempt has been made to evaluate agricultural production for domestic consumption in subsistence economies, but other household outputs for domestic consumption are generally omitted from these calculations.[7] Therefore, we must conclude that the lower the standard of living and the more primitive the economy, the more downward biased is the national product estimate.

There is a strong and significant correlation between per capita income and various indicators of the standard of living[8] — so, despite the above reservations, it seems justifiable to regard GNP per capita estimates as indicating differences in the standard of living between countries.

The following estimate of world income distribution in 1974 is based on U.N. and World Bank data on 169 countries (Table 10.1). It shows the wide gap between the developed part of the world (with approximately one-quarter of the population) and the developing part (with three-quarters of the population). The average per capita income of the developed part is about ten times larger than the average of the developing part. However, the gap between the least-developed African and Asian countries (with a per capita income of less than $150) and the most-developed countries like Sweden and the U.S.A. (with $7,000) amounts to a difference of 50 or 60 times. Taking into account the above reservations about cross-country GNP comparisons, S. Kuznets calculated various adjustments in the data for developing countries to narrow the gap by about 57% — i.e., to 22-26 times.[9]

Beckerman[10] uses seven indicators with a very high correlation to per capita private consumption in order to compare real incomes. He calculated an index for 57 countries in 1960. This index shows somewhat smaller gaps than do Kuznet's adjusted figures.

The development index based on 18 indicators calculated by the U.N. Research Institute for Social Development[8] showed also considerably smaller gaps than did per capita product for 1960 in 58 countries. Hence, real income

Table 10.1
Estimated World Income Distribution, 1974

	Population *million*	*%*	*GDP* *$ million*	*%*	*GDP per capita* *$*
Developing Countries					
Africa (excl. South Africa)	367.2	9.5	117.9	2.2	321
Latin America	301.0	7.7	312.5	5.8	1,038
Asia-Middle East	116.6	3.0	155.0	2.9	1,330
Asia-East and S.E. (excl. Japan)	1,124.9	28.9	219.2	4.0	193
TOTAL	1,909.7	49.1	804.6	14.9	421
Europe*	53.3	1.4	118.3	2.2	2,221
Socialist Countries**	927.4	23.8	255.4	4.7	275
Total Developing Countries	2,890.4	74.3	1,178.3	21.8	408
Developed Countries					
Market Economies	675.0	17.3	3,463.9	64.1	5,132
Socialist Countries	327.8	8.4	761.6	14.1	2,323
Total Developed Countries	1,002.8	25.7	4,225.5	78.2	4,214
World	3,893.2	100.0	5,403.8	100.0	1,388

*Spain, Portugal, Greece and Malta

**Republic of China, Mongolia, North Korea, North Vietnam, Albania, Rumania, Bulgaria, Yugoslavia, Cuba.

Source: U.N. Yearbook of National Account Statistics, 1975, N.Y.
U.N. Monthly Statistical Bulletin, May 1976.
World Economic Indicators, IBRD, 1976.
Finance and Development, IMF, IBRD, Sept. 1973.
The World in Figures. The Economist, 1976.

differences may be assumed to be smaller than those revealed by per capita product.

Table 10.1 shows that 74 percent of the world's population live in developing countries, but have only 22% of world income; the developed countries have 26 percent of population, and 78 percent of the income. Countries in Asia and Africa are poorest, with per capita income averaging about $200 and $300 respectively. With the exception of the Communist bloc, 38 percent of the world's population live in Africa and Asia (excluding the Middle East), but their income share is only 6 percent. If the Communist countries (including China) are added, these two continents comprise 61 percent of the population — with only 10 percent of the income, and an average per capita product of $250.

In 1974, about one billion people (about one-quarter of the world's population) lived in very poor countries where average per capita income was less than $200; their income share was about 2½ percent. 1,400 million (35 percent) lived in poor countries ($200 to $500); their income share was about 6 percent. Thus, 60% of the population received only 8½ percent of the income. About 800 million people (20 percent) lived in countries with an average income of $500 to $2500 receiving 21% of income; about 800 million people (20 percent) lived in relatively rich countries with a per capita income of over $2,500 receiving 70% of world income.

The economic inequality between countries may be observed when the world population is divided into 10 equal parts according to per capita income by countries (Table 10.2).

Table 10.2
Estimated Inequality Between Countries by Per Capita Income, 1974

Deciles	*Income Shares (%)*	*GNP per capita ($)*
1	0.8	108
2	1.0	135
3	1.2	172
4	1.5	206
5	1.5	211
6	2.5	354
7	6.4	639
8	14.7	2,052
9	24.6	3,422
10	45.8	6,378
TOTAL	100.0	1,393

The top ten percent received 46% of the income; the bottom tenth had less than one percent — that is, one-fiftieth of the top tenth. Half of the population received 94% of world income, while the other half had only 6%. Even according to adjusted figures, the poor half had only 9%.

Income inequality between countries is higher than inequality within countries: the inequality index (Gini coefficient) based on the above figures comes to 0.653, compared with 0.350 to 0.450 among families in developed countries and 0.400 to 0.600 in developing countries. Income inequality in developing countries is greater than in developed countries, because social polarity is higher in the former. Most of the population in developing countries lives in rural districts with low incomes; there is a relatively thin layer of rich people (property owners and merchants), and the middle class is relatively small. In developed countries, the weight of the middle class is greater, and there is less income inequality (see Chapter 9).

Since the national product estimates in poor countries are downward biased, inequality between countries is smaller than that reflected in Table 10.2.

In a comparison of standards of living, it should be taken into account that a larger proportion of the product is used for private consumption in developing countries than in developed countries — which means that differences in per capita private consumption will be lower than differences in per capita income.

Furthermore, most countries (even the poorest) have some redistribution of income through taxation and public services, which reduces inequalities within countries. In general, this reduction of income inequality is greater in the developed countries.

Income inequality in the world is a combination of inequality between countries and inequalities within countries. The greatest polarity naturally occurs between the large poorer groups in poor countries and the prosperous classes in rich countries. But even the less poor and rich countries have groups

Table 10.3
Changes in Income Distribution in the World
(by per capita incomes)

World Population (Percent)	1860	1913	1960	1967	1974
	(Accumulated percentage of world income)				
25 richest	57.8	68.9	72.1	75.8	80.0
50 richest	73.3	86.1	90.0	90.9	94.0
75 richest	87.5	93.9	96.8	96.8	97.6
25 poorest	12.5	6.1	3.2	3.2	2.4
Average per capita income (1967-69 $)*	120	260	520	700	862

*Based on the U.S. consumers' price index.

Source: 1860 to 1960: L.J. Zimmerman, op. cit.;
1967: Sources of Table 10.1; 1974: Table 10.2.

whose incomes are extremely low. While one billion people lived in poor countries where per capita income was less than $200 in 1974, more than 1,600 million (40% of the world's population) had incomes below $200. The top tenth of the world's population had a per capita income of $7,700, which was 170 times higher than per capita income of the poorest 10% which was only $56. The inequality index of income distribution in the world, between and within countries, was 0.711.[10]

Income inequality between countries has widened in recent years. Zimmerman[11] shows that one-quarter of the world's population had 58 percent of the income in 1860, and 72 percent in 1960; according to our estimate, their share rose to 80 percent in 1974. Table 10.3 shows the great decline in the income share of the poorest one-quarter of the population over one century — from 12½ percent to 2½ percent. One must, of course, use caution in comparing Zimmerman's data — which are based on 85 percent of the world population, and do not include Africa — with our figures, which are based on U.N. estimates of practically all countries. The declining trend in the income share of poor countries is also indicated by the comparative growth rates of per capita product.

The Pace of Growth

Kuznets describes the two centuries of modern economic growth[12] since about 1750, during which per capita product increased considerably, but the gap between poor and rich countries widened. During the first 100 years, per capita product went up relatively slowly. In England — the pioneer of economic growth — per capita product grew 0.2 percent annually between 1700 and 1780, 1.3 percent between 1780 and 1881, and 4 percent between 1850 and 1950.

Zimmerman's data make it possible to calculate the annual growth rate of per capita income between 1860 and 1960. Although these data do not include Africa, they apparently express the national product and population trends in both the developed and developing parts of the world. Per capita product in developed countries grew 1.6 percent annually during the second half of the 19th century, and 1.9 percent during the first half of the 20th century (Table 10.4).

In the fifties and sixties, the pace quickened: the world product doubled in 17 years, and grew 2.6 times between 1950 and 1975; per capita product grew about 75 percent. The growth of per capita product was more rapid in developed countries from 1860 up to the middle of the sixties. During 1950-1966, the national product of the developing countries reached the same growth rate as in the developing countries; however, the population upsurge in the developing countries caused their per capita growth to lag behind. In the last period (1966 to 1975) per capita product grew faster in developing countries — due to the rapid economic growth of oil producing countries and the recession in the developed countries.

Table 10.4
Annual Growth Rate of World Product, Population and Per Capita Product (Percent)

	1860 to 1913	*1913 to 1960*	*1950 to 1966*	*1966 to 1975*
Developed Countries				
National product	2.7	2.8	5.1	3.9
Population	1.1	0.9	1.3	1.0
Per capita product	1.6	1.9	3.8	2.9
Developing Countries				
National product	1.3	2.5	5.0	5.6
Population	0.5	1.0	2.0	2.3
Per capita product	0.8	1.5	3.0	3.2

Source: Calculated on the basis of Zimmerman's data, pp. 35-37; 1950 to 1966, UNCTAD, Proceedings of Second Session, Vol. IV, U.N., N.Y., 1968; 1966 to 1975, World Economic Indicators, IBRD, 1976.

Tables 10.2 and 10.3 showed inequality between countries in 1974, when the influence of the recession of the developed countries was only partly felt. Figures for 1975, which were not available in sufficient detail, may show somewhat less inequality. However, this does not appear to mark a change in the trend of increasing inequality, especially not for the least-developed countries.

Table 10A.1 (Appendix) shows the different growth rates by development stages. The lower the per capita income was, the smaller was economic growth. The oil producing countries constitute a special category with very high growth rates, even during the two recession years of 1974 and 1975 (although they, too, were negatively influenced by the recession). In contrast, the growth of the socialist countries was somewhat higher during 1974 and 1975 compared with the preceding period.

The quicker economic growth of the developed countries up to 1973 has widened the gap between them and the developing countries. This is liable to overshadow another fact — that the growth rate in the developing countries since the Second World War has been higher than it was in the developed countries during the 19th century (Table 10.4). At this rate, developing countries will be able to double their per capita income within about 25 years — an achievement which took 40 years for the developed countries in the preceding century. This annual growth rate of about 3 percent means a sixteenfold increase within 100 years — e.g., an increase from $200 to $3200.

If per capita income increases by the same percentage in rich and poor countries, the absolute gap widens.[13] What is more, the developed country's increment alone may be larger than the developing country's total per capita income.

The diverging growth rates in the developing countries (Appendix, Table 10A.1) have increased inequality among them to a considerable degree. Although there is a strong dividing line between countries above and below a per capita income of $1,500, the differences between countries above and below the $200 line are just as great. (The oil producing countries are in a special category; some of them have very high per capita incomes, and all of them have had a high growth rate in recent years.) Hence, the classification of developing countries into lower, middle, and higher income groups is important because it indicates the different stages of development of these countries.

The distribution of income illustrates the division between countries where most of the people enjoy a reasonable standard of living (and some of them even live in great comfort), countries where many of the people live in poverty, and countries where the majority are poor and a large proportion suffer from undernourishment and sickness. Furthermore, this division has political implications as well. Economic potential forms the basis of military and political power — so the growth of economic power affects the political situation of each country.

Causes for differences in the standard of living

Differences in per capita product can be explained by differences in economic production capacity — i.e., the quantity and quality of capital, labor and natural resources, the organization of the production factors, and the technological level. These factors and the degree of their exploitation determine the national product; growth of the national product is the result of growth in one or more factors and increased efficiency in their utilization.

Although natural resources are more or less given, their extent and location in developing countries are not sufficiently known — so it is possible to increase their utilization through surveys to discover additional resources and through more efficient production methods. These depend partly on technological improvements and partly on investment. Since the labor force will expand rapidly with the growth in population, the growth in per capita product will be largely the result of increases in the other factors, and of the qualitative improvement in the labor force.[14] A rising technological level is related to a rise in the ratio of human and physical capital to labor. It is possible to differentiate between product growth stemming from a quantitative growth of factor inputs, and product growth per input unit (or growth in productivity).

Denison[15] shows that 26 to 58 percent of the growth in product can be attributed to the increase in capital and labor inputs; the remaining 42 to 74 percent is due to increased productivity. Since 12 to 29 percent of the product growth comes from an increase in physical capital, the importance of physical capital appears to be smaller than is generally assumed. However, technical changes in production methods require changes in capital equipment; this qualitative change in capital cannot be measured, and therefore is not taken into account.

Increased productivity comes largely from a rise in the technological level. Kuznets[16] established that what characterizes economic development in modern times (compared with that in previous periods) is the application of science to production processes. Denison attributes increased productivity to three main factors: (1) advances in know-how, (2) economies of scale, and (3) improved allocation of resources, mainly transfer of resources from agriculture to other sectors.

There is an essential difference between the growth of developed and developing economies. The former undergo relatively mild structural changes that occur in the course of expansion — that is, the "growth" branches progress more rapidly, while the others expand more slowly. On the other hand, less-developed economies advance through revolutionary changes in their social and economic structure.

Krueger[17] shows that 50 to 70 percent of the difference in per capita income between the U.S. and 16 developing countries is due to the quality of manpower i.e., education and skills.

Psacharopoulos, too, comes to the conclusion "that differential income levels are better explained by means of differences in human capital endowments than by more traditional inputs such as physical capital and the number of persons employed", in an analysis of the data of 13 countries.[18]

To sum up: in order for less developed countries to reach a standard of living equal to that in developed countries, they must obtain the per capita stock of capital, the technological level and the quality of manpower that prevail in developed countries. While increased investment is important, the improvements in technology and manpower are even more important.

Thus far, we have expressed the differences between developed and less-developed economies in quantitative terms, but there are fundamental qualitative differences between them as well. These include life style, nutrition, dwellings, clothing, etc. — all of which make up the standard of living; the economies also show qualitative differences in their structure, the quality of their production factors, and their institutions.

The standard of living is, to a great extent, a function of the per capita product, but it also depends on the utilization of the product; the more product that is saved for investment, the less remains for consumption. Public consumption plays a role in the standard of living but per capita private consumption is a better indicator. In developing countries, the percentage of the product allocated to private consumption is relatively high — which is why the differences in per capita private consumption between developed and developing countries are smaller than the differences in per capita product.

Can the study of economic causes alone help us understand the factors necessary for accelerated development? Are the less-developed countries facing the same industrialization process undergone by the developed countries, and is it only necessary to accelerate it in order to attain a higher standard of living in a shorter period — or did special conditions prevail in the developed countries one or two hundred years ago which do not exist in the same form today in less-developed countries, which means the development process of the latter may have to be different? Some economists and sociologists, such as Weber, Sombart and Schumpeter, point to spiritual, psychological and sociological factors — particularly the utilitarian concept, the Protestant religion's view of labor as the performance of a duty to God, the use of science to increase output, and the development of an entrepreneurial class. Obviously, these values of the European-American culture within which today's modern economies developed are vastly different from the values of other cultures. The question is whether less developed countries must adopt at least some of these values in order to reach a similar level of development.

The less-developed countries which have grown rapidly over the last 15 years are those where the influence of European-American values has increased. On the other hand, this set of values is being increasingly attacked by the younger generation of Europeans and Americans, who question the need for rapidly swelling material wealth; some of them are seeking new values in other cultures. Therefore, should other cultures strive for modern development and all that is involved in it? Or will the attempt destroy a culture's old values without its being able to accept new values in their place?

Apparently, however, it is no longer a matter of choice. Technological development is indispensable, and all less-developed countries are already advancing in this direction; their very demographic growth presses them towards economic growth. The question is how these countries can adopt the necessary values (which may be foreign to them) while keeping their own special character and their cultural, religious and spiritual values. Such an adjustment is possible, as has been demonstrated by countries such as Japan, Taiwan, China and others. Nevertheless, whoever wants to eat the fruit of modern progress must also shoulder the inherent risks.

NOTES

1. Excluding oil producing countries.
2. W. Leontieff, "The Structure of Development", *Technology and Economic Development*, "Scientific American" book, New York, 1963.
3. Fanny Ginor, "The Impact of Capital Imports on the Structure of Developing Countries", *Kyklos*, January 1969.
4. For a justification of per-capita national product as an indicator of development, see Harvey Leibenstein, *Economic Backwardness and Economic Growth*, N.Y., 1957.
5. Milton Gilbert and Irving B. Kravis, *An International Comparison of National Products and the Purchasing Power of Currencies", OEEC*, 1954.
6. Milton Gilbert and Associates, *Comparative National Products and Price Levels, OEEC*, 1959.
7. S.H. Frankel, in his book *The Economic Impact on Underdeveloped Countries*, Oxford, 1933, rejects the possibility of comparing the income of a developed market and monetary economy with that of a primitive subsistence economy, because of the different tenor of life and the different set of values.
8. See a list of development indicators and their correlation with per-capita GNP in D.V. McGranahan, *Contents and Measurement of Socio-economic Development*, UNRISD Report No. 70.10, Geneva, 1970. The development index showed a somewhat different ranking than the per-capita GNP for 58 countries.
9. S. Kuznets, *Modern Economic Growth*, London, 1966. p. 385.
10. W. Beckerman, *International Comparisons of Real Incomes*, OECD, Paris, 1966.
11. L.J. Zimmerman, *Poor and Rich Lands: The Widening Gap*, The Hague, 1964.
12. S. Kuznets, op. cit.
13. A 10% rise in a country with $200 per-capita income amounts to $20, while in a country with $3000 per-capita income a 10% rise amounts to $300 — which means that the absolute gap between the two countries has gone up from $2800 to $3080, even though the income ratio between the two countries has remained the same (15 times).
14. Connected, of course, with structural changes in the economy and urbanization.
15. Edward F. Denison, *Why Growth Rates Differ*, N.Y. 1967.
16. S. Kuznets, *op. cit.*
17. A.O. Krueger, "Factor Endowments and Per Capita Income Differences Among Countries", *The Economic Journal*, September 1968.
18. G. Psacharopoulos, op. cit. p. 104.

CHAPTER 11

SUMMARY AND CONCLUSIONS

The atmosphere on which social tensions and feelings of deprivation are based is created by tradition, religious attitudes, historical developments and views on social justice, as much as it is created by economic, social and political inequality. Hence, the tensions caused by socio-economic disparities are not necessarily correlated with them and often appear to have little correlation with factual developments, and the degree to which inequality is tolerated differs from society to society and from period to period.

Sensitivity to such disparities is especially great in Israel, whose society is being formed by people of different ethnic origins and historical and cultural backgrounds. The coincidence of socio-economic disparities with ethnic and cultural differences is likely to increase tensions and to reduce the tolerance of inequality.

The character and degree of socio-economic disparities are outcomes of historical developments. Hence, we investigated developments and trends from the beginning of the Mandatory period, when two distinct sectors were formed: the mainly traditional Arab sector and the more modern Jewish sector. To some extent the society and economy during the Mandatory period can be regarded as developing according to the pattern of a "dual" economy. The Jewish sector enjoyed economic growth and a rapid rise in the standard of living, primarily because of immigration and capital imports; these developments influenced the Arab sector, in which there was some quickening of the slow pace of advance.

There were considerable differences between the sectors in life style, mentality and living standards; the standard of living in the Jewish sector was about twice as high as that in the Arab sector. But disparities within each sector were much larger. There was a large gap between town and village in the Arab sector and urban inequality was quite high; inequality in the Jewish sector was relatively low. The two sectors clearly showed the characteristics of a traditional society (high inequality) and of a more modern society (relatively low inequality).

Socio-economic developments after independence in 1948 were along the same lines as those of the pre-State Jewish sector — rapid economic growth, a rising standard of living and relatively low socio-economic disparity. Structural changes, on the other hand, were marked.

The share of agriculture in the labor force and in the national product declined and that of industry rose, and there was a great increase in capital intensity. Capital per employed rose five and a half times during 1950-1976, indicating the quick pace of technological advance.

Mass immigration made the Jewish population more heterogeneous. The large influx of immigrants from the traditional societies of North Africa and Asia strengthened the traditional elements in Israeli society, such as the extended family; it raised birth and death rates, increased the proportion of children in the population, and reduced the average educational level. The ensuing greater educational inequality and occupational diversification increased socio-economic disparities.

As the economy progressed, the standard of living of all strata of the population rose. The traditional sectors underwent a process of modernization — slower among Arabs, quicker among Jews. Birth and especially death rates declined, life expectancy lengthened, educational level rose and skills increased.

Though income inequality steadily declined after its rise due to mass immigration and its subsequent considerable rise during the recession 1966/67, feelings of deprivation became stronger and more outspoken. This led to the government's greater emphasis on social targets in the seventies. The marked decline in income inequality in the mid-seventies can be partly attributed to the government's social policy.

Functional income distribution as expressed in the shares of labor and capital in the national income shows a rising trend in the share of capital because of the increase in capital intensity in all branches of the economy. The rate of return to capital was mainly influenced by the fluctuations of the business cycle, but appears to have risen somewhat over the period.

The business cycle had also a remarkable influence on the shares of labor and capital in the national income. The share of labor rose in years of recession, and the rate of return to capital fell drastically. In years of rising economic activity and low unemployment, the share of labor declined, as the share of capital rose and its rate of return.

Functional income distribution was only partly indicative of income inequality. Income differences between wage and salary earners and employers and self-employed were relatively small and only partly determined by the returns to labor and capital, since wage and salary earners own some capital and employers and self-employed pay interest on loans, and the self-employed receive remuneration of labor.

Furthermore, a considerable part of the incomes of the economically inactive (one fifth of all family heads did not belong to the labor force) is not included in the functional income distribution. Transfer payments constituted about one half of the total income of these families.

The factors influencing income inequality showed diverging trends over time. There was a constant rise in some of the factors that increased inequality — aging of the population, the weight of small families, labor force participation of married women. Some factors increased statistical income inequality without increasing welfare differences — such as the rising share of old people and students living in separate family units, and the increased labor force participation of married women (since only part of their earnings increased family welfare).

Other factors increased or reduced inequality intermittently. The decline in the educational level and the increase in educational inequality increased inequality during the period of mass immigration. Since the demand for skilled manpower rose constantly, the subsequent rise in the educational level was slow in raising the supply of skills to the required level; not until the late sixties did supply overcome demand, and then educational advancement reduced inequality.

The negative impact of the unemployment rate on socio-economic disparities was obscured by other factors until the late fifties — but its great influence on inequality became obvious in the sixties and seventies, raising it considerably during the recession. Inflation and measures to attract foreign capital appear to have increased inequality.

The forces reducing inequality were full employment, direct taxes, subsidies, social transfer payments, and the rise in the educational level overtaking technological advance. Their combined impact and the spectacular rise in social benefit payments caused a remarkable decline in income inequality in the mid-seventies.

A comparison with the Mandatory period showed that earnings differentials between men and women and between blue and white collar workers seem to have been larger in the Mandatory period than at present. The socio-economic differences between the two main Jewish groups (Ashkenazi and Oriental) remained quite similar, but declined in the mid-seventies; the great change was the large increase in the proportion of the Oriental communities, which together with their relatively small political weight led to feelings of deprivation.

The life style, the standard of living and the pattern of income distribution among Arabs in Israel underwent dramatic changes. Urbanization and full employment increased the standard of living and the levels of education and health. Income differences between town and village were reduced, and inequality was considerably smaller than during the Mandatory period. Income differences between the Arab and the Jewish population had become remarkably smaller. Evidently, rapid development of a traditional society as part of an economy developing along modern lines need not lead to an increase in inequality when it is economically integrated under full employment.

The situation at the end of the 1960s and the beginning of the 1970s showed that employment volume, education (connected with occupation) and work experience (age) were the most important determinants of income from work. Other factors (such as immigration status, country of origin, sex and dwelling locality) were less important. All these factors together explained half of earnings differentials; the remaining half must be attributed to factors not available in the data (such as personal ability, state of health, family background and luck).

Income inequality attributable to age-income differences may be regarded as not belonging to social inequality, which the comparison of life-time incomes may reflect better. But an income curve by age (peaking at age group 45-54) at a certain point in time does not represent lifetime income in a dynamic society, where the per capita product constantly increases. The assumption of rising per capita product and of changes in demand and supply of skills yields a more rapid rise to a later peak (age 55-64) and a much slower decline.

In Israel, however, age-income differences are part of socio-economic disparities, as a considerable part of the poor are old people.

The determinants of family income were similar to those found for earnings of individuals, but with different weights and two additional factors: family size and number of earners. Examination of family income by family type (husband-wife families, independent individuals and one-parent families) revealed the importance of the wife's educational level and her work outside her home for family income. This reflected two kinds of income differences: (a) between husband-wife families and families composed of individuals or one parent, and (b) between husband-wife families with working wives and those with non-working wives.

In one-quarter of all husband-wife families, the wife was working. Incomes of families with working wives were 57% higher on the average than those of families in which the wife was not working. But part of this difference was illusory (because of the expenses involved in enabling the wife to work outside her home), and therefore inflated statistical family income inequality. The earnings of married women increased income inequality in 1968/69 by 7%.

The separate analysis of husband-wife families showed the great influence of the wife's education on family income which stood also for the husband's educational level because of its high correlation with that of his wife. However, the analysis revealed that labor force participation was of no less importance.

For the income of individuals and one-parent families, labor force participation was more important than educational level or other characteristics. To a great extent, low labor force participation in this category (especially among women) was due to advanced age, and was found mainly among individuals living alone. A considerable percentage of this category belonged to the lower income brackets.

The low income categories consisted of two distinct groups: those who did not work because of old age or some disability; and those who worked, but had low earning power because of low educational and occupational levels. The first group consisted mostly of independent individuals or small families; the second group consisted mainly of large families.

Low income per standard equivalent adult in families whose heads did not work was due to the lack of labor force participation of the family head because of old age or infirmity and his low educational level. Low income per standard equivalent adult in families whose heads were working was caused by low-paid occupations due to low educational level, partial employment and large family size. In most cases, there was a combination of these causes.

The percentage of the population living in poverty and near-poverty declined from 20% in 1968/69 to 15% in 1975-76 — owing to the improvement in the employment situation, the general rise in the educational level of the population, and increased social transfer payments. This estimate is based on the relative poverty concept, according to which the poverty band rises with the standard of living. The standard of living rose by about one-fourth during this period. Hence, only 9% of the population and 7% of the families in 1975/76 lived below the poverty and near-poverty line of 1968/69.

The great impact of labor force participation on family income underlines the importance of a situation of full employment as well as of a social security system, caring for the old and the disabled.

In view of the great influence of education on income level, the question arises whether the increase in secondary and higher education and professional training can reduce income inequality. It does indeed seem so. It should, in any case, reduce the number of the economically active who had very low earning power. We also saw that education is more profitable to employees than to the self-employed. The increase in the percentage of employees which may be expected in the process of future technological developments, together with the expansion of education, are also likely to contribute towards reducing income inequality.

However, feelings of deprivation among the population relate not only to income inequality but also to other forms of inequality — such as status, prestige, and political and economic power. Greater equality in education should also be able to influence these other forms of inequality.

The great importance of the wife's education not only for family income, but also for the family's standard of living and the children's education, requires attention. Expansion of women's education throughout the population may guarantee, more than any other factor, the equality of opportunities so necessary to the coming generations.

An international comparison showed the well-known phenomenon that inequality is higher in countries with a low standard of living, and lower in the developed countries with high standards of living. Israel compared well even with countries with higher standards of living.

Inequality appears to widen in the first stages of development, and starts to decline from a certain level of development. The rise or decline in total inequality during urbanization depends on changes in income inequality between and within the rural and urban sectors.

There is a great gap in living standards between developed and developing countries, and among the developing countries. Rapid economic growth led to a five-fold increase in per capita world income over the last 100 years, but the gap between the developed and developing countries widened due to the quicker economic advance of the former. After 1950, the economic growth of the less-developed countries reached the same pace as in developed countries — but the quicker populaion growth in the less-developed countries caused lower per capita income growth.

Economic inequality (as reflected in income distribution) appears to be the result of the distribution of human and physical capital (including natural resources). Therefore, the transfer of physical capital and technical assistance are efficient means for reducing income inequality between countries, when used in sufficient measure.

It appears that the differences in human capital were more decisive for differences in standards of living among countries than were differences in physical capital. The acquisition of human capital requires time. This appears to be the reason for the relatively small results of foreign assistance in some of the developing countries, while quite spectacular results were obtained in countries in which there was already a considerable stock of human capital.

Redistribution of income within countries by means of redistribution of human and physical capital also requires time. Redistribution of physical capital without revolutionary measures is possible by land reform and by redirection of investments (in the form of government credits to small farmers and artisans and mortgages to low-income groups, etc.). A reduction in educational inequality resulting from the wider spread of education may take generations to become effective, since it requires the creation of a suitable environment for the poorer groups. The lack of aspirations, encouragement and suitable home surroundings prevents a considerable proportion of the children of poor families from continuing their education beyond primary school.

It appears that for the modern economy, the more important educational achievements are those of post-compulsory education — which develop the ability to use facts stored in books, journals or computers, and the capacity to formulate and solve problems.[1] Statistical evidence shows that the percentage of university graduates in population groups is correlated with income and social status in the mature economies. Since the proportion of employees among the employed increases during development, the distribution of human capital is more important for income inequality the more advanced a country is; the educational level influences the earnings of employees much more than it does those of the self-employed.

Government policies designed to achieve some redistribution of physical and human capital can influence inequality only in the long run. Redistribution in the short run is attainable by various policy measures such as taxes, subsidies, social benefits and relief payments. The great importance of full employment for reducing income inequality calls for a policy encouraging economic growth and full employment.

Economic growth is necessary to provide the additional means needed for successful long-term and short-term policies for reducing socio-economic gaps. Full employment in a dynamic society with population growth is attainable only by high investment activity and economic growth. Some redistribution of human and physical capital can be attained by directing additional capital to the poor to raise their earning capacity. Additional income from economic growth raises government revenue from taxes more than proportionally, and therefore increases the ability to improve income distribution by expanding educational and health services and social benefits.

Social Policy in Israel

Social policy can be divided into two categories:

1. Policy designed to increase equality of opportunity and equality of income from economic activity, through full employment and more equal distribution of human and physical capital.
2. Policy designed to redistribute income through taxes, subsidies and social payments.

The first category provides a basis for a more equal (or even "optimal") income distribution — increasing equality mainly among the economically active population. The second category can reduce income gaps between the rich and the poor in the short run, and improve the situation of the economically inactive population — mainly the old and the disabled and their dependents.

Raising the standard of living of disadvantaged groups and reducing social gaps are among the targets set out in national development plans and the national budget.

While the full employment policy helped reduce socio-economic disparities, the influence of expanded and improved health and educational services and improved housing conditions is less clear. Though there was a decline in general educational inequality as measured by years of schooling, the percentage of disadvantaged population groups with university education rose little. In Israel, as in other countries with a similar level of social services, the middle and higher income groups apparently utilize the educational facilities much more extensively than do low-income groups.

Measures were taken to raise school attendance rates of children from disadvantaged groups, and to facilitate the continuation of their studies by scholarships and subsidies. Priority was also given to housing for large families living in sub-standard housing, in order to improve the home surroundings of the children. But this is a long,drawn-out process, and the low educational and occupational levels of the parents and their low aspirations hamper the educational achievements of their children.

Increasing the educational level of the Oriental communities was an important policy goal, designed to reduce inequality between ethnic groups. However, the educational levels of all groups rose — so the educational gap remained quite considerable.

Though there was a decline in educational inequality among ethnic groups in the lower age groups (which points to an improvement in the future), the low percentage of young Orientals with higher education shows that further efforts are needed to increase their motivation in order to raise their school attendance rates and achievements.

Educational and occupational levels are also important to social and political status. Consequently, the failure of second-generation low-income groups to significantly raise their educational level perpetuates their inferior social and political status — even if their incomes are supplemented by social transfer payments. This also perpetuates feelings of deprivation in spite of an increase in relative incomes.

It appears that short-term measures were more successful than long-term measures in Israel. The 1975 tax reform, combined with an extended system of social transfer payments linked to average wages increased income redistribution considerably. Since part of the social transfer payments were universal, this increased their burden on the government budget and contributed to inflationary pressures (caused mainly by high security expenditures). Inflation increased inequality, as did various measures for attracting foreign capital.

There are conflicting targets in this respect. The universality of social transfer payments removes the stigma and assures that they reach all of the needy. But greater inflationary pressures can increase inequality. Tax benefits, concessionary loans and other measures for increasing investments to accelerate economic growth and increase employment obviously benefit the wealthy and increase inequality — but full employment reduces inequality.

An effective long-term policy for more equal distribution of physical and especially human capital can offset the negative effects of measures for attracting foreign capital, and increasing investments.

To increase equality of opportunity, parents in disadvantaged population groups must be taught how to create the aspirations and the home environment necessary for successful school attendance. The importance of education to social and economic success can be brought home to wide parts of the public through the mass media — especially through television, which has become widely popular.

One of the difficulties of long-term policy is that several years must pass before its fruits can be reaped — but a government elected for a four-year term wants to be able to show results while it is still in office. It takes courage for a government to initiate long-term policies which may show tangible results only after it has left office — unless it is a stable government based on a major party which can hope to remain in power for a relatively long period.

The remarkable decline in income inequality and the reduction of the proportion of the population living in poverty in the mid-seventies was in the main the result of full employment, the high level of social transfer payments and the rise in the educational level of the population.

NOTE

1. A.E. Anderson, "Redistribution and the Social Policy in Market Economies", in *Distribution Policies in Long-Term Development Planning*, U.N., New York, 1973.

APPENDIXES

Tables and Regressions

APPENDIX 0

Table 0A.1
Income Distribution by Deciles

Deciles	*A*	*B*	*C*	*D*	*E*	*F*	*G*	*H*	*I*
Lowest	1	3	2	1	4	1	2	5	3
Second	2	3	3	2	4	2	4	5	5
Third	2	3	5	3	5	3	5	5	6
Fourth	3	4	6	4	5	4	6	5	7
Fifth	4	4	6	6	6	8	7	7	8
Sixth	5	5	6	9	6	12	9	7	9
Seventh	6	6	6	13	6	13	10	8	11
Eight	7	6	6	15	6	14	12	9	13
Ninth	10	6	20	18	6	18	18	15	15
Highest	60	60	40	29	52	25	27	34	23
TOTAL	100	100	100	100	100	100	100	100	100
Gini Coefficient	0.622	0.566	0.466	0.454	0.454	0.414	0.372	0.360	0.298
40 lowest %	8	13	16	10	18	10	17	20	21
40 medium %	22	21	24	43	24	47	38	31	41
20 highest %	70	66	60	47	58	43	45	49	38
% transfer needed for equal distribution	50	50	40	35	42	32	27	29	22

LORENZ CURVES

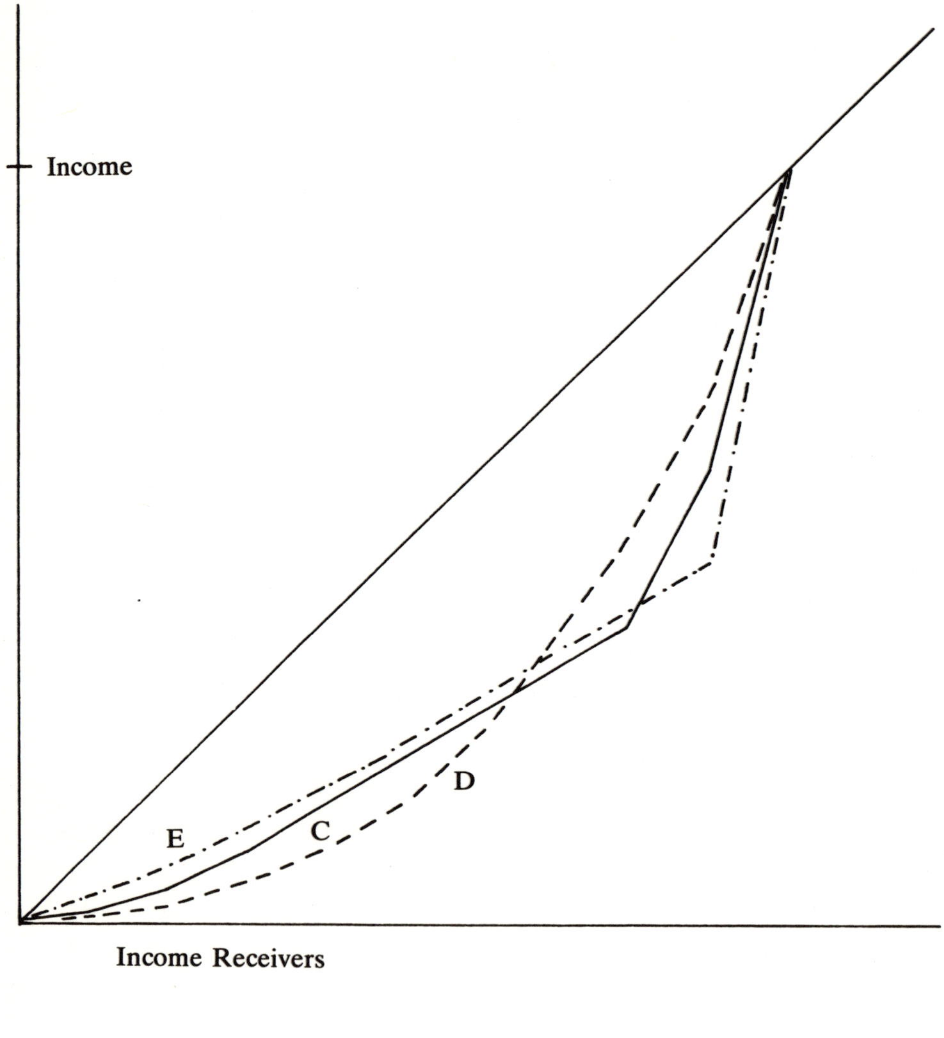

Figure 0A.1

APPENDIX 1

Table 1A.1
Mortality Rates and Life Expectancy at Birth

1. *Mortality rates per 1000 of mean settled population*

Year	*Moslems*	*Christians*	*Jews*	*Total Population**
1926/28	29.4	18.7	12.4	25.3
1932/34	25.7	15.4	9.4	21.4
1938/40	20.3	12.1	8.0	15.8
1941/43	20.1	11.6	8.1	15.6
1944/45	16.8	10.0	6.9	13.1
Decline in % from				
1926/28 to 1938/40	−31	−35	−36	−38
From 1926/28 to				
1944/45	−43	−47	−44	−48

2. *Infant mortality rates (deaths under 1 year of age per 1000 births)*

1926/28	174.2	162.3	105.8	164.2
1932/34	165.5	140.8	81.4	151.8
1938/40	132.1	103.9	57.2	115.6
1941/43	128.4	91.9	52.6	111.7
1944/45	98.4	72.5	36.0	83.6
Decline in % from				
1926/28 to 1938/40	−24	−36	−46	−30
From 1926/28 to				
1944/45	−44	−55	−66	−49

3. *Life expectancy (in years) at birth*

	Moslems		*Christians*		*Jews*	
	M.	*F.*	*M.*	*F.*	*M.*	*F.*
1926/27	37.1	37.9	...	...	54.1	54.7
1933/35	42.0	42.0	52.6	54.2	59.5	61.8
1939/41	46.1	46.8	57.2	59.4	62.3	64.5
1942/44	49.3	50.4	57.4	60.1	64.1	65.9

*Including others
Source: 1 and 2 — Vital Statistics, Tables 1922-45. Jerusalem, 1947.
3 — Statistical Abstract of Palestine, 1944-45. Jerusalem.

Table 1A.2
Infant Mortality Rates and Life Expectancy

1. *Infant mortality rates (per 1000 births)*

*Egypt**		*Trans-Jordan*		*Arab population (Palestine)*	
Year		*Year*		*Year*	
1930/32	209	1929/31	209	1926/28	173
1939/41	198	1939/41	171	1938/40	129

2. *Life expectancy at birth*

Egypt			*Moslem population (Palestine)*		
Year	*M.*	*F.*	*Year*	*M.*	*F.*
1917/27	31	36	1926/27	37.1	37.9
1936/38	35.7	41.5	1936/38	46.7	48.5

Source: 1. Statistical Handbook of Middle Eastern Countries, Economic Research Institute, Jewish Agency, 1945, Jerusalem.
2. Statistical Abstract of Palestine, 1944/45. Jerusalem 1945.

*The Statistical Yearbook of the United Nations in 1954 gives the following figures for Egypt: 1930-34: 162.5; 1935-39: 162.9 (i.e., lower figures, but no change).

Table 1A.3
Income and Expenditure of Jewish Urban Workers' Families
August 1926

Decile	*Income per family* %	*Family size*	*Expenditure per family* %	*Family size*	*Expenditure per standard equivalent adult* %
1	5.8	2.9	5.0	3.4	4.9
2	6.5	3.9	6.8	2.9	6.8
3	7.8	4.1	7.6	3.7	7.8
4	8.6	3.4	8.5	3.4	8.7
5	9.7	3.6	9.2	3.1	9.3
6	9.7	3.4	9.7	3.8	10.1
7	10.7	3.0	10.5	3.2	10.6
8	11.6	3.5	11.2	3.4	11.7
9	12.7	3.7	12.8	4.5	13.1
10	16.9	4.4	18.7	4.4	17.0
Total	100.0	3.6	100.0	3.6	100.0
Gini Coeff.	0.170		0.191		0.179

Source: Report on Investigation of Cost of Living of Jewish Workers' Families, Aug. 1926. *Palestine Zionist Executive Statistical Bulletin*, No. 14, Jerusalem.

Table 1A.4
Monthly Earnings of Jewish Wage and Salary Earners, 1930

Decile	*% of Earnings*	*Average Monthly Earnings LP*
1	2.6	1.94
2	4.3	3.25
3	5.6	4.21
4	6.7	5.00
5	7.6	5.67
6	8.8	6.60
7	10.2	7.69
8	12.1	9.05
9	14.8	11.07
10	27.3	20.52
Total	100.0	7.50
Gini Coefficient	0.340	

Source: Census of Jewish Wage and Salary Earners, *Commerce and Trade*, Sept. 1931.
Remark: It was assumed that daily wage earners worked 25 days per month, and that the value of food for those receiving monthly salaries with food was LP1 per month.

Table 1A.5
Income Distribution of Jewish Urban Families, 1930

Monthly Income L.P.	*Ashkenazim*	*Sephardim*	*Yemenites*	*Other Oriental Communities*	*Total*	*% of families*	*% of Income*
3— 3.9	—	—	2	1	3	4.1	2.1
4— 4.9	2	5	5	6	18	24.3	16.4
5— 5.9	2	4	5	6	17	23.0	18.9
6— 6.9	8	4	1	—	13	17.6	17.5
7— 7.9	1	2	2	1	6	8.1	9.3
8— 8.9	4	1	—	2	7	9.5	12.4
9— 9.9	1	—	—	—	1	1.3	2.0
10—10.9	3	2	—	—	5	6.8	11.0
11—11.9	1	—	—	—	1	1.3	2.4
12+	3	—	—	—	3	4.0	8.0
TOTAL	25	18	15	16	74	100.0	100.0
Average Income per Family LP	7.6	6.0	4.8	5.1	6.1		
Average Family Size	5.0	5.9	4.9	5.3	5.3		
Monthly Income per Person LP	1.52	1.02	0.98	0.96	1.15		
Persons per Room	2.5	3.5	3.7	3.3	3.16		

Source: J. Kligler, A. Geiger, Sh. Bromberg, D. Gurevitz, "An Inquiry into the Diets of the Population of Palestine," *Commerce and Industry*, No. 20-21, October 1931.

TABLE 1A.6
Consumption Expenditure per Member in Collective Settlements

	1929	*1935*	*1937*
Number of Settlements	20	38	81
Expenditure per Member, LP			
Lowest	37	30	26
Highest	56	61	54
Average	44.6	45.6	36.9
Gini coefficient	0.062	0.089	0.122

Source: Brit Pikuah for the agricultural cooperatives, *Yalkut*, August 1938.

Table 1A.7
Distribution of Income and Living Expenditure in Three Smallholders' Settlements

	1935			1936		
Gross Income Group LP	*% of Farms*	*% of Net Income**	*% of Living Expenditure*	*% of Farms*	*% of Net Income**	*% of Living Expenditure*
70—150	5.0	1.9	2.2	3.4	1.7	1.5
150—200	14.6	10.6	10.9	13.5	7.6	5.8
200—250	27.0	21.4	21.0	22.6	17.1	16.0
250—300	20.2	21.1	20.3	23.7	21.9	21.6
300—350	13.5	16.4	17.3	14.7	16.8	18.3
350—400	4.0	4.5	4.7	12.4	17.1	17.1
400—450	7.9	11.3	11.5	5.1	7.8	9.4
450—500	5.0	7.8	7.7	2.3	4.9	5.1
500—615	2.8	5.0	4.4	2.3	5.1	5.2
TOTAL	100.0	100.0	100.0	100.0	100.0	100.0
Average per Farm, LP		168	132		154	113
Gini Coefficient		0.169	0.167		0.205	0.250

*Including investments made on the farm; living expenditure is defined as net income less investments.

Source: I. Elazari-Volcani, *Planned Mixed Farming*, Rehovot, 1938.

Table 1A.8
Estimated Distribution of Income in 1936

	Urban Population	*Settled Agric. Population*	*Beduin*	*Total*
Jews				
% of population	86	14	—	100
% of income	90	10	—	100
LP per capita	48.1	34.0	—	46.2
LP per family*	187	99	—	170
Non-Jews				
% of population	33	60	7	100
% of income	70	28	2	100
LP per capita	32.6	7.0	4.5	15.3
LP per family*	195	42	27	92
Total Population				
% of population	49	46	5	100
% of income	81	18	1	100
LP per capita	40.7	9.4	4.5	24.3

Source: L. Gruenbaum (now A.L. Gaathon), *National Income and Outlay in Palestine*, 1936. Jerusalem, 1941.

*Calculated by us on the basis of family size as follows: In the Jewish sector: 3.9 in the urban population, 2.9 in the rural population, in the Arab sector 6.

Remark: The non-Jewish sector did not include the British administration; it did include other Europeans in the urban population and the Templer settlements in the agricultural population, but the weight of these was very small.

Table 1A.9
Income Distribution of the Jewish Population, 1936

METHOD OF ESTIMATE

Source of Data	*Weight (%)*	*Average Income per Family 1936 values LP*	*Inequality Index*
Family survey (1939), urban employees	50	155.5	0.224
Family survey (1926), urban employees	20	188.4	0.191
Nutrition survey (1930)	10	102	0.195
Survey of wage and salary earners (1930)	10	124.8	0.340
Self-employed with high incomes (est.)	10	420	—
Total, Urban Population	100 = 75	180	0.301*
Family survey (1939) rural employees	40	106.2	0.180
Kibbutzim (1936)	25	67	0.122
Moshavim (1936)	15	113	0.250
Survey of wage and salary earners (1930)	10	125	0.340
Citrus grove owners and other self-employed with high incomes	10	288	0.346
Total, Rural Population	100 = 25	117.5	0.317*
Total Population	100	164.4	0.320*

*The total inequality index was calculated by combining the deciles of all the surveys used ordered by average income into new deciles according to their weights.

Data Used and Method of Calculation

The nearest family survey in time is that of 1939; however, it is representative only of typical employees' families, and does not include unemployed and single persons, and 1939 was a year of economic recession and considerable unemployment. We therefore added the data of other surveys which represent single persons (the workers' survey of 1930), the poorer strata of the population (the nutrition survey of 1930), and urban workers in a more prosperous time (the 1926 survey of urban workers' families). None of these surveys included self-employed. It was assumed that the incomes of about three-quarters of the self-employed were similar to those of wage and salary earners; for about one-quarter (10% of the urban population), a higher income figure was assumed. All data were translated into 1936 values according to the national product per capita at current prices, as calculated by Szereszewski. The inequality index was 0.301.

For the rural population, we used the consumption data of the kibbutzim in 1937; the distribution of living expenditure in smallholders' settlements in 1936 shown by Elazari-Volcani; the distribution of citrus groves for citrus grove owners and other self-employed; the 1939 survey of rural workers' families for agricultural and non-agricultural workers and self-employed with low and medium incomes and the 1930 survey of wage and salary earners. This combination yields an inequality index of 0.317 in the Jewish rural population.

Table 1A.9 shows the method used. The weights allotted to the various surveys were based on detailed population figures and family size according to statistics and census figures, as well as on the representativeness of the various surveys. The estimated distribution of the national income (Table 1A.8) served as the framework of the calculation.

Table 1A.10
Estimated Distribution of Land Holdings and Income in 1929 in 104 Arab Villages

Size of Holding (dunams)	*% of Families*	*% of Area Owned*	*% of Estimated Income**
up to 2	29.4	1.7	12.1
2— 5	4.7	0.7	3.2
5— 10	10.7	2.4	9.0
10— 15	8.9	3.0	6.6
15— 20	7.1	3.6	7.7
20— 30	8.9	6.3	8.6
30— 40	7.0	7.3	7.2
40— 60	6.8	9.8	8.4
60— 80	5.5	11.0	8.2
80—100	3.2	8.2	5.3
100—150	3.5	12.4	7.1
150—200	1.7	8.8	4.3
200—300	1.6	11.5	5.6
300—400	0.5	5.1	2.5
400+	0.5	8.2	4.2
TOTAL	100.0	100.0	100.0
Gini Coefficient		0.662	0.327

Remark: The distribution of the 800,000 dunams of cultivated land owned by 23,573 families in 104 villages has been estimated on the basis of the data given by Johnson-Crosbie and the distribution of land holdings in 322 villages in 1936, published in the national income estimate for 1944 by the government statistician.

Source: 1) *Report of a Committee on the Economic Conditions of Agriculturists in Palestine*, W.J. Johnson and Crosbie, Jerusalem, 1930. Table 24.
2) P.J. Loftus, *National Income of Palestine,* 1944. Jerusalem, 1946.

*On the basis of the Johnson-Crosbie report and the distribution of land holdings, the distribution of income has been estimated as follows: It has been assumed that the 370,000 dunams owned by absentee landlords and leased from other villages were rented mainly by farmers who owned 5-60 dunams; those owning less than 5 dunams were landless, working as laborers or in some other occupation. ("The smallholder or tenant who has not the necessary minimum holding must supplement his income either by hiring himself out as a labourer inside or outside the village or by engaging in transport work, in charcoal or lime-kiln burning or some other occupation". Johnson-Crosbie Report, p.22. It has been assumed that landless laborers and small tenant farmers worked for a wage of about 50 mils in some of the villages, and for 80-120 mils in villages near the cities and the areas inhabited by Jews. See Abramovich and Gelfat, *The Arab Economy,* 1944, p.56). It has been further assumed that the average net return from 100 dunams of land was LP35 to an owner-cultivator, and LP20 to a tenant farmer, as calculated by Johnson-Crosbie on the basis of villagers' declarations. Though there seems to have been quite some underreporting by the villagers, since the purpose of the report was to examine the tax burden of the farmer, the various indicators of income distribution are estimated to be valid.

Table 1A.11
Literacy and Life Expectancy

	Percentage of Literate Persons Aged 7 or over, 1931			Life Expectancy at Birth 1933-35 (years)	
	Male	*Female*	*Total*	*Male*	*Female*
Moslem	25.1	3.3	14.4	42.0	42.0
Christian	71.5	44.1	57.7	52.6	54.2
Arab population	29.7	7.4	18.7	43.1	43.2
Jewish population	93.4	78.7	86.1	59.5	61.8
Total population	42.8	22.1	32.6	47	48

Source: Statistical Abstract of Palestine, 1937/38, 1944/45.

Table 1A.12
Monthly Income and Expenditure of Jewish Urban Families
January – March 1946

Monthly Income (LP)	*% of Families*	*% of Income*	*% of Expenditure*
Up to 15	3.0	0.9	1.1
16 — 20	3.4	1.4	1.6
21 — 30	18.7	11.2	12.2
31 — 40	26.6	21.8	22.5
41 — 50	23.1	24.2	24.4
51+	25.2	40.5	38.2
TOTAL	100.0	100.0	100.0
Gini Coefficient*		0.229	0.198

*Calculated by deciles.
Source: Dr. Cyderovich, *Standard of Living Survey*, Jewish Agency, 1947.

Table 1A.13
Monthly Income by Towns and Communities, Family Survey, 1946

	Monthly Income (LP)		*Average Family Size*	*Housing Density No. of Persons per room*
	per family	*per capita*		
Tel Aviv				
Ashkenazi	44.1	10.10	4.1	2.6*
Other Communities	38.6	6.46	6.0	4.3*
Haifa				
Ashkenazi	50.5	10.92	4.6	3.0
Other Communities	42.8	6.86	6.2	4.6
Jerusalem				
Ashkenazi	39.4	8.00	4.9	2.7
Other Communities	27.4	3.99	6.9	4.9
All Three Cities				
Ashkenazi	44.9	10.32	4.3	2.7
Other Communities	35.3	5.58	6.3	4.5

*A census of housing conditions in Tel Aviv in March 1943 showed an average density of 2.41 persons per room. The difference seems to indicate that the above survey included mainly middle and lower income classes, but there was also an increase in housing density during the war years.

Table 1A.14
Distribution of Family Expenditure by Deciles, 1942
(Vickers' Survey)

Deciles	*Arab and Jewish Families* % of Expenditure	*Arab and Jewish Families* Family Size	*Arab Families* % of Expenditure	*Arab Families* Family Size	*Jewish Families* % of Expenditure	*Jewish Families* Family Size
1	4.7	5.6	4.3	6.1	4.9	5.6
2	6.3	5.3	6.3	5.8	6.2	5.0
3	7.2	6.2	7.3	7.0	7.0	5.7
4	7.9	6.3	8.0	7.1	7.9	5.3
5	8.6	6.3	8.5	7.0	8.7	6.2
6	9.3	5.7	9.3	6.1	9.3	4.7
7	10.1	6.4	10.2	7.6	10.0	5.3
8	11.7	6.1	11.3	7.3	12.1	5.4
9	14.5	5.6	14.3	6.2	14.6	6.0
10	19.7	8.4	20.5	9.7	19.3	7.6
TOTAL	100.0	6.2	100.0	7.0	100.0	5.7
Gini Coeff.	0.222		0.229		0.221	
Average Monthly Expenditure						
per family LP		14.267		14.043		14.372
per person LP		2.300		2.014		2.545

Source: W.J. Vickers, *A Nutritional Survey of Wartime Palestine.* Department of Health, Jerusalem, 1944.

Table 1A.15
Weights Used for Calculation of Inequality Index

1. Jewish Urban Population

Source of Data	*Weight (%)*	*Average Income per Family (LP at 1944 values)**
1944 tax data	40	606
1946 family survey	30	403
1943 Vickers' survey	10	312
1942 Vickers' study of unskilled labor	10	180
1943 industrial workers	10	250
TOTAL	100	438**

2. Arab Urban Population

Source of Data	*Weight (%)*	*Average Income per Family (LP at 1944 values)**
1944 tax data	40	586
1942 Vickers' survey	40	217
1942 special study of unskilled labor	20	150
TOTAL	100	351***

*Incomes deflated by the increase in the consumers' price index and in real incomes between 1944 and 1946, or inflated between 1943 and 1944 or 1942 and 1944.

**Income per capita in the Jewish urban sector in 1944 was estimated at LP134 (according to Loftus, excluding undistributed company profits). Average family size, including single persons, is estimated at 3.7 (i.e. income per family was about LP496). The above LP438 is 12% smaller — which may be regarded as the result of underreporting, but may also indicate the lack of the highest income groups.

***According to national income data, income per family of 6 in urban areas was LP366 in 1944. The above combination shows an average of LP351, an underestimate of 4%.

APPENDIX 2

Table 2A.1
Annual Rates of Births, Deaths, Natural Increase and Population Growth
(%)

	Jews				Non-Jews			
Year	*Births*	*Deaths*	*Natural Increase*	*Population Growth*	*Births*	*Deaths*	*Natural Increase*	*Population Growth*
1941-45	2.63	0.75	1.88	3.5	4.80	1.76	3.04	3.2
1950-52	3.24	0.66	2.58	12.9	4.51	0.99	3.52	4.0
1960-62	2.27	0.57	1.70	3.6	5.00	0.72	4.28	4.6
1966-68	2.22	0.66	1.56	1.9	4.65	0.61	4.04	3.9*
1974-76	2.49	0.70	1.79	2.0	4.37	0.54	3.83	4.0

Source: Statistical Abstract of Israel, 1977.
*Excluding the addition of the East Jerusalem population in 1967.

Table 2A.2
Gross Reproduction Rates

Year	Jews, by mother's continent of birth: Europe America	Asia Africa	Israel	Total	Non-Jews, by religion: Moslems	Christians	Total*
1944-46	...	...	...	1.69	...	...	...
1949-50	1.57	2.46	1.82	1.77	...	...	...
1951-53	1.47	3.03	1.64	1.92	...	...	...
1955-57	1.27	2.71	1.37	1.77	3.92	2.31	3.49
1964-66	1.23	2.21	1.38	1.66	4.75	2.24	4.06
1974-76	1.40	1.81	1.49	1.55	3.83	1.67	3.38
Composition of population (%)							
8.11.48	54.8	9.8	35.4	100.0	68.6**	22.5**	100.0
31.12.76	26.4	21.5	52.1***	100.0	77.3	14.8	100.0

* Including Druze and others
** At the end of 1951
*** Father born in Europe or America, 16.4%; in Asia or Africa, 24.7%; in Israel, 11.0%.

Source: Statistical Abstract of Israel 1963 and 1977.

Table 2A.3
Age Composition (in %)

	End of 1944	8.11.48	1955	1965	1976
Jews					
0-14	28.4	28.7	33.9	32.3	30.1
15-64	66.9	67.5	61.4	61.4	61.0
65+	4.7	3.8	4.7	6.3	8.9
Non-Jews					
0-14	42.5	...	45.7	50.0	49.4
15-64	53.3	...	48.8	45.7	47.2
65+	4.2	...	5.5	4.3	3.4

Source: Statistical Abstracts of Israel

Table 2A.4
Education of Population Aged 14 and Over
(by years of schooling, in %)

	Years of Schooling	*0*	*1-4*	*5-8*	*9-12*	*13-15*		*16+*
Jews	1961 (census)	12.6	7.5	35.4	34.6		9.9	
	1976	7.2	4.4	25.8	45.2	10.4		7.0
Non-Jews	1961 (census)	49.5	13.9	27.5	7.6		1.5	
	1976	22.7	12.4	37.3	23.4	3.0		1.2
	Jews by continent of birth, 1976							
Continent of Birth								
Asia-Africa		20.8	6.5	33.5	32.1	5.0		2.1
Europe-America		2.4	6.5	29.3	39.4	11.8		10.6
Israel, father: Israel		1.4	0.8	15.9	61.4	12.9		7.6
Asia-Africa		0.7	0.8	25.6	65.9	5.7		1.3
Europe-America		0.4	0.3	6.4	57.3	21.6		14.0

Source: Statistical Abstract of Israel 1977.

Table 2A.5
Net Domestic Product at Factor Cost, by Economic Branch

	Jewish Sector 1936	*1952*	*Average 1961-65*	*1976*
Agriculture	9.5	11.5	9.5	7.3
Industry and Mining	22.0	21.8	24.3	25.3
Construction, Electricity & Water	8.6*	10.7	11.1	10.7
Transport and Communication	**	7.0	8.1	9.5
Trade, Finance & Personal Services	34.4	25.1	22.6	20.0
Public and Community Services	14.2	18.7	17.7	19.8
Ownership of Dwellings	11.3	5.2	6.7	7.4

*Electricity and water included in industry and agriculture.
**Included in Trade, etc.

Source: Statistical Abstracts of Israel.
L. Gruenbaum, *National Income and Outlay in Palestine*, 1936.

Table 2A.6
Capital Stock in Fixed Assets (in %)

	Jewish Sector 1937	*(at 1955 prices) 1950*	*1960*	*1970*	*(at 1975 prices) 1976*
Agriculture	48.2	32.7	23.2	14.1	10.7
Industry	39.4	20.3	22.9	20.9	21.4
Electricity & Water	...*	16.6	16.9	13.3	9.6
Construction Equipment	1.1	1.8	2.0	2.2	1.9
Transport		16.5	17.6	23.2	27.3
Public Services	11.3**	6.1	13.2	17.5	22.1
Commerce & other services		6.0	4.1	8.7	7.0
Total without housing	100.0	100.0	100.0	100.0	100.0
Housing	54.6	40.1	39.2	36.9	38.6
Other branches	45.4	59.9	60.8	63.1	61.4
Grand Total	100.0	100.0	100.0	100.0	100.0

* Water is included in agriculture; electricity is included in industry.
** Part of transport and communications was in the Government sector (post, trains, harbor facilities), and is therefore not included in the Jewish sector.

Source: Statistical Abstracts of Israel; Annual Reports, Bank of Israel; R. Szereszewski, op. cit.

Table 2A.7
Capital – Output Ratios
(at constant prices)*

	Total Economy	*All Economic Branches Excluding Housing Sector*	*% of Unemployment*
1936 (Jewish sector)	2.25	...	...
1947 (Jewish sector)	1.95	...	2
1950	2.46	1.55	6.9**
1955	2.75	1.71	7.4
1960	3.03	1.95	4.6
1965	3.11	2.10	3.6
1970	2.51	1.59	3.8
1975	2.94	1.92	3.1
1976	3.09	2.02	3.6

* Ratio of capital stock to gross domestic product. 1936 and 1947 at 1936 prices; 1950-65 at 1955 prices; 1970-1976 at 1971 prices.
** Without potential labor force in immigrants' camps.

Table 2A.8
Composition of Domestic Use of Resources (%)
(in 1970 prices)

	Jewish sector of Palestine 1936	1950	1960	1966	1970	1976
Private Consumption	62.3	48.5	56.9	58.0	48.4	48.0
Public Consumption	6.1	17.3	18.1	20.2	28.7	30.8
Gross Investments	31.6	34.2	25.0	21.8	22.9	21.2
TOTAL	100.0	100.0	100.0	100.0	100.0	100.0
GNP	72.1	67.6	86.1	86.8	79.3	80.2
Import Surplus	27.9	32.4	13.9	13.2	20.7	19.8

Source: Statistical Abstracts of Israel.
Jewish Sector 1936: R. Szereszewski, op. cit., p.9. Import surplus includes excess of purchases from non-Jewish sector over sales to non-Jewish sector. Import surplus from abroad was approximately 20%.

Table 2A.9
Balance of Payments, 1950-1976
(Annual Averages, $ million)

Years	*Imports* of goods and services	*Exports* of goods and services	*Import surplus*	*Exports as % of imports*	*% of unilateral transfers in import surplus*	*% of import surplus in resources for local uses**
1950-52	384	63	321	16	43	28.7
1953-55	389	127	262	33	82	20.7
1956-58	548	206	342	37	73	18.5
1958-61	699	334	365	48	82	16.1
1962-64	1,050	556	494	53	70	17.0
1965-67	1,289	798	491	62	78	15.1
1968-70	2,210	1,282	928	58	56	18.8
1971-73	3,946	2,293	1,653	58	81	19.9
1974	7,035	3,648	3,387	52	51	23.3
1975	7,816	3,766	4,050	48	44	24.2
1976	7,690	4,422	3,268	58	69	19.8
1977	7,967	5,410	2,557	68	78	16.2

Source: Statistical Abstracts; Annual Reports, Bank of Israel.
*At 1970 prices. At 1975 prices the percentage was 28.6% in 1975, 24.6% in 1976 and 20.1% in 1977.

Table 2A.10
Families Possessing Durable Consumer Goods by Continent of Birth (%) in 1975/76

	Jews						Non-Jews
			Born in Asia-Africa		Born in Europe-America		
	Total	Born in Israel	Total	Immig. after 1961	Total	Immig. after 1961	
Gas range and/or oven	49.2	42.0	49.5	42.5	52.0	35.8	76.7
Electric range and/or oven	33.3	30.1	37.2	28.1	32.1	16.5	43.0
Combined gas/electric system	51.8	58.7	52.9	60.2	48.2	63.0	9.1
Electric refrigerator	99.0	98.7	98.7	99.6	99.0	97.7	82.3
Electric washing machine	74.6	75.3	79.3	79.3	68.6	69.6	41.2
Telephone	59.4	66.1	40.6	24.4	69.9	50.9	12.7
TV set	89.5	86.3	89.9	86.5	90.5	91.6	71.8
Radio	84.2	86.5	77.0	72.3	88.2	81.9	52.6
Radio-tape	14.2	15.9	18.1	21.5	10.9	11.2	14.4
Private car	31.2	47.8	18.7	15.1	32.9	39.0	12.7

Source: Family Expenditure Survey 1975/76, Special Series No. 563, 1978.

Table 2A.11
Housing Density and Family Size by Population Groups, 1976*

Population Group	*No. of persons per room*	*Average family size*	*Average No. of rooms per family*
Jews	1.27	3.5	2.76
Continent of Birth			
Israel	1.27	3.5	2.76
Asia and Africa	1.64	4.5	2.74
Europe and America	0.99	2.7	2.73
Non-Jews	2.76	6.4	2.32

* Housing density of the total population (urban and rural) excluding kibbutzim, institutions and Beduin.
Source: Statistical Abstract of Israel No. 28, 1977.

Table 2A.12
Participation in the Labor Force (in %)
(Population aged 14 and over)

		1955	1960	1965	1970	1975	1976
All ages	Total	53.6	52.9	52.8	49.3	48.1	48.1
	Males	80.1	78.1	76.1	69.2	64.9	64.6
	Females	26.5	27.3	29.4	29.3	31.6	31.9
Aged 14-17	Total	37.2	26.8	32.8	22.8	14.9	14.2
	Males	42.2	32.1	38.1	27.3	18.5	17.6
	Females	31.7	21.1	27.1	18.1	11.3	10.6
Aged 18-24	Total	...	...	...	45.4	40.4	39.5
	Males	...	...	...	46.0	40.3	39.0
	Females	...	...	...	44.9	40.4	40.0
Aged 18-34	Total	56.8	56.6	57.0	54.0	56.0	56.6
	Males	80.9	79.5	76.3	74.3	71.9	72.7
	Females	32.2	33.2	37.5	40.1	42.4	42.8

Source: Statistical Abstracts of Israel.

Table 2A.13
Employed Persons by Years of Schooling and Sex, and Labor Force Participation by Schooling (in %)

Year	Years of Schooling	0	1-4	5-8	9-12	13+	*Total*
	Total						
1961 (Census)			51.6*		35.2	13.2	100.0
1965		7.3	8.3	36.3	35.6	12.5	100.0
1970		5.9	7.0	34.3	36.6	16.2	100.0
1976		3.8	4.7	26.5	41.8	23.1	100.0
1961	Labor force participation (%)	27.4	52.1	56.3	54.4	69.7	53.5
1976	Labor force participation (%)	20.8	40.9	47.2	47.6	70.0	48.1
	Males						
1961 (Census)			54.8*		33.0	12.2	100.0
1965		7.0	9.6	39.3	33.0	11.1	100.0
1970		5.7	8.3	38.0	34.4	13.6	100.0
1976		3.8	5.7	31.0	40.1	19.4	100.0
1961	Labor force participation (%)	68.5	83.6	81.8	68.7	78.8	79.0
1976	Labor force participation (%)	49.7	66.8	71.4	58.4	73.9	64.5
	Females						
1961 (Census)			42.3*		41.5	16.2	100.0
1965		8.1	5.1	28.4	42.2	16.2	100.0
1970		6.4	3.8	25.6	41.6	22.6	100.0
1976		3.9	2.6	17.3	45.1	31.1	100.0
1961	Labor force participation (%)	11.7	18.4	26.7	38.3	57.8	27.6
1976	Labor force participation (%)	9.7	14.6	21.4	36.1	65.6	31.9

* 0 - 8

Source: Statistical Abstracts of Israel.

APPENDIX 4

4A COMPARABILITY OF SURVEYS

How far do the consumption surveys of Jewish urban employees' families made between 1950/51 and 1968/69 reflect the changes in income distribution during this period?

The surveys clearly show growing inequality during the 18-year period (Table 4A.1), but their comparability must be questioned, because of changes in coverage and survey methods and the low representativeness of the first survey in the series.

The 1950-51 survey shows less inequality than does the last peacetime survey in 1939. Hence, it obviously does not reflect the changes brought about by mass immigration. Social and economic disparities — especially between old-timers and newcomers — apparently were quite considerable, according to indicators of unemployment, health, education and housing. But since the new immigrants were not represented in the 1950/51 survey, these differences were not reflected.

The purpose of the survey was to provide the basis for a cost of living index. It included only families with an "orderly household"; it excluded single persons and the unemployed. Furthermore, it was conducted in only eight localities with over 10,000 inhabitants, and seems to have included only employees with regular jobs.[1] Thus, the survey represented only well-established Jewish urban employees. The austerity period also influenced the results of the survey, since fixed prices and rationing reduced consumption differences between families.

Later surveys gradually widened the population represented (smaller urban localities, single persons, etc.). In addition, the general rise in the standard of living brought the poorer strata of the population into the scope of the family surveys — since they became "orderly households".

Most of the consumption surveys show higher average expenditures than incomes; this is assumed to indicate underreporting of income. The difference between average expenditure and net income (after deduction of direct taxes) was especially high in the 1950/51 survey, indicating some unreliability of the income figures.[2] The difference declined from 20% in 1950/51 to about 10% in 1959/60 and 7% in 1968/69 — another gradual improvement in the surveys.[3] In 1975/76 net income was by 3% higher than expenditure.

Savings surveys and income surveys are also available. These can be regarded as a combined series, since their methods were similar. When savings surveys were conducted at the same time as consumption surveys (1957/58 and 1963/64), the savings surveys showed more income inequality than did the consumption surveys (Table 4A.1). From a difference of 20% in their inequality indexes in the late fifties, the gap between the two types of surveys narrowed to about 5% in the mid-sixties and to no difference at the end of the sixties, and in the seventies.

The savings surveys, which required less constancy from the families surveyed,[4] apparently included a wider spectrum of the population than did the consumption surveys. Over the years, improved survey methods and the rise in the standard of living widened the scope of the consumption surveys, impairing comparability within the series, but improving their comparability with the savings surveys. Thus, the savings and income surveys apparently reflect historical development more consistently than do the consumption surveys.

NOTES

1. See G. Hanoch, *Income Differences in Israel*, Falk Institute, Report No. 5, Jerusalem, 1961.
2. *Report of the Index Committee*, Statistical News No. 15, 1951 (Hebrew). The report assumes that the expenditure figures were more accurate than the income figures.
3. Another difference between the 1950/51 survey and the others is that the former includes income data only on families whose heads worked during the survey months; thus, family heads who worked part of the year, but not the survey months, were not included. Such families were included in later surveys based on annual income. The 1959/60 survey includes both annual and monthly income data; the monthly figures show higher inequality than do the annual data, because the survey includes family heads who worked part of the year but *not* the survey months. (C.B.S., Special Series No. 200, p.45). This is another way in which the scope of the surveys has been widened.
4. In a consumption survey, a family is asked to record all details of its consumption for an entire month.

Table 4A.1
Income Inequality in Jewish Urban Families and Jewish Urban Employees' Families (Gini Coefficient)

	Consumption Surveys			*Savings or Income Surveys*	
Year	*Urban Employees' Families*	*Urban Families*	*Year*	*Urban Employees' Families*	*Urban Families*
1926	0.191		1954	0.260	0.298**
1939	0.224		1957/58	0.311	0.355
1946		0.229**	1963/64	0.309	0.361
1950/51	0.182		1965	0.304	0.355
1956/57	0.255		1967	0.358	0.409
			1969	0.314*	0.384*
1959/60	0.273		1970	0.304	0.373
1963/64	0.288		1973	0.300*	0.373*
1968/69	0.313	0.373	1974	0.315*	0.386*
1975/76	0.276*	0.334*	1975	0.289*	0.360*
			1976	0.281*	0.350*
			1977	0.290*	0.341*

* Including Arab population, which had little influence on the index. In 1970, the inequality index of employees' families including Arab families was 0.305.

** Families whose heads did not belong to the labor force (19% of all families in 1968/69) were not included.

Source; Statistical Abstracts, C.B.S.

Inequality in Jewish Urban Families and Urban Employees' Families

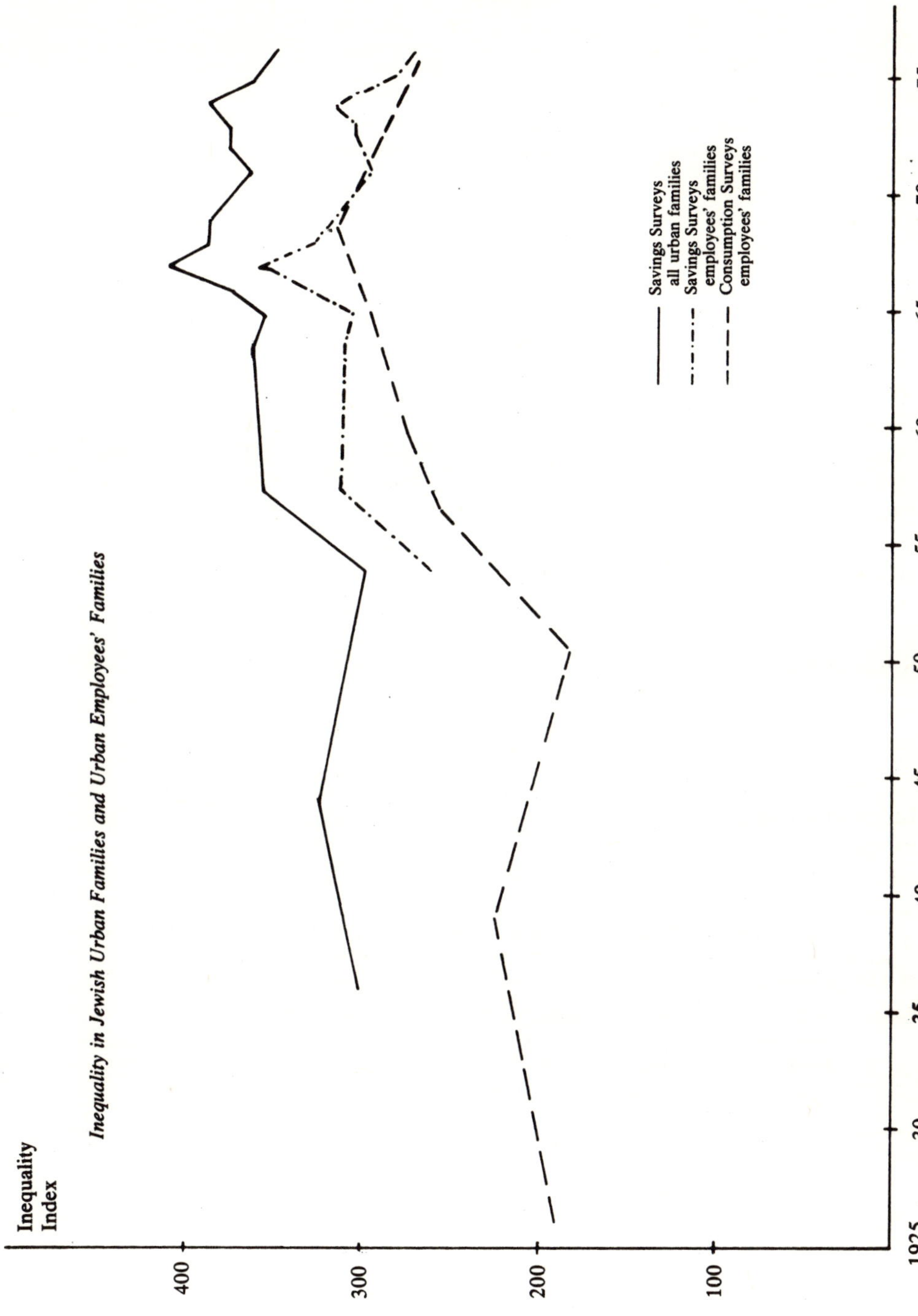

Figure 4A.1

Source: Tables 4A.1, 4.1

Table 4A.2
Income of Employees by Educational Level
(% of average)

Years of Schooling	*Income of Unit Head from Work* 1957/58	*Income of Employees from Work* 1963/64	*Employees' Annual Earnings* 1968	1976
0	55	52	59	63
1— 4	69	67	70	79
5— 8	89	87	81	86
9—12	112	108	106	98
13—15	. . .		119	106
	(125)	134**		
16+	164*		178	142
	(175)			
Ratio of highest to lowest level	3.0		3.0	2.3
	(3.2)			
Sum of deviations	163 (199)		193	122
Index of income inequality by educational level	0.158		0.144	0.092

* 15+ years of schooling. Figures in parentheses are adjusted figures to 13-15 and 16+ years of schooling.
** 13+ years of schooling.

Source: 1957/58 Savings Survey, according to R. Klinov, op. cit., p. 28.
Employee Earnings 1968-1972, CBS, Special Series, No. 435 and Supplement to Monthly Statistical Bulletin No. 9, 1977.
Family Expenditure Survey 1963/64, Special Series No. 200.

Table 4A.3
Income Distribution of Urban Population, 1968/69 and 1975/76
(% of Income by Deciles)

	All Urban Families				*Employees' Families*		*Income per Standard Adult (All Families) Total Net Income*		
Deciles	*Gross Monetary Income*		*Net Monetary Income*		*Gross Monetary Income*		*Family Income*	*S.A. Income*	
	1968/69	1975/76	1968/69	1975/76	1968/69	1975/76	1975/76	1968/69	1975/76
1	1.5	1.9	1.8	2.3	2.3	3.1	4.4	2.6	2.9
2	3.2	3.7	3.8	4.3	4.5	5.0	6.1	4.2	4.9
3	5.0	5.5	5.6	6.1	5.9	6.3	6.9	5.6	5.9
4	6.4	6.9	7.1	7.5	7.1	7.4	7.5	6.7	7.0
5	7.9	8.3	8.4	8.7	8.2	8.5	8.6	7.8	8.2
6	9.3	9.7	9.8	10.0	9.4	9.8	10.2	9.2	9.5
7	10.9	11.3	11.3	11.4	10.8	11.1	11.1	10.7	10.9
8	13.1	13.2	13.3	13.1	12.8	12.8	12.3	12.9	12.9
9	16.5	16.0	16.2	15.5	15.6	15.2	14.6	15.9	15.5
10	26.2	23.5	22.7	21.1	23.4	20.8	18.3	24.4	22.3
Gini Coeff.	0.371	0.334	0.327	0.296	0.314	0.276	0.224	0.328*	0.297

Source: Statistical Abstracts; C.B.S., Family Surveys 1968/69 and 1975/76; Report of the Committee on Income Distribution, Tel-Aviv, 1971, p. 23.

*Jewish families: net income calculated by deciles of gross total income per S.A.

Table 4A.4
*Regression Equations for Inequality Index (Gini Coefficient)**

No. of Regres-sion	*Depend-ent Variable*	*Inter-cept*		D/S_{13}	D/S_9	u	A	LMW	SF	R^2	*No. of Observa-tions*
1	Gini UP	0.199	Coefficient		0.0042	−.0033	−.0604	0.0095	−.0073	0.823	14
			significance		(0.0011)	(.0029)	(.026)	(0.0064)	(.0074)		
			add. explan. (%)		55.2	1.0	16.8	7.2	2.1		
			beta coefficient		3.142	−.316	−2.781	1.020	−.778		
2	Gini UP	0.1151	Coefficient	0.0015				0.0026		0.579	14
			significance	(.0004)				(.0018)			
			add. expl. (%)	50.4				7.5			
			beta coeff.	0.662				0.278			
3	Gini UP	0.200	Coefficient			0.0061			0.0045	0.676	13
			significance			(.0014)			(.0014)		
			add. explan. (%)			34.9			32.7		
			beta coefficient			0.823			0.618		
4	Gini UE	0.1455	Coefficient	0.0012		0.0027				0.495	14
			significance	(.0004)		(.0019)					
			add. explan. (%)	39.9		9.6					
			beta coefficient	0.627		0.309					
5	Gini UE	0.239	Coefficient		0.0044	−.0024	−.0653	0.0103	−.0112	0.826	14
			significance		(.0009)	(.0025)	(.0219)	(.0054)	(.0063)		
			add. explan. (%)		16.9	2.0	45.5	13.4	4.8		
			beta coefficient		3.891	−.273	−3.529	1.300	−1.400		
5a	Gini UE	0.0184	Coefficient		0.0034		−.0773	0.0129		0.758	14
			significance		(.0007)		(.0207)	(.0055)			(3 steps
			add. explan. (%)		16.9		45.5	13.4			only)
			beta coefficient		2.995		−4.178	1.628			
6	Gini UE	0.2426	Coefficient	0.0003		0.0066				0.831	13
			significance	(.0002)		(.0011)					
			add. explan. (%)	2.7		80.4					
			beta coefficient	0.174		0.836					
7	Gini UE	0.2593	Coefficient		0.0006	0.0056	−.0090			0.837	13
			significance		(.0005)	(.0018)	(.0084)				
			add. explan. (%)		1.2	80.4	2.1				
			beta coefficient		0.548	0.712	−.514				
8	Gini UE	0.2820	Coefficient		0.0003	0.0064		−.0014		0.826	13
			significance		(.0002)	(.0015)		(.0019)			
			add. explan. (%)		1.2	80.4		1.0			
			beta coefficient		0.225	0.812		−.183			

*(1) D/S_{13} represents the ratio of capital per employed (D) to the percentage of the labor force with 13 years of schooling (S_{13}) and D/S_9 with 9 years of schooling (S_9); u represents the percentage of unemployed. A is the percentage of the Jewish population aged 65 and over; LMW is the percentage of married women in labor force; SF is the percentage of one and two person families.
(2) Gini UP represents the inequality index of the urban population; Gini UE, that of urban employees' families.
(3) Figures in parentheses are standard errors.

Table 4A.5
Correlation Matrix of Explanatory Variables

I. *1954 – 1975 (14 observations)*

	% of aged 65+	*% of small families*	*Labor part. of M.W.*	*Demand/ Supply Skilled* L/13	*Demand/ Supply Skilled* L/9	*% of unemploy-ment*
SF	0.947	1.000	0.830	0.582	0.956	−.550
LMW	0.944	0.830	1.000	0.173	0.774	−.672
D/S_{13}	0.425	0.582	0.173	1.000	0.714	0.016
D/S_9	0.920	0.956	0.774	0.714	1.000	−.360
u	−.593	−.550	−.672	0.016	−.360	1.000

II. *1957/58 – 1975 (13 observations)*

	% of aged 65+	*% of small families*	*Labor part. of M.W.*	*Demand/ Supply Skilled* L/13	*Demand/ Supply Skilled* L/9	*% of unemploy-ment*
SF	0.923	1.000	0.756	0.406	0.932	−.377
LMW	0.921	0.756	1.000	−.134	0.668	−.560
D/S_{13}	0.198	0.406	−.134	1.000	0.587	0.350
D/S_9	0.883	0.932	0.668	0.587	1.000	−.082
u	−.447	−.377	−.560	0.350	−.082	1.000

Table 4A.6
Beta Coefficients

1954-1975				1957/58-1975			
Inequality Index of*				*Inequality Index* of*			
Urban Families		*Urban Empl. Families*		*Urban Families*		*Urban Empl. Families*	
	Regr. 1		*Regr. 5*		*Regr. 3*		*Regr. 6*
D/S_9	3.142	D/S_9	3.891	u	0.823	u	0.836
A	−2.781	A	−3.529	SF	0.618	D/S_{13}	0.174
LMW	1.020	SF	−1.400	R^2	0.676	R^2	0.831
							Regr. 7
u	−.316	u	−.273			u	0.712
R^2	0.823	R^2	0.826			D/S_9	0.548
						A	−.514
	Regr. 2		*Regr. 4*			R^2	0.837
D/S_{13}	0.662	D/S_{13}	0.627				
LMW	0.278	u	0.309				
R^2	0.579	R^2	0.495				
							Regr. 8
						u	0.812
						D/S_9	0.225
						LMW	−.183
						R^2	0.826

* Dependent variable
Source: Results of Regressions. Table 4A.4.

APPENDIX 5

Table 5A.1
Educational Capital per Capita
(Jewish population aged 14 and more)

*Country of Origin**	*1961* *% of Population*	*Ed. Capital per capita Index*	*1972* *% of Population*	*Ed. Capital per capita Index*	*Rise from 1961-1972 (%)*
AA	33.8	50	33.8	54	32.6
IAA	3.2	81	11.5	79	18.7
EA	49.2	121	35.5	121	23.0
II	4.0	122	4.5	122	20.7
IEA	9.8	165	14.7	162	19.3
	100.0	100	100.0	100	21.7
Inequality Index**	0.203		0.213		

* AA — born in Asia-Africa; IAA — Israel born, father from Asia-Africa;
EA — born in Europe-America; II — Israel born, father Israel born;
IEA — Israel born, father from Europe-America.

** Calculated by us as Gini index.

Source: Calculated on the basis of Z. Hercovitz, *Educational Capital in Israel*, Falk Institute, Jerusalem 1976; Table 7, p. 24.

Table 5A.2

Share of Oriental Employees by Occupation of Family Head

Occupation	1946 Monthly Income per family	1946 Monthly Income per capita	1946 % of Oriental Community	Occupation	1974 Income per family	1974 Income per capita	1974 % of Asian-African born
Liberal Professions	129	140	9	Scientific & Academic Workers	152	175	11
				Professional & Technical Workers	119	129	25
Employees (clerks)	105	108	16	Administrators & Managers	161	170	20
				Clerical Workers	102	117	35
				Salesmen	92	106	34
Workers	91	94	38	Agricultural Workers	68	48	43
Transport Workers	137	149	12	Skilled Workers	91	85	52
				Unskilled Workers	74	60	62
Policemen	70	74	44	Service Workers	68	65	59
Miscellaneous	53	36	82				
TOTAL	100	100	35	TOTAL	100	100	41

Source: 1946 — Survey of Urban Jewish Families; 1974 — Income Survey of Employees' Families. % of Asian-African born (including Israel born whose father came from Asian-African countries) according to labor force survey of 1974 (Jewish employees).

Table 5A.3
Income Distribution Among Kibbutzim
(Income shares of quintiles in %)

Quintiles	1955	1957	1961	1968
1	10.9	11.3	12.7	10.5
2	16.7	17.1	16.6	16.4
3	19.6	19.7	18.7	19.1
4	22.1	22.1	23.1	23.0
5	30.7	29.8	28.9	31.0
Gini Coeff.*	0.190	0.180	0.163	0.204
% of unemployment (for agricultural years)	7.8	7.1	3.8	7.2

*Calculated on the basis of deciles.

Source: 1955 and 1961 — Report of Committee, 1966, p. 182.
1957 and 1968 — J. Simchoni, S. Shmueli, op. cit. 1974.

Table 5A.4
Income Distribution in Moshavim

Deciles	*All Moshavim* 1954	*Veteran Moshavim* 1959	*All Moshavim* 1970	*% of Veteran Moshavim* 1970	*% of Farm Income* 1970
1	1.6	3	1.6	35	14
2	3.1	5	3.4	57	65
3	4.8	6	5.1	49	66
4	6.0	6	6.5	62	58
5	7.7	7	7.6	35	43
6	9.3	8	8.9	46	57
7	10.3	10	10.4	70	58
8	13.0	14	12.3	76	67
9	18.2	18	15.3	83	81
10	26.0	23	28.9	78	88
Gini Coeff.	0.381	0.324	0.378	59	59

Source: 1954: G. Kaddar, Family Farms in Cooperative Villages, Tel Aviv 1956.
from: M.I. Klayman, *The Moshav in Israel*, N.Y., 1970.
1959: Y. Lowe and I. Riemer, *Profitability of Veteran Moshavim*, Tel Aviv, 1960.
1970: Calculated by A. Katri, Institute of Farm Income Research, Tel Aviv (negative incomes excluded), 1976.

APPENDIX 6

Table 6A.1
Average Monthly Cash Income, per Family, by Age of Family Head

	All families		Wage and salary earners		
Age of head of family	*%*	*Average monthly income per family (% of average)*	*%*	*Average monthly income per family (% of average)*	*Income from work of family head (% of average)*
up to 24	3.0	70	3.5	71	68
25 — 34	16.4	107	21.5	97	103
35 — 44	22.9	114	28.1	106	109
45 — 54	21.1	119	23.8	115	114
55 — 64	19.4	101	17.4	89	84
65+	17.2	56	5.7	69	53
TOTAL	100.0	100	100.0	100	100
IL		905		989	766
Inequality index, by age groups		0.111		0.071	0.083
Inequality index for all families		0.373		0.313	0.238*

*Heads of families who worked 43 or more weeks.
Source: Computed from data of the *Survey of Family Expenditure*, 1968/69.

Table 6A.2
Average Monthly Cash Income per Family, by Years of Schooling of Family Head

	All families		Wage and salary earners		
Years of schooling of head of family	*% of families*	*Income per family (% of average)*	*% of families*	*Income per family (% of average)*	*Income from work of family heads who worked 43 or more weeks (% of average)*
0 — 4	19.6	57	14.6	62	59
5 — 8	32.5	81	32.1	79	83
9 — 12	30.6	119	33.7	108	108
13+	17.3	150	19.6	148	144
TOTAL	100.0	100	100.0	100	100
IL		905		989	799
Inequality index by educational groups		0.177		0.154	0.148
General inequality index		0.373		0.313	0.238

Source: See Table 6A.1

Table 6A.3
*Inequality Indices of the Income of Homogeneous Groups**

		All families		*Wage and salary earners*			
						Income from work of head of family	
Age of head of family	*Number of years of schooling*	*% of all families*	*Inequality index of family income*	*% of all families*	*Inequality index of family income*	*yearly income*	*weekly income*
1. 25-34	0-4	1.1	0.304	1.3	0.275	0.181	0.178
2. 35-44		3.7	0.270	4.4	0.240	0.227	0.204
3. 45-54		3.9	0.300	3.7	0.210	0.152	0.149
4. 25-34	5-8	5.2	0.274	6.7	0.259	0.217	0.205
5. 35-44		8.1	0.236	9.3	0.204	0.157	0.147
6. 45-54		7.3	0.251	8.0	0.229	0.168	0.158
7. 25-34	9-12	6.3	0.238	8.7	0.230	0.170	0.163
8. 35-44		7.3	0.250	9.3	0.234	0.161	0.142
9. 45-54		7.4	0.267	7.7	0.271	0.202	0.189
10. 25-34	13+	3.9	0.278	4.8	0.216	0.187	0.165
11. 35-44		3.8	0.235	5.0	0.221	0.150	0.144
12. 45-54		3.3	0.279	4.5	0.259	0.222	0.203
All families			0.373		0.313	0.238**	0.238**
Percentage differences			20-37		17-35		14-40

Source: See Table 6A.1
*The index was computed from ten income groups on a rising scale, each consisting of one tenth of the population.
**Income of heads of families, who worked at least 43 weeks.

Table 6A.4
Results of Multiple Regressions on Income from Work by Wage Earning Heads of Families
(1564 Observations)

No. of regres-sion	*Dependent variable*	*Intercept*		*Years of schooling of head*	*Weeks worked*	*Years of schooling × traders agents salesmen*	*Years of schooling × farmers and com-mon laborers*	*Years of schooling × indust-rial workers*	*Sex of head of family*	*Eur.-Am. origin, old-timers*	*Age of head of family, squared*	*Age of head of family*	*Years of schooling × mana-gerial and clerical workers*	R^2
				INDEPENDENT VARIABLES										
1	Income from work of head of family	−1,633.88	Order of app.	1	2	3	4	5	6	7	8	9	10	
			Additional explanation (%)	26.45	9.14	2.50	1.80	1.97	1.94	1.13	1.05	3.78	0.89	
			Coefficient	48.827	15.826	−28.451	−41.498	−19.092	266.901	129.629	−0.572	49.81	−9.89	0.506
			Significance	(1.867)	(1.104)	(2.93)	(4.957)	(2.248)	(33.505)	(22.813)	(0.048)	(4.453)	(1.865)	
2	Income from week of work by head of family	−207.321	Order of app.	1		2	3	4	5	6	7	8	9	
			Additional explanation (%)	28.45		2.76	2.37	2.24	2.24	1.22	1.25	4.17	1.07	
			Coefficient	11.757		−6.957	−10.724	−4.743	65.804	31.598	−0.139	12.104	−2.508	0.458
			Significance	(0.453)		(0.711)	(1.198)	(0.545)	(8.114)	(5.532)	(0.012)	(1.075)	(0.452)	
						Age × farmers and common laborers	Age × traders, agents, salesmen	Age × industr-rial workers						
3	Logarithm of income from work of head of family	0.843	Order of app.	2	1	4	5	6	3	7	8	9		
			Additional explanation (%)	19.19	24.58	3.67	3.54	1.68	4.12	0.73	1.19	4.15		
			Coefficient	0.0191	0.0186	−0.0048	−0.0034	−0.0016	0.2299	0.0687	−0.0004	0.035		0.629
			Significance	(0.0012)	(0.0007)	(0.0004)	(0.0003)	(0.0003)	(0.0206)	(0.0137)	(0.0000)	(0.0027)		
4	Logarithm of income from week of work of head of family	1.1166	Order of app.	1		3	4	5	2	6	7	8		
			Additional explanation (%)	25.29		5.24	4.47	2.35	5.75	0.98	1.60	6.10		
			Coefficient	0.0191		−0.0049	−0.0033	−0.0017	0.2374	0.0684	−0.0004	0.0369		0.518
			Significance	(0.0012)		(0.0004)	(0.0003)	(0.0003)	(0.0205)	(0.0137)	(0.0000)	(0.0026)		

The regressions were computed on the basis of ten steps. | × denotes interaction between two explanatory variables. | Figures in parentheses denote standard error.

Table 6A.5
Coefficients of Correlation between Number of Years of Schooling of the Wage Earning Family Head and His Earnings per Work Week, with his Continent of Origin

Continent of Origin and arrival in Israel	*Coefficient of correlation* with education of wage earning head of family	with income from week of work by wage earning head of family
Asia and Africa		
arrived before 1948	−0.080	0.017
1948 — 1957	−0.260	−0.206
after 1957	−0.197	−0.184
Europe and America		
arrived before 1948	0.195	0.233
1948 — 1957	0.074	0.045
after 1957	0.082	−0.035

Reference group: Jewish native-born Israelis.
Source: see Table 6A.1

APPENDIX 7

Table 7A.1
Composition of Total Monthly Income of Urban Families by Employment Status of Family Head (%) 1968/69

	Total Population	*Wage and Salary Earners*	*Self-Employed*	*Not in Labor Force*	*Total 1975/76*
No. of families (000)	614.2	395.5	103.2	115.4	777.4
Income from work					
of family head	63.9	69.5	72.3	—	58.8
of his wife	10.2	11.2	4.7	14.1	9.6
of other family members	6.5	5.1	7.8	17.2	5.1
Imputed income from housing, vehicles, etc.	10.6	10.0	9.7	16.0	14.3
Income from pensions, allowances and support	7.8	3.5	4.5	49.0	9.6
from property	1.0	0.7	1.0	3.7	2.6
Total Income* IL	1,010	1,097	1,265	482	4,835
Index	100	109	125	48	
Average family size	3.65	3.9	4.0	2.4	
Total income per person IL	277	281	316	201	
Earners per family	1.3	1.5	1.5	0.4	

Source: Family Expenditure Survey 1968/69, Part IV, Special Series 388, CBS, Jerusalem 1972. Family Expenditure Survey 1975/76, Special Series No. 563, 1978.

*Total gross money income and income in kind (i.e., imputed income from use of privately owned dwelling or vehicle, as well as the value of goods taken from business for personal use or received by wage-earners without payment).

Table 7A.2
Husband-Wife Families with Working Wives and with Non-Working Wives

	(1) *Total*	(2) *Wife Working*	(3) *Wife not Working*	(4) *(2) as a % of (3)*
Average Monthly Income – IL				
Total family income	1,102	1,520	967	157
Net cash family income	827	1,136	727	156
Income from family head's work	737	854	699	122
Income from wife's work	111	451	—	—
Earners per family	1.39	2.08	1.17	178
Family size	4.02	3.71	4.13	90
Family Head				
Weeks worked	44.8	46.8	44.2	106
Age	47.2	42.4	48.7	87
Years of schooling	9.0	11.1	8.3	133
Continent of Birth – %				
Asia-Africa	36.6	25.8	40.1	64
Europe-America	48.5	52.7	47.2	112
Israel — Jews	12.9	21.5	10.0	215
Arabs	2.0	—	2.7	—
New Immigrants after '58 %	14.0	11.9	14.7	81
Wife of Family Head				
Weeks worked	12.8	45.0	—	—
Age	41.8	37.3	43.3	86
Years of schooling	8.0	10.5	7.2	147
Children per family				
up to 17 years	1.64	1.43	1.97	73
up to 5 years	0.55	0.48	0.57	84
No. of families surveyed	1,988	488	1,500	

Source: Family Expenditure Survey 1968/69.

Notes to Tables 7A.3 – 7A.16:

1. The regressions are presented in ten steps.
2. Standard errors in parentheses.
3. × denotes interaction between two explanatory variables.
4. *Reference Groups*
   Occupation: Agents, traders, salesmen.
   Country of origin and year of Immigration: Israel, Jews.
   Dwelling locality: Tel Aviv.
5. The beta coefficient (regression coefficient in standard form) shows the average number of units of the standard deviations' increase or decrease in the dependent variable (income) which occur with each increase of one unit of the standard deviation in the independent variable.

Table 7A.8 (cont.)

Results of Multiple Regressions on Incomes of One-Parent Families and Individuals (Men, 122 observations)

No. of Regres-sion	*Depen-dent Variable*	*Intercept*		*Independent Variables*											R^2
				Weeks worked	*School.*	*Member of coop.*	*Eur.-Am. Veteran*	*Schooling × (Age)²*	*Age × not in lab. force*	*Age × School.*	*Age × constr. workers*	*Constr. workers*	*Schooling × unskill. workers*		
13	Income from work	−487.0	Order of appear.	1	2	3	4	5	6	7	8	9	10		0.720
			Add.Expl.(%)	50.89	5.27	3.96	1.87	2.42	2.65	1.14	1.12	1.63	1.01		
			coefficient	16.72	−4.69	923.8	157.0	−0.028	6.11	2.14	21.77	−861.0	−26.6		
			significance	(2.25)	(18.74)	(235.8)	(64.9)	(0.009)	(1.79)	(0.85)	(6.88)	(335.7)	(13.3)		
			beta coeff.	.903	−.058	.198	.129	−1.584	.450	1.630	.393	−.317	−.104		
				No. of earners	*School.*	*Child. 6-13*	*Age × constr. worker*	*Arab*	*Immigr. Settl. up to 10,000*	*Eur.-Am. Veteran*	*Jeru-salem*	*School. × trans. worker*	*Child. up to 5*	*Age × Serv. Work.*	
14	Net Family Cash Income	−30.66	Order of appear.	1	2	3	4	5	6	7	8	9	10	11	0.747
			Add.Expl.(%)	34.18	10.39	12.79	2.93	3.24	3.47	1.95	1.81	1.55	1.21	1.13	
			coefficient	284.7	30.52	451.5	16.88	−615.5	−388.8	200.4	−208.5	27.43	−204.8	−3.53	
			significance	(35.7)	(4.6)	(61.7)	(3.1)	(196.6)	(95.1)	(61.2)	(80.7)	(10.8)	(81.6)	(1.59)	
			beta coeff.	.458	.370	.607	.296	−.181	−.209	.160	.144	.126	−.214	−.112	

Table 7A.4

Results of Multiple Regressions on Income of "Husband-Wife" Families (1,988 families)

No. of Regression	Dependent Variable	Intercept		Schooling Wife	Earners in Family	Age × Liberal Prof. H.	Eur.-Am. Veteran H.	Weeks Worked H.	Age × not working H.	Family Size	Schooling × Man.Clerk. H.	Weeks worked W.	Not in labor force W.	R^2
	Net		Order of appear.	1	2	3	4	5	6	7	8	9	10	
	Family		Add.explan.(%)	19.17	15.39	3.52	1.64	1.44	2.15	1.17	1.12	0.93	1.08	0.476
3	Cash	−892.1	coefficient	32.84	190.4	7.55	166.5	11.89	8.10	35.9	12.14	9.12	343.0	(0.499
	Income		significance	(2.3)	(13.7)	(0.6)	(21.9)	(1.07)	(0.87)	(4.84)	(1.97)	(1.1)	(53.6)	with
			beta coeff.	0.293	0.301	0.226	0.130	0.399	0.337	0.141	0.109	0.394	0.311	19 steps)

Employees (1.365 families)*

No. of Regression	Dependent Variable	Intercept		Schooling W.	Earners in family	Weeks worked H.	Schooling × lib. prof. H.	Schooling × Man. clerks H.	Eur.-Am. Veteran H.	Family Size	Weeks worked W.	Not in labor force W.	Age × not work. H.	R^2
	Net		Order of appear.	1	2	3	4	5	6	7	8	9	10	
	Family		Add.explan.(%)	23.11	14.12	4.18	4.11	2.57	1.77	1.63	1.74	1.47	0.72	0.554
4	Cash	−865.5	coefficient	27.95	183.9	11.78	22.15	13.76	176.8	36.71	9.50	334.9	9.30	(0.585
	Income		significance	(2.42)	(15.3)	(1.14)	(1.72)	(1.84)	(23.0)	(4.75)	(1.02)	(49.6)	(1.99)	with
			beta coeff.	.280	.285	.189	.278	.155	.146	.158	.466	.349	.087	19 steps)

*Members of cooperatives not included.

Table 7A.3

Results of Multiple Regressions on Family Income – All families (2,412 observations)

No. of Regres-sion	*Depen-dent Variable*	*Intercept*		*Schooling Wife*	*No. of earners*	*Age × liberal prof.* H.	*Schooling × Manag. clerks* H.	*Eur.-Am. Veteran* H.	*Schooling family head*	*Family Size*	*Schooling × Liberal profess.* W.	*Age × Manag. clerks* W.	*Weeks worked Head*	*Age × not in lab. force* H.	R^2
	Total		Order of appear.	1	2	3	4	5	6	7	8	9	10	11	
	family	−522.1	Add. Expl. (%)	21.45	7.82	3.94	1.76	1.09	0.52	0.36	0.41	0.39	0.45	1.10	
1	Income		coefficient	29.44	215.5	10.15	14.54	222.8	20.56	31.29	20.79	6.58	12.64	8.62	0.392
			significance	(3.55)	(20.6)	(1.10)	(3.45)	(34.8)	(3.85)	(7.29)	(4.30)	(1.63)	(1.62)	(1.31)	(0.412 with
			beta-coeff.	.183	.218	.178	.078	.107	.122	.079	.091	.071	.314	.270	19 steps)
				Schooling Wife	*No. of earners*	*Schooling Head*	*Weeks worked Head*	*Eur.-Am. Veteran Head*	*Family Size*	*Age × not in lab. for Head*	*Schooling × service workers Head*	*Eur.-Am. 1948-57 Head*	*(Age)*^{2} *Head*	*Age Head*	
	Log.		Order of appear.	1	2	3	4	5	6	7	8	9	10	11	
	total		Add. Expl. (%)	30.34	16.73	4.74	3.78	1.37	1.59	1.02	0.59	0.51	0.60	0.90	
2	family	1.718	coefficient	0.014	0.127	0.018	0.008	0.129	0.020	0.005	−0.010	0.058	−0.0002	0.015	0.622
	income		significance	(0.001)	(0.006)	(0.001)	(0.001)	(0.012)	(0.002)	(0.000)	(0.002)	(0.011)	(0.000)	(0.002)	(0.657 with
			beta coeff.	.210	.318	.272	.489	.154	.126	.405	−.073	.076	−.806	.675	25 steps)

Table 7A.6

Results of Multiple Regressions on Income of H.-W. Families in which Wife was not working (1,500 families)

No. of Regression	Dependent Variable	Intercept		Earners in family	Schooling H.	Age × Lib. Prof. H.	Schooling W.	Weeks worked H.	Age × not in labor force H.	Persons in family	Eur.-Am. Veteran H.	Schooling × Man. Clerk H.	Eur.-Am. 1948-57 H.	R^2
				Independent Variable										
	Net		Order of appear.	1	2	3	4	5	6	7	8	9	10	
	Family		Add.Expl.(%)	11.79	13.06	2.30	2.26	1.19	2.27	1.00	1.27	0.66	0.51	0.363
7	Cash	−530.0	coefficient	193.0	11.15	6.67	20.37	11.22	7.77	34.29	165.9	10.30	84.07	(0.383
	Income		significance	(14.8)	(3.13)	(0.79)	(3.25)	(1.33)	(1.06)	(5.44)	(27.4)	(2.59)	(24.3)	with
			beta coeff.	.318	.113	.203	.190	.434	.383	.157	.141	.091	.079	16 steps)

Employees (972 families)

No. of Regression	Dependent Variable	Intercept		Schooling H.	Earners in family	Weeks worked H.	Schooling × not working W.	Schooling × lib. prof. H.	Schooling × Man.Cl. H	Persons in family	Eur.-Am. Veteran H.	As.-Afr. Veteran H.	Eur.-Am. 1948-57 H.	R^2
	Net		Order of appear.	1	2	3	4	5	6	7	8	9	10	
	Family		Add.Expl.(%)	14.17	10.35	5.75	2.63	2.19	1.95	1.95	1.22	0.84	1.11	0.421
8	Cash	−531.2	coefficient	8.47	191.8	10.96	19.97	18.54	12.34	36.27	165.6	179.0	104.2	(0.457
	Income		significance	(3.2)	(15.5)	(1.30)	(2.96)	(2.47)	(2.39)	(5.09)	(28.3)	(41.8)	(24.3)	with
			beta coeff.	.104	.323	.209	.228	.243	.151	.201	.158	.107	.115	18 steps)

Table 7A.7

Results of Multiple Regressions on Earnings of Family Head's Wife (488 observations)

No. of Regression	*Dependent Variable*	*Intercept*												R^2
				Schooling	*Weeks Worked*	*Prof. Scient. worker*	*Manag. cleric. worker*	*Veteran settl. up to 10,000*	*Afr.-As. Veteran*					
9	Wife's income from work	−294.1	Order of appear.	1	2	3	4	5	6					0.445
			Add.Expl.(%)	25.39	16.71	0.83	0.65	0.49	0.45					
			coefficient	25.0	9.5	111.3	69.4	−145.2	156.4					
			significance	(3.4)	(0.8)	(33.0)	(30.0)	(66.2)	(79.3)					
			beta coeff.	.338	.405	.169	.099	−.075	.067					
				Schooling W.	*(Age)²* W.	*Children up to 5 years*	*Weeks worked* H.	*Afr.-As. new imm.* W.	*Family income less W. earnings*	*Children aged 13-17*				
10	Wife worked outside home (1968 observations)	0.322	Order of appear.	1	2	3	4	5	6	7				0.152
			Add.Expl.(%)	10.61	2.05	1.33	0.44	0.29	0.25	.021				
			coefficient	0.030	−0.0001	−0.064	−0.002	−0.093	−0.00003	(0.032)				
			significance	(0.002)	(0.0000)	(0.013)	(0.001)	(0.033)	(0.00000)	(0.014)				
			beta coeff.	.306	−.250	−.128	−.067	−.060	−.060	.048				
				(Age)² W.	*Children up to 5 years*	*Wife's more years of school. than H.*	*Af.-As. new imm.* W.	*Af.-As. 1948-57* W.	*Arab* W.	*Age* W.	*Af.-As. Veteran* W.	*Weeks worked* H.	*Eur.-Am. 1948-57* W.	
10a	Wife worked outside home	0.845	Order of appear.	1	2	3	4	5	6	7	8	9	10	0.117
			Add.Expl.(%)	3.81	2.87	1.01	0.95	1.15	0.89	0.37	0.25	0.19	0.17	
			coefficient	−0.00002	−0.082	0.077	−0.239	−0.152	−0.315	−0.010	0.156	−0.0013	−0.047	
			significance	(0.00005)	(0.013)	(0.021)	(0.036)	(0.024)	(0.066)	(0.005)	(0.057)	(0.0006)	(0.024)	
			beta coeff.	−.050	−.165	.077	−.155	−.154	−.104	−.295	−.059	−0.051	−.047	

Table 7A.8

***Results of Multiple Regressions on Incomes of One-Parent Families and Individuals* (Women: 302 observations)**

No. of Regression	Dependent Variable	Intercept		*Independent Variables*									R^2
				Weeks worked	*Age × service workers*	*Age × industr. workers*	*Unskill. workers*	*Transport & commun. workers*	*Not in labor force*	*Veteran settl. up to 10,000*	*Farmer*	*Jerusalem*	
11	Income from work	358.75	Order of appear.	1	2	3	4	5	6	7	8	9	0.741
			Add.Expl.(%)	53.00	10.40	3.54	1.85	1.76	1.58	0.90	0.72	0.37	
			coefficient	6.33	−8.26	−7.73	434.7	−686.7	−357.9	−176.8	−415.7	59.5	
			significance	(1.53)	(0.6)	(1.02)	(89.3)	(151.1)	(79.8)	(57.5)	(151.1)	(29.3)	
			beta coeff.	.530	−.550	−.244	−.149	−.137	−.599	−.092	−.083	−.063	
				No. of earners	*Schooling*	*Age × Serv. Work.*	*Eur.-Am. Veteran*	*Family Size*	*Immigr. Settl. over 10,000*	*Managers Clerks*			
12	Net Cash Family Income	80.64	Order of appear.	1	2	3	4	5	6	7			0.540
			Add.Expl.(%)	32.71	10.64	4.41	2.40	1.73	1.12	1.00			
			coefficient	218.3	15.17	−2.69	136.2	45.48	−91.1	147.4			
			significance	(23.8)	(3.1)	(0.79)	(35.6)	(11.9)	(34.1)	(58.2)			
			beta coeff.	.506	.227	−.152	.166	.198	−.112	.110			

Table 7A.5

***Results of Multiple Regressions on Income of Husband-Wife Families in which Wife was Working* (488 families)**

No. of Regression	Dependent Variable	Intercept		*Schooling* W.	*Weeks Worked* H.	*Weeks Worked* W.	*Eur.-Am. Veteran* H.	*Persons in Family*	*Schooling × Lib. Prof.* H.	*Schooling × Age* H.	*Age × not working* H.	*Schooling × (Age²)* H.	*Schooling* H.	R^2
	Net		Order of appear.	1	2	3	4	5	6	7	8	9	10	
	Family		Add.Exp.(%)	25.06	9.92	7.46	5.29	4.63	1.54	0.83	0.68	0.78	1.82	0.580
5	Cash	−794.0	coefficient	39.89	12.91	9.77	238.4	54.41	8.80	4.20	5.28	−0.04	−76.20	(0.604
	Income		significance	(5.41)	(1.74)	(1.21)	(41.2)	(11.43)	(2.9)	(0.75)	(1.62)	(0.008)	(16.78)	with
			beta coeff.	.329	.360	.254	.188	.163	.111	1.930	.157	−1.383	−.655	15 steps)

***Employees* (392 families)**

No. of Regression	Dependent Variable	Intercept		*Schooling* W.	*Weeks worked* W.	*Schooling × (Age)²* W.	*Persons in Family*	*Eur.-Am. Veteran* H.	*Weeks worked* H.	*Schooling × Lib. Prof.* H.	*Schooling × Age* H.	*Age × not working* H.	*Schooling × not working* H.	R^2
	Net		Order of appear.	1	2	3	4	5	6	7	8	9	10	
	Family		Add.Expl.(%)	31.8	6.37	5.66	4.40	3.42	3.53	2.63	1.20	1.04	1.28	0.610
6	Cash	−766.1	coefficient	1.98	9.30	−0.026	55.06	219.1	13.07	10.03	0.41	36.55	−80.96	(0.625
	Income		significance	(0.26)	(1.14)	(0.004)	(10.9)	(40.8)	(2.09)	(2.73)	(0.011)	(8.44)	(22.9)	with
			beta coeff.	.799	.275	−.591	.169	.186	.204	.145	.196	.474	−.387	12 steps)

Table 7A.9
Regression No. 15
All Families (including independent individuals)
(2,412 observations)

Dependent Variable: Net Cash Income per Standard Equivalent Adult

Steps	*Independent Variables*	*Expl. Power %*	*Coefficient*	*Beta Coefficient*
1	Schooling, Family head	20.67	8.74 (0.80)	.213
2	Weeks worked, wife	5.42	3.49 (0.46)	.354
3	Eur.-Am., Veteran, fam. head	3.90	82.6 (8.4)	.162
4	Number of children	2.46	−23.4 (1.9)	−.207
5	Weeks worked, fam. head	4.29	3.54 (0.39)	.361
6	Age × liberal prof., fam. head	1.85	2.56 (0.26)	.185
7	Age × manag., clerk, fam. head	0.81	1.15 (0.20)	.100
8	Age × not working, fam. head	0.63	1.91 (0.31)	.246
9	Number of earners	0.84	33.0 (5.0)	.137
10	Not belonging to labor force, wife	0.47	98.2 (22.4)	.210
	TOTAL	41.34	Constant −125.1	
	with 25 steps	45.22		

Table 7A.10
Regression No. 16
All Husband-Wife Families
(1988 observations)

Dependent Variable: Net Cash Income per S.E.A.

Steps	*Independent Variables*	*Expl. Power %*	*Coefficient*	*Beta Coefficient*
1	Schooling, Wife	23.72	4.31 (1.53)	.096
2	Weeks worked, Wife	4.64	1.64 (0.19)	.177
3	Age × lib. prof., Husband	3.83	3.00 (0.25)	.224
4	Eur.-Am., Veteran, H.	2.83	60.7 (9.5)	.118
5	Weeks worked, H.	2.03	4.05 (0.45)	.340
6	Number of children	3.16	−17.8 (2.11)	−.161
7	Age × schooling, W.	1.00	0.15 (0.03)	.158
8	Schooling × manag., clerk, H.	0.76	4.31 (0.82)	.097
9	Age × not working, H.	0.68	2.06 (0.37)	.215
10	Number of earners	0.80	28.13 (5.33)	.111
	TOTAL	43.44	Constant −65.6	
	with 19 steps	45.55		

Table 7A.11
Regression No. 17
Husband-Wife Families with Working Wives
(488 observations)

Dependent Variable: Net Cash Income per S.E.A.

Steps	*Independent Variables*	*Expl. Power %*	*Coefficient*	*Beta Coefficient*
1	Schooling × age, wife	30.33	0.342 (0.042)	.347
2	Weeks worked, husband	8.37	5.21 (0.67)	.376
3	Weeks worked, w.	5.15	3.29 (0.47)	.222
4	Number of children	3.49	−32.4 (4.52)	−.234
5	Schooling × lib. prof., h.	2.84	5.31 (1.03)	.173
6	Europe-Am., Veteran, h.	3.41	103.8 (16.0)	.212
7	$(Age)^2$, wife	1.30	−0.034 (0.009)	.153
8	Age × not working, h.	0.79	1.79 (0.64)	.137
9	Schooling × farmer, gardener, w.	0.47	−18.4 (7.85)	−.071
10	Schooling × service worker, w.	0.41	−4.17 (1.97)	−.066
	TOTAL	56.55	Constant −70.4	
	with 13 steps	57.93		

Table 7A.12
Regression No. 18
Husband-Wife Families with Non-Working Wives
(1500 observations)

Dependent Variable: Net Cash Income per S.E.A.

Steps	*Independent Variables*	*Expl. Power (%)*	*Coefficient*	*Beta Coefficient*
1	Schooling × age, wife	18.05	0.235 (0.024)	.269
2	Age × lib. prof., husb.	4.39	3.15 (0.31)	.235
3	Weeks worked, husb.	3.36	3.71 (0.56)	.351
4	Number of children	2.44	−18.1 (2.51)	−.187
5	Eur.-Am., new immigr., h.	0.93	−53.2 (17.1)	−.069
6	Schooling × manag., clerk, h.	0.81	4.40 (1.04)	.096
7	Number of earners	0.69	30.1 (6.11)	.122
8	Age × not working, h.	0.68	2.07 (0.47)	.250
9	Eur.-Am., veteran, h.	0.56	42.7 (11.5)	.089
10	$(Age)^2$, husb.	0.21	−0.008 (0.004)	−.065
	TOTAL	32.12	Constant −17.89	
	with 13 steps	33.00		

Table 7A.13
Regression No. 19
Individuals and One-Parent Families (Women)
(302 observations)

Dependent Variable: Net Cash Income per S.E.A.

Steps	*Independent Variables*	*Expl. Power (%)*	*Coefficient*	*Beta Coefficient*
1	Schooling	26.80	6.82 (2.21)	.206
2	Age × Manager, clerk	8.30	4.19 (0.75)	.299
3	No. of earners	4.39	54.3 (10.3)	.254
4	Eur.-Am., Veteran	5.41	85.9 (19.1)	.212
5	Imm. Settl., 10,000 +	1.55	−52.2 (17.8)	−.129
6	Lib. Prof.	1.09	120.4 (38.7)	.161
7	Schooling × not working	0.68	4.96 (2.52)	.135
	TOTAL	48.22	Constant 101.17	

Regression No. 20
Individuals and One-Parent Families (Men)
(122 observations)

Steps	*Independent Variables*	*Expl. Power (%)*	*Coefficient*	*Beta Coefficient*
1	Schooling	23.14	16.8 (2.63)	.386
2	Weeks worked	14.69	3.55 (0.62)	.353
3	Age × construction worker	8.01	26.0 (5.76)	.863
4	Eur.-Am. Veteran	7.04	162.4 (39.7)	.246
5	Schooling × constr. w.	4.20	−94.3 (33.2)	−.558
6	Schooling × farmer	1.53	−17.8 (8.4)	−.127
7	Arab	1.38	−230.3 (116.0)	−.128
	TOTAL	59.99	Constant 21.32	

Table 7A.14
Regression No. 21
Families Whose Heads Did not Belong to the Labor Force
(434 observations)

Dependent Variable: Net Cash Income per S.E.A.

Steps	*Independent Variables*	*Additional Expl. Power (%)*	*Coefficient*	*Beta Coefficient*
1	Schooling × age, head	16.55	0.288 (0.08)	.656
2	Europe-America, veteran, head	6.56	89.1 (15.8)	.247
3	Number of earners	4.23	44.8 (8.68)	.217
4	Africa-Asia, immigr. after 1958, head	0.91	−51.7 (22.4)	−.096
5	Family head woman	0.73	46.9 (13.8)	.161
6	Schooling × $(age)^2$, wife	1.22	0.001 (0.000)	.157
7	New towns, over 10,000 inhabitants	0.79	−28.9 (14.3)	−.085
8	Schooling × $(age)^2$, head	0.64	−0.002 (0.001)	−.387
	Total explanation (%)	31.63	Constant 69.5	

Table 7A.15
Regression No. 22
Employee Families
(1,535 observations)

Dependent Variable: Net Cash Income per S.E.A.

Steps	*Independent Variables*	*Additional Explan. Power (%)*	*Coefficient*	*Beta coefficient*
1	Schooling, head	24.80	7.39 (0.92)	.198
2	Weeks worked, wife	9.27	3.54 (0.43)	.419
3	Number of children	6.97	−26.1 (1.83)	−.263
4	Weeks worked, head	3.72	4.39 (0.43)	.183
5	Europe-America, veteran, head	2.88	71.4 (8.9)	.149
6	Age × liberal profession, head	1.46	2.06 (0.25)	.188
7	Schooling × manager, clerk, head	1.16	4.37 (0.76)	.124
8	Age × liberal prof., wife	0.72	1.72 (0.35)	.106
9	Wife not belonging to lab. force	0.50	100.3 (20.4)	.253
10	Number of earners	0.63	25.6 (5.7)	.098
	Total ten steps	52.11	Constant −148.7	
	(Total explanation with 25 steps 56.57%)			

Table 7A.16
Regression No. 23
Self-Employed Families
(441 observations)

Dependent Variable: Net Cash Income per S.E.A.

Steps	*Independent Variables*	*Additional Explan. Power (%)*	*Coefficient*	*Beta coefficient*
1	Schooling × age, head	13.30	.180 (0.06)	.158
2	Age × liberal profession, head	4.00	3.99 (0.91)	.204
3	Schooling × manager, clerk, wife	3.08	16.8 (4.16)	.169
4	Number of children	2.77	−25.0 (6.8)	−.163
5	Weeks worked, head	1.05	4.77 (2.07)	.096
6	Europe-America, veteran, head	0.89	63.7 (27.8)	.103
7	Liberal profession, wife	0.66	117.9 (60.1)	.083
	Total explanation	25.75	Constant −8.94	

Table 7A.17
Years of Schooling and Labor Participation

Years of Schooling	*% of females aged 14+ in labor force*		*% of males aged 14+ in labor force*	
	1969	1976	1969	1976
0	12	10	63	50
1—4	18	15	79	67
5—8	27	21	79	71
9—10		29		56
11—12	37	41	61	60
13—15		61		69
16+	57	76	74	80
TOTAL	30	31.9	70	64.5

Source: Statistical Abstract 1977.

Table 7 A.18
Independent Individuals and One-Parent Families

Average Monthly Income	*Men*		*Women*	
	Individuals	*One-Parent Families*	*Individuals*	*One-Parent Families*
Total family income IL	609	917	355	741
Income from work of family head IL	429	512	103	234
Earners in family	0.69	1.27	0.29	1.19
Persons in family	1	3.36	1	3.16
Children aged 0-17	—	1.17	—	1.12
Family head				
Age	52.7	44.1	63.3	49.5
Years of schooling	9.0	8.6	6.3	5.9
Weeks worked	33.3	41.2	14.1	23.3
Continent of Birth (in %)				
Asia-Africa	31.2	54.0	25.1	50.6
Europe-America	54.0	31.2	65.2	35.5
Israel — Jews	14.8	10.7	8.0	12.2
Arabs	—	4.1	1.7	1.7
Employment Status (in %)				
Employee	56.8	68.8	25.7	39.5
Self-employed	12.1	14.6	3.4	8.6
Not belonging to labor force	31.1	16.6	70.9	51.9
New immigrants arriving after 1958 (%)	9.5	14.3	15.5	16.5
No. surveyed	74	48	175	127

Source: Family Expenditure Survey 1968-1969.

Table 7A.19
Incomes and Earnings by Occupation

Occupation	Total Family Income by Occupation of Family Head 1968/69 — % of families	Average monthly total income (% of average)	Weekly earnings of employees in 1968 (% of average) — Males	Females
Professional and scientific workers	11.0	172	150	140
Administrative, executive, managerial and clerical workers	15.4	137	121	134
Transport and communicationworkers	5.9	117	113	80
Traders, agents and salesmen	6.7	109	82	74
Construction workers, quarrymen and miners	5.2	92	86	—
Industrial workers and craftsmen	21.6	91	86	72
Services, sports and recreation workers	9.7	79	75	64
Farmers, fishermen and related workers	2.9	68	52	64
Unskilled workers	1.9	57	...	...
Not in labor force and did not work	19.4	52	—	—
Occupation unknown	0.3	150	—	—
Total (IL)	100.0	1,010	155	99

Source: Family Survey 1968/69, Income of Employees, 1968-1972, CBS.

Table 7A.20
Urban Families by Deciles of Gross Money Income by Continent of Birth and Period of Immigration of Family Head

Continent of birth and period of immigration	*Lowest decile*	*Second lowest decile*	*Ninth decile*	*Highest decile*	*Total*	*Monthly total income per fam. (% of average)*
Asia-Africa						
up to 1947	6.2	3.4	4.7	3.7	4.6	
1948-1954	20.4	19.2	13.4	8.0	20.1	85
1955-1960	8.3	4.3	2.4	1.4	5.0	
1961 +	6.6	12.4	1.6	0.8	6.2	66
Europe-America						
up to 1947	12.0	12.6	27.9	36.5	19.5	
1948-1954	20.2	27.4	21.7	18.5	20.8	116
1955-1960	7.7	3.4	5.2	4.2	4.6	
1961 +	8.4	6.5	2.5	4.8	4.6	90
Israel – Jews	7.2	6.6	20.1	21.7	12.6	122
Non-Jews	3.1	4.2	0.5	0.4	2.0	60

Source: CBS Special Series, No. 388.

APPENDIX 8

Table 8A.1
Scales of Differential Weights for Standard Equivalent Adults

	Number of Standard Equivalent Adults per Family	
No. of Persons in Family	*Income Distr. Committee*	*Bank of Israel*
1	1.25	1.20
2	2.00	2.00
3	2.65	2.70
4	3.20	3.30
5	3.75	3.80
6	4.25	4.30
7	4.75	4.70
8	5.20	5.00
9	5.60	5.30
Each additional person	0.40	0.30

Source: Report of the Committee on Income Distribution and Social Inequality, Tel-Aviv, 1971, p. 39; Bank of Israel, Worksheets (see also: Patterns of Poverty in Israel, R. Rotter and N. Shamai, in *Social Security*, February 1971).

Table 8A.2
Characteristics of Low Income Groups

	Poverty Group (Up to IL100)*	*Near-Poverty Group* (IL100-125)*	*Others* (Over IL125)*
No. of families (000)	75.6	38.4	500.2
%	12.3	6.2	81.5
No. of persons (000)	287.8	158.6	1,792.5
%	12.9	7.1	80.0
% of families with children below age 17	48.1	50.7	59.8
children below 17, % of persons	48.8	47.5	37.0
Family size (%) 1-2	50.7	43.7	30.6
3-4	15.9	17.7	45.8
5-6	14.8	15.7	17.1
7+	18.6	22.9	6.5
Employment Status of Family Head (%)			
Employee	35.6	58.6	69.2
Self-employed	10.3	9.4	18.4
Not in labor force	54.1	32.0	12.4
Age of Family Head (%)			
18-34	12.8	18.1	20.5
35-54	29.0	35.6	46.8
55+	58.2	46.3	32.7
65+	40.1	31.3	12.8
Education of Family Head (%)			
0-4	52.6	40.6	12.9
5-8	32.0	39.7	32.0
9-12	9.5	12.3	35.3
13+	5.9	7.4	19.8
Country of Origin of Family Head (Jewish Families)			
Asia-Africa	59.8	60.1	31.6
Europe-America	33.3	33.1	54.2
Israel	6.9	6.8	14.2
Women heads of families, %	27.4	20.9	10.6
Family heads immigrated after 1959, %	21.3	22.5	10.8
% of food in consumption expenditure	48.4	46.1	27.3
% of food in consumption expenditure (Incl. imputed cons. exp.)	42	41	25

Source: Family Expenditure Survey 1968/69.
*Monthly gross cash income per standard adult in 1968/69.

Table 8A.3
Deciles of Families by Total Consumption per Standard Adult, 1968/69

	Lowest Decile	*Second Lowest Decile*	*Second Highest Decile*	*Highest Decile*	*Total*
Total Consumption per Standard Adult in IL	up to 130	130-170	475-602	602+	337
Family Size					
1	18.0	13.4	11.4	19.4	10.9
2	32.4	17.8	29.0	37.1	23.0
3-4	21.0	19.3	49.9	39.8	40.4
5-6	11.8	26.0	8.1	3.7	16.7
7+	16.8	23.5	1.6	—	9.0
Average family size	3.69	4.62	3.02	2.49	3.65
No. of standard adult (average)	2.8	3.3	2.6	2.3	2.9
Employment Status of Family Head					
Employee	41.0	54.9	74.7	66.4	64.4
Self-employed	11.5	17.8	15.9	23.1	16.8
Not in labor force	47.5	27.3	9.4	10.5	18.8
Age of Family Head					
up to 34	14.6	17.3	18.9	19.7	19.4
35-54	29.1	42.7	49.4	43.9	44.0
55+	56.3	40.0	31.7	36.4	36.6
% of children up to age 17	44.8	50.7	30.0	20.7	39.3
% of persons above 65	15.4	9.8	5.0	7.1	7.7
% of food in consumption expenditure	49	44	21	17	29

Source: Family Expenditure Survey 1968/69.
Note: Consumption data refer to September 1968 — August 1969, whereas the income data in Table 8A.2 refer to the 23-month period October 1967-August 1969, with the center of the period in September 1968. The above consumption data include imputed consumption (from owned dwellings, etc.).

Table 8A.4
Family Heads Not in the Labor Force
by Years of Schooling and Age 1968/9 (%)

	Poverty Group	*Near-Poverty Group*	*Others*
Years of Schooling			
0-4	65.4	48.4	26.3
5-8	23.5	29.3	29.5
9-12	6.1	9.8	27.5
13+	5.0	12.5	16.7
TOTAL	100.0	100.0	100.0
Age			
Up to 34	5.2	1.7	6.8
35-54	16.2	13.1	12.2
55-64	13.7	15.1	23.5
65+	64.9	70.1	57.5
TOTAL	100.0	100.0	100.0
% of families not in labor force	35.3	10.7	54.0
% of all families	12.3	6.2	81.5

Source: Family Survey 1968/69.

Table 8A.5
Family Heads Who Worked by Years of Schooling and Age (%)

	Employees			Self-Employed		
	Poverty Group	Near-Poverty Group	Others	Poverty Group	Near-Poverty Group	Others
% of families	6.8	5.7	87.5	7.6	3.5	88.9
Years of schooling						
0-4	40.9	35.7	11.2	26.7	44.8	10.4
5-8	37.5	44.0	30.9	57.5	48.2	37.8
9-12	13.7	14.5	36.5	12.6	7.0	36.0
13+	7.9	5.8	21.4	3.2	—	15.8
TOTAL	100.0	100.0	100.0	100.0	100.0	100.0
Age						
up to 34	20.1	28.8	25.1	26.9	7.0	12.7
35-54	45.0	43.1	53.1	41.1	65.1	46.8
55+	34.9	28.1	21.8	32.0	27.9	40.5
TOTAL	100.0	100.0	100.0	100.0	100.0	100.0

Source: Family Survey 1968/69.

Table 8A.6
Family Heads by Country of Origin and Years of Schooling (Jewish Families) (%)

Country of origin	*Years of schooling*	*Poverty Group*	*Near Poverty Group*	*Others*
Asia-Africa	0-4	57.6	49.2	24.3
	5-8	29.9	36.3	39.7
	9-12	8.3	9.9	27.8
	13+	4.2	4.6	8.2
	TOTAL	100.0	100.0	100.0
	%	18.9	10.0	71.1
Europe-America	0-4	49.0	30.4	8.8
	5-8	35.6	42.3	28.8
	9-12	10.7	17.3	38.9
	13+	4.7	10.0	23.5
	TOTAL	100.0	100.0	100.0
	%	7.7	4.0	88.3
Israel	0-4	32.1	21.0	3.5
	5-8	15.5	35.7	24.9
	9-12	20.1	18.7	38.9
	13+	32.3	24.6	32.7
	TOTAL	100.0	100.0	100.0
	%	6.2	3.2	90.6

Source: Family Survey 1968/69.

Table 8A.7
Families by Size and Country of Origin of Family Heads
(Jewish Families, in %)

Country of Origin	*Family Size*	*Poverty Group*	*Near Poverty Group*	*Others*
Asia-Africa	1-2	39.5	26.2	14.2
	3-4	16.5	19.9	39.3
	5-6	16.8	21.6	29.5
	7+	27.2	32.3	17.0
Europe-America	1-2	78.6	76.3	42.6
	3-4	15.1	14.5	46.2
	5-6	4.4	6.8	10.4
	7+	1.9	2.4	0.8
Israel	1-2	51.3	50.0	22.7
	3-4	20.2	17.1	59.7
	5-6	25.3	8.5	14.6
	7+	3.2	24.4	3.0

Source: Family Survey 1968/69

APPENDIX 9

Table 9A.1
Distribution of Pre-Tax Incomes

Deciles	*Australia* 1966/67	*Israel** 1975/76 (b)	*Japan* 1969	*United Kingdom* 1973	*Sweden* 1972	*Norway* 1970	*Israel** 1968/69 (a)	*Israel** 1968/69 (b)	*Canada* 1969	*Netherlands* 1967	*West Germany* 1973	*United States* 1972	*France* 1970
1	2.1	1.9	2.9	2.1	2.0	1.7	1.8	1.5	1.2	2.3	2.5	1.2	1.5
2	4.5	3.7	4.7	3.3	4.0	3.2	3.5	3.2	3.1	3.6	3.4	2.6	2.8
3	6.2	5.5	5.8	5.1	5.3	4.9	5.1	5.0	4.6	4.9	4.5	4.2	4.2
4	7.3	6.9	6.8	6.9	6.1	6.7	6.6	6.4	6.3	6.0	5.6	5.8	5.7
5	8.3	8.3	7.7	8.3	7.9	8.2	7.9	7.9	7.9	7.3	6.8	7.5	7.1
6	9.5	9.7	8.6	9.8	9.5	9.8	9.3	9.3	9.4	8.5	8.3	9.3	8.7
7	10.9	11.3	9.7	11.2	11.2	11.3	10.9	10.9	11.1	9.9	9.9	11.1	10.4
8	12.5	13.2	11.3	13.0	13.1	13.3	13.0	13.1	13.1	11.7	12.2	13.4	12.6
9	15.1	16.0	13.9	15.6	16.1	16.4	16.5	16.5	16.2	14.7	15.7	16.4	16.0
10	23.8	23.5	28.6	24.7	24.8	24.5	25.4	26.2	27.1	31.1	31.1	28.4	31.0
Gini Coeff.	0.313	0.334	0.335	0.344	0.346	0.354	0.357	0.371	0.382	0.385	0.396	0.404	0.416
Lowest 20%	6.6	5.6	7.6	5.4	6.0	4.9	5.3	4.7	4.3	5.9	5.9	3.8	4.3
Ratio of Highest 20% to lowest 20%	5.9	7.1	5.6	7.5	6.8	8.3	7.9	9.1	10.1	7.8	7.9	11.8	10.9

*(a) total income including computed rent; (b) gross money income.
Source: M. Sawyer, ''Income Distribution in OECD Countries'', *OECD Economic Outlook*, July 1976. Statistical Abstracts of Israel, 1971; C.B.S. data of Family Survey 1975/76.

Table 9A.2
Distribution of After-Tax Incomes

Deciles	Israel 1975/76	Sweden 1972	Norway 1970	Australia 1966/67	Japan 1969	United Kingdom 1973	Israel 1968/69	Canada 1969	Nether-lands 1967	Spain 1973/74	United States 1972	West Germany 1973	Italy 1969	France 1970
1	2.3	2.2	2.3	2.1	3.0	2.5	1.8	1.5	2.6	2.1	1.5	2.8	1.7	1.4
2	4.3	4.4	4.0	4.5	4.9	3.8	3.8	3.5	3.9	3.9	3.0	3.7	3.4	2.9
3	6.1	5.9	5.6	6.2	6.1	5.5	5.6	5.1	5.2	5.3	4.5	4.6	4.7	4.2
4	7.5	7.2	7.3	7.3	7.0	7.1	7.1	6.7	6.4	6.5	6.2	5.7	5.8	5.6
5	8.7	8.5	8.6	8.3	7.9	8.5	8.4	8.2	7.6	7.8	7.8	6.8	7.0	7.4
6	10.0	10.0	10.2	9.5	8.9	9.9	9.8	9.7	8.8	9.1	9.5	8.2	9.2	8.9
7	11.4	11.5	11.7	10.9	9.9	11.1	11.3	11.2	10.3	10.6	11.3	9.8	9.8	9.7
8	13.1	13.3	13.0	12.5	11.3	12.8	13.3	13.1	12.4	12.5	13.4	12.1	11.9	13.0
9	15.5	15.7	15.1	15.1	13.8	15.2	16.2	15.9	15.2	15.6	16.3	15.8	15.6	16.5
10	21.1	21.3	22.2	23.7	27.2	23.5	22.7	25.1	27.7	26.7	26.6	30.3	30.9	30.4
Gini Coeff.	0.296	0.302	0.307	0.312	0.316	0.318	0.327	0.354	0.354	0.355	0.381	0.383	0.398	0.414
Ratio of highest 20% to lowest 20%	5.5	5.6	5.9	5.9	5.2	6.2	6.9	8.2	6.6	7.0	9.5	7.1	9.1	10.9
Ratio of highest 10% to lowest 10%	9.2	9.7	9.7	11.3	9.1	9.4	12.6	16.7	10.7	12.7	17.7	10.8	18.2	21.7

Source: See Table 9A.1.

Table 9A.3
Income Distribution of Households with Heads Aged 25-54 Years (%)

Deciles	*West Germany** 1969	*Australia* 1966-68	*United Kingdom* 1973	*Norway* 1970	*Israel* 1968/69	*Canada* 1972	*United States* 1972
1	4.0	3.7	3.3	2.3	2.7	1.7	1.9
2	5.8	5.6	5.5	4.9	4.7	4.2	4.1
3	6.8	6.8	6.6	6.4	5.9	6.0	5.8
4	7.6	7.5	7.6	7.6	7.0	7.4	7.1
5	8.4	8.4	8.5	8.6	8.2	8.7	8.3
6	9.3	9.4	9.4	9.6	9.3	9.8	9.6
7	10.4	10.5	10.5	10.9	10.7	11.1	10.9
8	11.9	11.9	12.0	12.7	12.7	12.7	12.3
9	14.0	14.2	14.3	15.1	16.2	15.0	15.0
10	21.9	22.0	22.3	22.0	22.7	23.5	25.0
Gini Coeff.	0.252	0.260	0.269	0.290	0.307	0.317	0.329
Gini Coeff. of all households	0.314	0.313	0.344	0.354	0.371	0.382	0.404
Difference (%)	−20	−17	−22	−18	−17	−17	−19

*Calculated from after-tax data. All others calculated from pre-tax data.
Source: Sawyer, op. cit., Israel, survey data 1968/69.

Table 9A.4
Per-Capita Distribution of Income
(Income Shares in %)

	Pre-tax Data							*After-tax Data*		
Deciles	*Israel* 1968/69	*Norway* 1970	*United Kingdom* 1973	*Australia* 1966/67	*Canada* 1969	*United States* 1972	*France* 1970	*Sweden* 1972	*Germany* 1969	*Spain** 1973
1	3.5	3.5	3.5	3.5	2.2	1.8	2.0	3.5	3.6	2.3
2	4.3	4.7	4.8	4.8	4.0	3.7	3.8	5.8	5.2	4.0
3	5.9	5.6	5.9	5.5	5.2	5.0	4.8	6.8	5.9	5.2
4	7.0	6.6	6.6	6.5	6.2	6.3	5.7	7.6	6.6	6.3
5	8.3	7.7	7.5	7.8	7.4	7.5	6.9	8.5	7.7	7.4
6	9.4	9.2	8.9	8.8	8.7	8.6	8.0	9.5	8.7	8.7
7	10.7	11.0	10.4	10.0	10.2	10.1	9.7	10.7	10.0	10.3
8	12.9	12.9	12.6	12.0	12.4	12.6	11.9	12.4	12.4	12.5
9	15.7	15.5	16.0	15.4	15.9	15.8	15.4	14.7	15.5	15.9
10	22.3	23.5	23.9	25.6	27.8	28.6	31.8	20.5	24.5	27.4
Gini Coeff.	0.296	0.305	0.307	0.318	0.363	0.376	0.398	0.254	0.303	0.359
Per family distr. Gini Coeff.	0.371	0.354	0.344	0.313	0.382	0.404	0.416	0.302	0.312	. . .
Percentage difference in the share of the two bottom deciles compared with per household distr.	66	67	54	26	44	45	35	41	26	

*Not strictly comparable to figures in Table 9A.2.
Source: See Table 9A.3

Table 9A.5
Households of Given Size by Decile Shares

Deciles	Eight OECD Countries*					Israel 1968/69				
	1	2	3	4	5+	1	2	3	4	5+
1	35.7	7.5	2.4	1.5	1.2	43.7	17.3	3.0	1.9	1.4
2	22.3	12.1	4.5	2.9	2.8	19.8	18.7	6.5	2.9	6.9
3	13.0	12.6	6.9	5.1	5.3	10.9	10.5	8.6	7.1	13.1
4	9.7	11.2	9.1	7.6	7.0	7.7	9.9	11.7	8.0	11.1
5	7.0	10.2	10.7	10.3	8.3	5.3	9.3	8.8	10.1	13.7
6	4.4	10.0	12.1	12.3	10.7	5.1	6.9	13.3	10.4	12.2
7	2.9	10.0	13.0	13.8	12.4	3.6	4.8	11.1	13.2	14.2
8	2.0	9.7	13.3	14.5	14.1	3.0	8.3	12.0	12.8	10.9
9	1.4	8.9	14.3	15.0	16.3	0.9	7.1	12.4	16.6	9.2
10	1.6	8.0	13.8	17.2	22.3	—	7.2	12.6	17.0	7.3

(Column headings: Number of Persons in Household)

*Arithmetic means of the data of Australia, Canada, Germany, Spain, Sweden, United Kingdom and United States.
Source: T. Sawyer, op. cit., Israel, 1968/69 survey.

APPENDIX 10

Table 10A.1
Annual Growth Rates of World Product and Population 1967-75
(in %)

	1967-73			*1973-75*			
	Popula-tion	*GNP*	*GNP per capita*	*Popula-tion*	*GNP*	*GNP per capita*	*GNP per capita* $ in 1975*
Developing Countries							
Lower income (below $200)*	2.4	3.9	1.5	2.5	1.8	−0.6	91
Middle income ($200-375)*	2.6	5.7	3.0	2.7	3.7	1.0	253
Higher income (over $375)*	2.4	6.6	4.1	2.4	3.4	1.0	670
Total, excluding oil producers	2.5	5.8	3.2	2.5	3.4	0.9	255
Oil-producing countries	2.5	7.7	5.1	2.8	6.3	3.4	245
Developed Countries	1.0	4.6	3.6	0.8	−0.7	−1.5	3,095
*Centrally Planned Economies***	1.5	5.8	4.2	1.5	6.0	4.4	595
World	1.9	5.2	3.3	1.9	1.3	−0.6	852

*Per-capita income at 1967-69 prices.
**Including developed and developing countries.
Source: World Economic Indicators, IBRD, 1976.

BIBLIOGRAPHY

Adams, F.G., "The Size of Individual Incomes: Socio-Economic Variables and Chance Variation". *Review of Economics and Statistics,* Nov. 1958.

Adelman, I. & Morris, C.T., "An Anatomy of Patterns of Income Distribution in Developing Nations". *American Economic Review*, 1972.

———, *Economic Growth and Social Equity in Developing Countries.* Stanford, 1973.

Ahluwalia, M.S., "Income Inequality: Some Dimensions of the Problem" in: *Redistribution with Growth*, Oxford University Press, 1974.

———, "Inequality, Poverty and Development". *Journal of Development Economics.* Dec. 1976.

Amir, S., *Incomes of Wage and Salary Earners in Israel, 1968/69.* Falk Institute, Jerusalem, 1975.

———, "The Influence of Increased Social Benefits to Large Families on Labor Supply". *Bank of Israel Bulletin No. 47*, Nov. 1977.

Anderson, A.E., "Redistribution and Social Policy in Market Economies" in: *Distribution Policies in Long-Term Development Planning*, U.N., New York, 1973.

Anderson, C.A., "Employment, Occupation and Socio-Economic Status of Swedish Wives in Relation to Occupation and Status of Husbands". *Statistics Tidskrift* 6, 1957.

Arrow, Kenneth J., *Social Choice and Individual Values.* Yale U. Press, 1963 (2nd ed.).

———, "Some Ordinalist-Utilitarian Notes on Rawls's Theory of Justice". *The Journal of Philosophy*, May, 1973.

Atkinson, A.B., *The Economics of Inequality.* Oxford University Press, 1975.

———, "On the Measurement of Inequality". *Journal of Economic Theory*, Vol. 2, 1970.

Atkinson, A.B. (ed.), *The Personal Distribution of Incomes.* Allen & Unwin Ltd., London, 1976.

Avnimelech, M., *Influence of Public Expenditure on Social Services on Redistribution of Incomes in 1968/69.* Unpublished M.A. Thesis, Jerusalem 1973 (Hebrew).

Baharal, U., *The Influence of Mass Immigration on Wages in Israel.* Falk Institute, Jerusalem, 1965.

Bank of Israel, *Annual Reports*, 1956-1977.

Bardhan, Pranab K., "On the Minimum Level of Living and the Rural Poor". *Indian Economic Review*, Vol. 5, April 1970.

Baruch, J., "Educational Capital". *Bank of Israel Bulletin* No. 25, Jerusalem, 1966.

Bar-Yoseph, R., Padan, D., "Class Crystallization of the Immigrants from Islamic Countries in Israel". *Molad*, Nov. 1964 (Hebrew).

BIBLIOGRAPHY

Baster, Nancy, "Development Indicators". *Journal of Development Studies,* Vol. 8, 1971-72.

Bavly, Sara, *Level of Nutrition in Israel 1968 /69.* C.B.S., Jerusalem 1972 (Hebrew).

Becker, Gary S., *Human Capital.* Columbia University Press for NBER, New York, 1964.

______, *Human Capital and the Personal Distribution of Income* – Woytinsky Lecture No. 1. Univ. of Michigan, 1967.

Becker, G.S. & Chiswick, B.R., "Education and the Distribution of Earnings". *Am. Ec. Review*, May 1966.

Beckerman, W., *International Comparisons of Real Incomes.* OECD, Paris, 1966.

Bendix R. & Lipset S.M. (eds.), *Class, Status and Power.* Routledge and Kegan Paul, 1967.

Ben-Shahar, H., *Changes in Income Distribution of Employees* 1950-57. Ministry of Finance, Jerusalem, 1961. (Hebrew).

Ben-Shahar, H., Sandberg, M., "Economic and Institutional Effects of Income Distribution: The Case of Israel". *Public Finance*, No. 3, 1967.

Ben-Yosef, T., *Analysis of Earnings Differences between Men and Women in Israel, 1971.* Falk Institute, Paper No. 7610, Jerusalem, 1971. (Hebrew).

Berler, A., "The Regional Structure" in: *Urban-Rural Relations in Israel.* Rehovot, 1970.

Berry, R. Albert., "Land Reform and the Agricultural Income Distribution". Center Paper No. 184. Yale Univ. Economic Growth Center, New Haven, Conn.,1972.

Béteille André (ed.), *Social Inequality* – Readings. Penguin, 1969.

Blaug, Marc., *Education and the Employment Problem in Developing Countries.* I.L.O., Geneva, 1973.

______, "Human Capital Theory: A Slightly Jaundiced Survey". *Journal of Economic Literature*, Sept. 1976.

Bowen, Ian, *Acceptable Inequalities.* London, 1970.

Brit Pikuah for the Agricultural Cooperatives, *Yalkut.* Aug. 1938 (Hebrew).

Bronfenbrenner, M., *Income Distribution Theory.* Chicago, 1971.

Central Bureau of Statistics, *Employee Earnings 1965-1972*; 1973; 1974-1975. Special Series No. 435, Jerusalem, 1973.

______, *Family Expenditure Survey, 1968 /69.* Special Series No. 330, 368, 378, 388, Jerusalem, 1971-1973.

______, *Family Expenditure Survey 1963 /64.* Special Series No. 200.

______, *Savings Surveys 1963 /64*; 1964/65. Sp. S. No. 239, Jerusalem, 1967.

______, *Statistical Abstracts of Israel, 1950-1977.*

______, *Income of Employees' Families, 1972-1974.* Special Series No. 510, Jerusalem, 1976.

______, *Population Census 1972.* Jerusalem, 1975.

______, *Society in Israel.* Selected Statistics, Jerusalem, 1976.

______, *The Level of Education of the Population.* Special Series No. 66, 1955.

Chenery, H., Ahluwalia, M.S., Bell, C.L.G., Duloy, J.H., Jolly, R., *Redistribution with Growth.* Oxford University Press, 1974.

Chiswick, B.R., "Earnings Inequality and Economic Development". *Quarterly Journal of Economics*, No. 85, 1971.

Cohen, A., Shamgar, L., Levi, Y., *Immigrants' Absorption in Development Towns.* Hebrew University, 1964.

Committee for the Examination of the Distribution of National Income in Israel, *Report*. Tel-Aviv, 1966.

Committee on Income Distribution and Social Inequality, *Report*. Tel-Aviv, 1971.

Cyderovich, G. (Jewish Agency), *Standard of Living Survey 1946*. Jerusalem, 1947.

Dauley, R.A. & Ramsey, Ch.E., *Standardization and Application of a Level of Living Scale for Farm and non-Farm Families*. Cornell Univ., 1959.

David, M., "Time-Series Versus Cross-Section Lifetime Earnings Patterns in Different Occupational Groups". Paper No. 6941. *Social Systems Research Institute*, University of Wisconsin, Aug. 1969.

Denison, E.F., *Why Growth Rates Differ*. New York, 1967.

Deutsches Institut fuer Wirtschaftsforschung, *Economic Bulletin No. 7*, 1974.

Eisenstadt, S.N., *Israeli Society*. Weidenfeld and Nicholson, London, 1969.

Eisenstadt, S.N., Bar-Yosef, R., Adler, Ch. (eds.), *Integration and Development in Israel*. University Press, Jerusalem, 1970.

Elazari-Volcani, I., *Planned Mixed Farming*. Rehovot, 1938.

Elliott, Charles, "Income Distribution and Social Stratification: Some Notes on Theory and Practice". *Journal of Development Studies*, Vol. 8, 1971-72.

Ericson, Lars O., *Justice in the Distribution of Economic Resources*. Stockholm, 1976.

Ezekiel, M. & Fox, K.A., *Methods of Correlation and Regression Analysis*, New York, 1959.

Fair, R.C., "The Optimal Distribution of Income", *Quarterly Journal of Economics*, 85, 1971.

Feinstein, C.H., *Changes in the Distribution of National Income in the U.K. since 1860*. London, 1968.

Fishelson, G., Yuchtman, A., "Problems of Inequality in Income Distribution". *Economic Quarterly*, June 1970 (Hebrew).

Frankel, S.H., *The Economic Impact on Underdeveloped Countries*. Oxford 1933.

Franklin, N.N., "The Concept and Measurement of Minimum Living Standards". *International Labour Review*, April 1967.

Friedman, Milton. *A Theory of the Consumption Function*. Princeton, 1957.

——, "A Method of Comparing Incomes of Families Differing in Composition". *Studies in Income and Wealth*, Vol. 15, 1952.

——, "The Distributionn of Income". in: *Inequality and Poverty*, Budd E.C. (ed.), New York, 1967.

Fuchs, V.R., "Redefining Poverty". in: *Concept of Poverty*, Townsend P. (ed.), London, 1970.

Gaathon, A.L., *Economic Productivity in Israel*. Praeger, New York, Tel-Aviv, 1971.

——, "Erez-Israel", *Hebrew Encyclopaedia*, vol. 6, 1957.

——, *Changes in the Consumption of Urban Employee Families between 1959/60 and 1968/69*. Bank of Israel, Jerusalem, 1975.

Gabbai, J., "Changes in Public Finance and Fiscal Policy, 1949-72." *Israel Economic Quarterly*, April 1973 (Hebrew).

Gabbai, J. & Tawil, Y., *The Incidence of Value Added Tax and the Compensation of Low Income Groups*. National Insurance Institute, Jerusalem, 1976.

Gelfat, J. & Abramovich, *The Arab Economy*. Tel-Aviv, 1944 (Hebrew).

Gilbert, M. & Ass., *Comparative National Products and Price Levels*. OECD, Paris, 1959.

Gilbert, M. & Kravis, I.B., *An International Comparison of National Products and the Purchasing Power of Currencies.* OECD, Paris, 1954.

Ginneken, W. van, *Mexican Income Distribution.* ILO, WEP 2-23, WP 5, 1974.

Ginor, F., "The Impact of Capital Imports on the Structure of Developing Countries". *Kyklos*, January, 1969.

———, "Structural Changes in A Developing Economy: The Case of Israel". *Weltwirtschaftliches Archiv.* No. 1, 1970.

———, "Twenty Years — Israel's Economy." *Rivaon Lekalkala,* Aug. 1968 (Hebrew).

Ginsberg, Y., "The Sample". in: *Urban-Rural Relations in Israel.* Rehovot, 1970.

Government of Palestine, Department of Statistics, *Statistical Abstract of Palestine 1937/38; 1944/45.* Jerusalem, 1945.

———, "Investigation of Cost of Living". *Palestine Commercial Bulletin*, No. 23-24, 1922.

Griliches, Z. & Mason, "Education, Income and Ability". *Journal of Political Economy*, May-June 1972.

Gronau, R., "The Intrafamily Allocation of Time: The Value of the Housewives' Time". *American Economic Review*, Sept. 1973.

———, *The Measurement of Output of the Nonmarket Sector: The Evaluation of Housewives' Time.* Falk Institute, Jerusalem, 1974.

———, *The Allocation of Time of the Israeli Married Woman.* Falk Institute, Jerusalem, 1974.

Gruenbaum, L. (now A.L. Gaathon), *National Income and Outlay in Palestine, 1936.* Jerusalem, 1941.

Gurevitz, D., Gertz, A., *Survey of the Standard of Living, 1939.* Department of Statistics, Jewish Agency, Jerusalem, 1940.

Habib, Jack, *Horizontal Equity with respect to Family Size.* Falk Institute, Jerusalem, 1973.

———, "Poverty in Israel 1964-1974". *Social Security,* March, 1975 (Hebrew).

———, "Redistribution Through National Insurance". *Social Security*, Dec. 1975, (Hebrew).

———, *Income Maintenance in Israel.* Falk Institute, Jerusalem, 1977 (Hebrew).

Habib, Jack & Tawil, Y., *Equivalence Scales for Family Size.* National Insurance Institute, Jerusalem, 1974.

Habib, J., Kohn M., Lerman, R., "The Effect on Poverty Status in Israel of Considering Wealth and Variability of Income". *Review of Income and Wealth*, March, 1977.

Hanoch, G., *Income Differences in Israel.* Falk Institute, Report No. 5, Jerusalem, 1961.

———, *Personal Earnings and Investment in Schooling.* Unpublished Ph.D. dissertation, Univ. of Chicago, 1965.

Hansen, Lee W., "Education, Income and Human Capital". *Studies in Income and Wealth, No. 35*, N.B.E.R., New York, 1970.

Harrington, M., *The Other America: Poverty in the U.S.,* Pelikan Books, 1971.

Hawrylyshyn, Oli, "Value of Household Services". *Review of Income and Wealth*, June 1976.

Hercovitz, Z., *Educational Capital in Israel, 1961-1972.* Falk Institute, Jerusalem, 1976. (Hebrew).

Hill, T.P., "An Analysis of the Distribution of Wages and Salaries in Great Britain". *Econometrica*, 1959.

Hirschman, A.O. & Rothschild, M., "The Changing Tolerance for Income Inequality in the Course of Economic Development". *The Quarterly Journal of Economics, Nov. 1973.*

Horowitz, David, *The Abolition of Poverty*. Praeger, New York, 1969.

______, "The Social Test of Economic Policy". *Social Security*, No. 3, June 1972.

Horovitz, Ruth, "New Strategies for Social Development — the Role of Social Welfare", *Israel Report to the International Conference on Social Welfare,* 1970.

Institute of Farm Income Research, *The Profitability of Family Farms in Israel,* 1969/70. Tel-Aviv, 1973.

Institute for Research on Income and Output, *Reports* 1970-1976 (Hebrew).

International Bank for Reconstruction and Development (IBRD), *Economic Indicators,* 1976.

International Labour Office, *Equality of Opportunity and Treatment for Women Workers.* Geneva, 1974.

______, *Yearbook of Labour Statistics.* Geneva, 1975.

______, *Employment, Growth and Basic Needs: A One-World Problem.* Report to the World Employment Conference, Geneva, 1976.

Jackson, Dudley, *Poverty*. New York, 1972.

Jain, J., *Size Distribution of Incomes.* World Bank, 1975.

Jencks, Chr., *Inequality*. Basic Books, 1972.

Jewish Agency, Report on Investigation of Cost of Living of Jewish Workers' Families, Aug. 1926. *Palestine Zionist Executive Statistical Bulletin, No. 14,* Jerusalem, 1927.

______, (and Histadrut), Census of Jewish Wage and Salary Earners, 1930. *Commerce and Trade,* Sept. 1931 (Hebrew).

______, Economic Research Institute, *Statistical Handbook of Middle Eastern Countries*. Jerusalem, 1945.

______, Statistical Department, *Alon Statisti*. Jerusalem, 1946.

______, Economic Department, *Palestine, Facts and Figures*. Tel-Aviv, 1947.

Johnson, H.G., *The Theory of Income Distribution.* London, 1973.

Johnson, W.J. & Crosbie, *Report of a Committee on the Economic Conditions of Agriculturists in Palestine.* Jerusalem, 1930.

Johnston, J., *Econometric Methods*. McGraw-Hill, New York, 1972.

Kaddar, G., *Family Farms in Cooperative Villages.* Tel-Aviv, 1956 (Hebrew).

Klayman, M.I., *The Moshav in Israel.* Praeger, New York, 1970.

Kligler, J., Geiger, A., Bromberg, Sh., Gurevitz, D., "An Inquiry into the Diets of the Population of Palestine". *Commerce and Industry*, No. 20-21. Oct. 1931.

Klinov-Malul, R., *Returns on Investment in Education in Israel.* Falk Institute, Jerusalem, 1966.

Kravis, I., "Relative Income Shares in Fact and Theory". *American Economic Review*, 1959.

______, *The Structure of Income.* University of Pennsylvania Press, 1962.

Kuznets, S., "Quantitative Aspects of the Economic Growth of Nations: VIII. Distribution of Income by Size". *Economic Development and Cultural Change.* Chicago, 1963.

——, "Economic Growth and Income Inequality." *American Economic Review.* March 1955.

——, *Economic Growth and Structure.* W.W. Norton & Co., New York, 1965.

——, *Modern Economic Growth, Rate, Structure and Spread.* Yale University Press, New Haven, 1966.

Laumann, Edward O. (ed.), *Social Stratification.* N.Y., 1970.

Leibenstein, H., *Economic Backwardness and Economic Growth.* New York, 1957.

Lenski, G.E., *Power and Privilege: A New Theory of Stratification.* McGraw-Hill, 1966.

Leontieff, W., "The Structure of Development". in: *Technology and Economic Development.* Pelican Book, 1963.

Lerner, A.P., *The Economics of Control.* London, 1944.

Levi, Ch., *Wage Differentials of Employees in Israel, 1957 /58 and 1963 /64.* Bank of Israel, Jerusalem, 1968.

Lim Lin Lean, *The Pattern of Income Distribution in West Malaysia 1957-70.* ILO, WEP 2-23, Geneva, 1974.

Lipton, M., *Why Poor People Stay Poor.* Temple Smith, London, 1977.

Loftus, P.J., *National Income of Palestine, 1944.* Jerusalem, 1946.

Looney, Robert E., *Income Distribution Policies and Economic Growth in Semi-Industrialized Countries.* Praeger, New York, 1975.

Lowe, Y. & Riemer, I., *Profitability of Veteran Moshavim.* Tel-Aviv, 1960.

Lydall, Harold, *The Structure of Earnings.* Oxford, Clarendon Press, 1968.

——, *Income Distribution during the Process of Development.* ILO, WEP 2-23/WP 52, 1977.

Maital, S., *The Impact of Inflation.* Foerder Institute, Tel-Aviv, 1976.

Mark, N., "Investment in Education and Ethnical Income Difference". in: *Economic Studies,* 1976. Israel Economic Association, Jerusalem, 1977 (Hebrew).

Marx, E., "Some Special Contexts of Personal Violence". in: *The Allocation of Responsibility,* Gluckman M. (ed.), Manchester University Press, 1972.

Marx, Karl, *Critique of the Gotha Programme,* 1875.

McGranahan, D.V. et al., *Contents and Measurement of Socio-economic Development.* New York, 1972.

Menseli, Y., "Price Developments of Consumption Baskets of Different Income Groups in Israel". *Bank of Israel Bulletin* No. 41, Jerusalem, 1973.

Metcalf, L.E., "The Size Distribution of Personal Income during the Business Cycle". *American Economic Review.* Vol. 59.

Miller, H.P., "Annual and Lifetime Income in Relation to Education 1939-59". *Amer. Econ. Rev.,* Dec. 1960.

——, *Rich Man, Poor Man.* New York, 1971.

Mills, John, *Growth and Welfare.* London, 1972.

Minchas, B.H., "Rural Poverty, Land Redistribution and Development". *Indian Economics Review,* Vol. 5, April 1970.

Mincer, Jacob, *Schooling, Experience and Earnings.* NBER, New York, 1974.

——, "Investment in Human Capital and Personal Income Distribution". *Journal of Political Econ.,* August 1958.

——, "Schooling, Age, and Earnings" in: *Human Capital and Personal Income Distribution.* National Bureau of Econ. Research, 1969.

——, "The Distribution of Labor Incomes: A Survey with Special Reference to the

Human Capital Approach". *The Journal of Economic Literature*, March 1970.

Ministry of Finance, Bank of Israel, *National Budget for 1977.* Jerusalem, 1977 (Hebrew).

Morgan, J.N., "The Anatomy of Income Distributions". *Review of Economics and Statistics*, August 1962.

Morgan, J.N., Cohen, D., Brazer, *Income and Welfare in the United States.* McGraw-Hill, N.Y., 1962.

Muellbauer, J., "Inequality Measures, Prices and Household Composition". *Review of Economic Studies*, Oct. 1974.

National Insurance Institute, *Summary of Developments and Trends in Social Security, 1975.* Jerusalem, 1976.

Orshansky, Mollie, "Who is Who Among the Poor". *Social Security Bulletin*, Washington, July 1965.

———, "Counting the Poor: Another Look at the Poverty Profile". *Social Security Bulletin*, Jan. 1965.

———, "Who is Who Among the Poor? A Demographic View of Poverty". *Social Security Bulletin*, April, 1966.

Paglin, M., "The Measurement and Trend of Inequality: A Basic Revision". *American Economic Review*, Sept. 1975.

Paukert, Felix, "Social Security and Income Distribution: A Comparative Study". *International Labour Review*, 98:5, 1968.

———, "Income Distribution at Different Levels of Development". *International Labour Review*. Aug.-Sept. 1973.

Paukert, Felix, Skolka, J. & Maton, J., *Redistribution of Income Patterns of Consumption and Employment* (A Case Study for the Philippines). ILO, WEP 2-23, 1974.

Pen, Ian, *Income Distribution.* Penguin Press, London, 1971.

Peres, Y., "Ethnic Differences in Israel". *Megamoth*, Jan. 1974.

———, *Ethnic Relations in Israel.* Sifriat Poalim, Tel Aviv, 1976 (Hebrew).

Podder, N. & Kalswani, N.C., "Distribution of Wealth in Australia". *Review of Income and Wealth*, March 1976.

Prime Minister's Committee on Youth in Distress, *Report.* Oct. 1972 (Hebrew).

Psacharopoulos, G., *Returns to Education,* New York, 1973.

———, "Schooling, Experience and Earnings: The Case of an LDC". *Journal of Development Economics*, March 1977.

———, *Earnings and Education in OECD Countries.* OECD, Paris, 1975.

Rajaraman, Indira, *Constructing the Poverty Line: Rural Punjab 1960-61.* Woodrow Wilson School, Princeton, March 1974. (Paper 43).

Rawls, John, *A Theory of Justice.* Clarendon Press, Oxford, 1972.

Reder, M.W., "A Partial Survey of the Theory of Income Size Distribution". in: *Six Papers on the Size Distribution of Wealth and Income.* Soltow L. (ed.), London, 1969.

Rein, M., "Problems in the Definition and Measurement of Poverty". in: *Poverty in America.* Ferman, Kornblush, Haber (eds.), Michigan, 1968.

Rosenfeld, Y., *The Parents' Education and the Social Situation of the Family.* Democratic Center, Lecture. Jerusalem, 1971. (Hebrew).

Rotter, R. & Shamai, N., "The Reform of Taxation and Transfer Payments in Israel, July 1975". *Social Security*, March 1977 (Hebrew).

———, "Patterns of Poverty in Israel". *Social Security*, February 1971 (Hebrew).

Royal Commission on the Distribution of Income and Wealth, *Report No. 1 – Initial Report*. London, 1975.

Runciman, W.G., *Relative Deprivation and Social Justice*. Berkeley, 1966.

Sahota, Gian Singh, "Theories of Personal Income Distribution: A Survey". *Journal of Economic Literature*, March 1978.

Sandberg, M., (Sanbar) *Income Distribution in Israel, 1954*. Institute for Sociological Research, Jerusalem, 1956 (Hebrew).

Sawyer, M., "Income Distribution in OECD Countries". *OECD Economic Outlook*, July 1976.

Schnitzer, Martin, *Income Distribution*. A Comparative Study of the U.S., Sweden, West Germany, East Germany, the U.K. and Japan. New York, 1974.

Segre, V.D., *Israel – A Society in Transition*. Oxford University Press, 1971.

Sen, A.K., *Collective Choice and Social Welfare*. Holden-Day Inc., San Francisco, 1970.

———, *On Economic Inequality*. Oxford, 1973.

Seneca & Taussig, "Family Equivalence Scales and Personal Income Tax Exemptions for Children". *Review of Economics and Statistics*, Aug. 1971.

Simchoni, J. & Shmueli, Sh., *Inequality in Communal Settlements, 1957-68*. Tel-Aviv, 1974. (Economic Training Unit) (Hebrew).

Singer, Hans & Jolly, R., "Unemployment in an African Setting". *International Labour Review*, Vol. 107, No. 2, 1973.

Singer, Hans et al., *Employment, Incomes and Equality in Kenya*. ILO, Geneva, 1972.

Soltow, L., *Towards Income Equality in Norway*. Madison, 1965.

Szereszewski, R., *Essays on the Structure of the Jewish Economy in Palestine and Israel*. Falk Institute, Jerusalem, 1968.

Thurow, Lester C., *Poverty and Discrimination*, Washington, 1969.

———, *Generating Inequality*. Basic Books, London, 1976.

The Economist, *The World in Figures*. London, 1976.

Tinbergen, Jan, *Income Distribution*. Amsterdam, 1975.

Titmuss, R.M., *Income Distribution and Social Change*. Unwin University Books, 1962.

Townsend, Peter, *The Social Minority*. Allen Lane, Penguins, London, 1973.

Turnham, D.J., *Income Distribution: Measurement and Problems*. SID Document, Paris, May 1971.

United Nations, Department of Economic and Social Affairs, *Social Policy and the Distribution of Income in the Nation*. New York, 1969.

United Nations, *Statistical Yearbook 1975*. New York, 1976.

———, *Yearbook of National Accounts Statistics*. New York, 1968, 1975.

Urff, W.v., "Das Problem der Armut in der Indischen Entwicklungsplanung". *Internationales Asienforum* 5, 1974.

Vickers, W.J., (Government, Department of Health), *A Nutritional Economic Survey of Wartime Palestine*. Jerusalem, 1944.

Weber, Max, *Wirtschaft und Gesellschaft*. Mohr, Tuebingen, edition 1956.

Wedderburn, D., *Poverty, Inequality and Class Structure*. London, 1974.

Weintraub, D., *Immigration and Social Change*. Israel University Press, Jerusalem, 1971.

Wolff, E.N., "Occupational Earnings Behavior and the Inequality of Earnings by Sex and Race in the U.S". *Review of Income and Wealth*, June 1976.

Zimmerman, L.J., *Poor and Rich Lands: The Widening Gap*. Random House, New York, 1965.

Zussman, Z., *Wage Differentials and Equality Within the Histadrut*. Tel-Aviv, 1974. (Hebrew).

Author Index

Adams, F.G., 133, 134n
Adelman, Irma, 18n, 185, 192n
Adler, Ch., 64n
Ahluwalia, M.S., 36, 43n, 185, 192n
Amir, S., 87, 100n, 107, 117n
Anderson, A.E., 213n
Anderson, C.A., 163n
Arrow, Kenneth J., 192n
Atkinson, A.B., 11, 18n, 72n, 73n, 117n
Avnimelech, M., 100n

Baharal, U., 99n
Bank of Israel, 51n, 77n, 86n, 99n, 118n
Baruch, J., 83, 86n, 99n
Bar-Yoseph, R., 64n
Bavly, Sara, 64n
Becker, Gary S., 133n
Beckerman, W., 195
Bell, C.L.G., 8, 18n
Berler, A., 111, 118n
Blaug, Marc, 125, 133n, 163n
Bowen, Ian, 15, 19n
Brazer, H.E., 163n
Bromberg, Sh., 43n
Budd, E.C., 19n

Central Bureau of Statistics, 77n, 78n, 81n, 83n, 86n, 92n, 99n, 102n
Chan, L.S., 191n
Chenery, H., 18n, 19n, 43n
Committee for the Examination of the Distribution of National Income in Israel, 72n, 73n, 118n
Cohen, W.I., 163n
Committee on Income Distribution and Social Inequality, 18n, 28, 43n, 81n, 94, 117n
Crosbie, 35, 43n

Dauley, R.A., 163n
David, M.H., 163n
Denison, E.F., 202, 204n
Deutsches Institut fuer Wirtschaftsforschung, 118n
Duloy, J.H., 8, 18n

Eisenstadt, S.N., 64n
Elazari-Volcani, I., 33, 43n
Ezekiel, M., 162n

Fair, R.C., 189, 192n
Feinstein, C.H., 72n
Ferman, 18n
Fox, K.A., 162n
Frankel, S.H., 204n
Friedman, Milton, 18n, 19n
Fuchs, V.R., 12, 18n

Gaathon (Gruenbaum), A.L., 18n, 33, 34, 35, 42, 43n, 86n, 51n
Gabbai, J., 100n
Geiger, A., 43n
Gertz, A., 43n
Gilbert, M., 195, 204n
Ginneken, W. van, 192n
Ginor, F., 64n, 204n
Ginsberg, Y., 118n
Gronau, R., 140, 162n
Gruenbaum, L., see Gaathon
Gurevitz, D., 43n

Haber, 18n
Habib, J., 18n, 73n, 100n
Hanoch, G., 107, 117n, 133
Hercovitz, Z., 86n, 99n, 108, 117n
Hill, T.P., 133
Hirshman, A.O., 16, 19n, 104, 117n
Horovitz, Ruth, 100n
Hsia, R., 191n

AUTHOR INDEX

Institute of Farm Income Research, 117n, 118n
Institute for Research on Income and Output, 68, 69n
International Bank for Reconstruction and Development, IBRD,195, 196n, 200n
International Labour Office, ILO, 67n, 117n
Jackson, Dudley, 12, 18n
Jain, J., 179, 180n, 191n
Jewish Agency, 25, 30, 40, 43n, 44n, 46, 64n, 91
Johnson, W.J., 35, 43n

Kligler, J., 43n
Klinov-Malul, R., 70, 73n, 99n, 133n
Kohn, M., 73n
Kornblush, 18n
Kravis, I., 195, 204n
Krueger, A.O., 202, 204n
Kuznets, S., 36, 43n, 70, 72n, 118n, 179, 185, 186, 189, 192n, 195, 199, 202, 204n
Lean, Lim Lin, 19n, 191n
Leibenstein, H., 204n
Leontieff, W., 194, 204n
Lerman, R., 73n
Lerner, A.P., 189, 192n
Levi, Ch., 86n, 87, 100n
Lissak, M., 64n
Loftus, P.J., 42, 43n

Maital, S., 100n
Marx, Karl, 19n
McGranahan, D.V., 18n, 204n
Menseli, Y., 100n
Metcalf, L.E., 78, 99n
Miller, H.P., 133n
Mincer, Jacob, 133, 133n, 134n, 163n
Ministry of Health, 89
Ministry of Social Welfare, 90
Morgan, J.N., 12, 18n, 133, 134n, 144, 148, 163n
Morris, C.T., 18n, 185, 192n

National Insurance Institute, 75, 89, 90

Orshansky, Mollie, 18n

Paglin, M., 123
Paukert, Felix, 43n, 185, 191n, 192n
Peres, Y., 107, 117n
Prime Minister's Committee on Youth in Distress, 87, 90
Psacharopoulos, G., 70, 73n, 184n, 202, 204n

Rajaraman, Indira, 18n
Ramsey, Ch.E., 163n
Rawls, John, 14, 19n
Rein, M., 18n
Rosenfeld, Y., 163n
Rotter, R., 18n
Runciman, W.G., 15, 18n, 19n
Ruskin, 19n

Sawyer, M., 179, 180n, 182, 183, 188, 189, 191n
Schumpeter, Joseph, A., 203
Segre, V.D., 64n
Sen, A.K., 189, 192n
Seneca, 18n
Shamai, N., 18n
Shmueli, Sh., 43n
Simchoni, J., 43n
Singer, Hans, 19n
Soltow, L., 78, 99n, 185, 189, 192n
Sombart, Werner, 203
Szereszewski, R., 32, 38, 43n, 51n, 64n

Taussig, 18n
Tawil, J., 18n, 100n
Thurow, Lester C., 14, 19n, 100n, 162n
The Economist, 196n
Tinbergen, Jan, 84, 100n
Townsend, Peter, 18n

UNCTAD, United Nations Conference for Trade and Development, 200n
United Nations, 58n, 67n, 195, 196n, 199, 200
U.N. Research Institute for Social Development, 8, 195
U.N. Social Development Divison, 9, 18n
Urff, W.v., 19n

Vickers, W.J., 39, 40, 43n

Wada, 179, 180
Weber, Max, 18n, 203
Weintraub, D., 64n
World Bank, see International Bank for Reconstruction and Development

Zimmerman, L.J., 198n, 199, 200n, 204n
Zussman, Zvi, 103, 106, 117n

Subject Index

Africa and Asia, family heads, immigrants from, 46, 48, 50, 60, 113, 132, 139, 160, 166, 171, 196, 206
Age: composition, 48, 80, 81, 189; structure, 60, 79, 84, 85, 182
Age-income: differences, 123, 208; profile, 79
Aged (people), 17, 62, 90, 91, 97, 98, 166, 168, 174
Agrarian reform, 188, 210
Agricultural: holdings, distribution of, 35, 40, 41; workers, see Workers
Arab: families, 35, 39, 41, 114; population, 25, 26, 34-37, 40, 41, 43n, 49, 50, 62, 113-116, 207; sector, 23-25, 27, 33, 35-37, 40-42, 101, 115, 117, 205; society, 24, 114; villages, 89, 110
Argentina, farm incomes, 112
Ashkenazi: communities, 37, 43n; families, 30, 37, 39, 105, 107
Austerity: period, 60; regime, 45
Australia: farm incomes, 112; income distribution, 181, 182

Balance of payments, 47, 55, 60
Bangladesh, inequality index, 180, 191n
Beduin, 24
Belgium: food consumption, 57; women's earnings, 104
Beta coefficients, 98, 100n, 134n, 137, 141, 142, 145-149, 151-153, 155-158, 160, 162n
Birth rates, 26, 46-48, 80, 183, 206
Business: cycle, 68-70, 76, 78, 101, 206; sector, 68, 70, 72

Canada: income distribution, 182, 183; labor share, 66, 70
Capital: equipment, 202; human, 16, 17, 70, 71, 101, 201, 210-212; imports, 23, 45, 53-55, 84, 88, 194, 195, 205; intensity, 51-53, 68, 206; owners, 65; physical, 17, 70, 71, 201, 202, 210-212; rate of return to, 69, 70, 72, 206; returns to, 65, 67, 68, 206; stock, 50-53, 68, 202
Capital-output ratio, 51-53
Causes of poverty, see Poverty
Children: in poverty, 165, 167, 170, 174, 176; number of (in family), 147-149, 151-154, 160, 163n, 176n
Children's allowances, 76, 85, 90, 95, 153, 191
China: development, 203; per capita income, 197
Christians, 25, 36, 37, 43n, 48, 62
Coefficient: of determination, 133; of variation, 146; see also: Correlation, Regression
Communities, see Ashkenazi, Oriental, Traditional
Consumption: basket, 10, 93, 176n; defined, 8; expenditure, 9, 10, 33, 57, 59, 92, 165, 184; functions, 10; per standard adult, 164, 166; private, 25, 47, 53, 54, 56, 64n, 195, 198, 203; public, 53, 54, 202; surveys see Surveys
Continent of birth, of origin, 48, 50, 59, 130, 131
Correlation: coefficients, 76, 99n, 143, 144; matrix, 96; of age with income, inverse, 157; of education with income, 124, 143, 145, 156; of inequality with unemployment, 76, 96, 98; of labor force participation with education, 61, 82, 138, 139, 149
Cost of living, 27, 28, 30, 37, 76, 90, 93, 94, 162, 176n; allowance, 94
Countries: developed, 70, 179, 183-186, 191, 194-196, 198-203, 209, 210;

developing, less developed, 36, 70, 105, 115, 179, 184-186, 191, 193-196, 198-203, 210; least developed, 193, 195, 200; oil producing, 200, 201, 204n; socialist, communist, 197, 200
Country of origin, 85, 87, 107, 113, 122, 132, 134n, 136, 138, 141, 142, 145-147, 149, 151-154, 159, 160, 163n, 170, 171, 174, 208
Cultural: background, 7, 45, 205; heritage, 63
Currency's purchasing power, 194, 195

Denmark: inequality, 185; labor share, 70
Deprivation, feelings of, 13, 15, 46, 63, 105, 111, 205-207, 209, 212
Deprived homes, 88, 176
Determinants: of family income, 135, 152, 154, 171, 208; of income per standard adult, 152-154, 176n
Development: indicators, 8, 204n; towns, see New towns
Disadvantaged: groups, population, 11, 15, 46, 89, 211, 212; children, 63
Druze, 62, 89
Durable consumers' goods, 8, 59

Earners: number in family, 9, 76, 81, 136, 141, 142, 145, 151, 154, 155; percentage of, 48, 60
Earning power, 164, 165, 170, 209
Earnings: annual, 108; differences, differentials, 85, 126, 131, 157, 183, 184, 207, 208; hourly, 139, 157, 159, 170; inequality, 184; weekly, 38, 107, 159; wife's, 138, 147
Economic: growth, 9, 13, 24, 47, 50-52, 55, 56, 76-78, 87, 88, 101, 185-187, 194, 199, 200, 203, 205, 206, 210-212; inequality, see Inequality; structure, 15, 24, 112, 190, 194, 202
Economically: active (population), 65, 83, 135, 136, 209, 211; inactive, 65, 206, 211
Economies of scale, 9, 10, 162, 164, 202
Education: compulsory, 49, 50, 88, 124; national expenditure on, 88; quality of, 107, 124, 160; rate of return to investment in, 70, 126; university, 50, 89, 108, 138, 157, 184, 211
Educational: achievements, 17, 122, 130, 144, 165, 170, 173, 210, 212; capital, 51, 66, 83, 87, 100n, 108, 117n; inequality, 18, 82-84, 100n, 105, 108, 115, 183, 189, 206, 207, 210-212; reform, 88; services, 17, 89, 100n, 191, 211; system, 49, 50
Egalitarian, Egalitarianism, 15, 62, 101, 104, 189
Egypt, standard of living, 26
Elasticity of substitution, 70, 72n
Employees, 29-31, 38, 61, 62, 66, 68, 72, 78, 83-85, 87, 100n, 102-104, 107, 108, 139, 140, 143, 145-147, 157-159, 169, 170, 176n, 209, 210; compensation, 66-69; families, 30-32, 66, 75-78, 80-82, 91, 95-98, 99n, 114, 135, 144, 145, 154, 163n, 173
Employment: level, 16, 60, 76, 117, 189; partial, 168, 169, 209; status, 66, 122, 135, 139, 141, 142, 147, 151, 154-158
England, see United Kingdom
Equal citizenship, 14
Equality, 15, 32, 89, 93, 94, 112, 188, 209, 211; before the law, 14; of opportunities, 14, 88, 170, 176, 209, 211, 212
Equivalence scales, 10, 153, 164
Ethnic groups, 10, 16, 63, 104-107, 110, 160, 212
Europe and America, family heads, immigrants from, 48, 50, 60, 113, 132, 134n, 139, 160, 165, 166, 170
Explanatory variables, 95-98, 130-132, 136, 137, 141, 143, 145, 149, 155

Families: extended, 26, 46, 62, 101, 206; multi-problem, 63, 90, 176; urban, 35, 79, 80, 84, 97-100, 113, 114, 133; see also Arab, Employees, Husband-wife, Jewish, One-parent
Family: budget, 12, 13, 27, 29, 30, 39, 144; expenditure, 28, 39, 102, 121; incomes, 8, 10, 28, 30, 32, 35, 38, 67, 71, 76, 80-82, 91, 92, 95, 99n, 100n, 107, 111, 112, 114-117, 121, 124, 126-130, 133n, 135-141, 143-148, 151-160, 162, 170, 173, 183, 208, 209; size, 9, 10, 30, 37, 39, 48, 60, 65, 79-81, 84, 93, 99n, 105, 117n, 121, 133, 136, 141, 142, 145, 146, 150, 152, 153, 160-164, 167, 168, 170, 171, 182, 208, 209; survey, see Surveys;

types, 9, 12, 208
Farmers, 24, 26, 32, 40, 42, 68, 101, 112, 113, 118n, 187, 188
Finland, standard of living, 57
Food consumption, 57-59, 165
Foreign currency reserves, 54, 55
Fractile groups, 10, 11
France: food consumption, 58; income distribution, 183; labor share, 70

GDP (GNP) per capita, 8, 53, 66, 76, 173, 182, 195, 204n
Generation, see Second generation
Germany: income distribution, 183; labor share, 70; restitution payments, 55
Gini coefficient, 11, 28, 38, 40, 43n, 99n, 179, 190, 191n, 197
GNP, see GDP
Great Britain, see United Kingdom
Greece, standard of living, 57, 58

Haifa, 28, 38
Health: insurance, 90; national expenditure on, 89; services, 17, 24-26, 56, 89, 100n, 191, 211
Histadrut, 43n, 62, 101, 104
Homogeneous groups, 28, 39, 129-131, 155
Hong Kong, inequality by education, 184
Households, 8-10, 14, 30, 81, 95, 115, 118n, 121, 152, 179, 182, 184, 188, 189, 195
Housing: conditions, 17, 30, 46, 53, 109, 176, 211; density, 30, 37, 39, 53, 59, 60, 105, 172, 176; temporary, 46
Human capital, see Capital
Husband-wife families, 81, 135, 138-141, 143-150, 153, 155-158, 160, 167, 168, 176n, 208

Ideologies, 14, 101, 104; social, 14, 62
Immigrants: absorption, 54, 59, 87, 91; new, 45, 49, 53, 55, 59, 60, 88, 95, 109-113, 160, 166; society of, 104
Immigration, 23, 47, 54, 101, 116, 205; mass, 45, 47-51, 56, 62, 63, 75, 83, 107, 206, 207; year of, 85, 87, 107, 136, 141, 142, 145, 147, 151, 159, 160, 171
Import surplus, 53-55
Incentives, 15, 110, 189
Income(s): after-tax, 182, 189, 191; curves, 124, 127, 208; defined, 8-9; differences, differentials, 9, 16, 30-38, 41, 52, 62, 65, 67, 76, 80-87, 95, 100n, 103-107, 112-115, 121-123, 129, 131-138, 140-143, 145, 147, 151-157, 159, 160, 162, 184, 186, 188, 189, 206-208; from work, 121-124, 126-133, 135, 151, 157, 161, 163n, 165, 208; functional distribution of, 65, 67, 68, 206, 207; imputed, 9, 135, 164, 174, 176n; life-time, 71, 123, 127, 129, 189, 208; lower brackets, groups, 10, 11, 40, 41, 53, 55, 93, 94, 99n, 105, 135, 156, 157, 160, 161, 169, 176, 183, 191, 208; median, 12, 13, 173, 176n, 190; per capita, 25, 33, 40, 57, 65, 105, 111, 179, 181, 183, 185-187, 194-202, 204n, 210; per family, see Family income; per farm, 111, 112; per standard adult, 10, 34, 93, 164, 165, 168-176, 183, 189, 191n, 209; pre-tax, 71, 181, 182; redistribution of, 91, 121, 193, 198, 210, 212; rural, 24, 42, 110, 111, 114, 115, 186, 187; surveys, see Surveys; transfer, 68
Income inequality, 18, 60, 65, 80-85, 87, 91-96, 105, 112-116, 123, 129, 132, 146, 156, 173, 179-186, 188, 189, 193, 197-199, 206-211, 213; between communities, 108; between countries, 197-199, 210; by age, 80, 123; by education, 84, 100, 123; by occupation, 85
Independent individuals, 135, 138, 149, 153, 154, 160-162, 168, 208, 209
India: income distribution, 80, 191n; labor share, 70; poverty, 13
Industrialization, industrial development, 52, 58, 187, 191, 194, 203
Inequality: economic, 7, 8, 14, 15, 27, 46, 197, 205, 210; forms of, 7, 8, 209; income, see Income inequality; of family income, 91, 92, 130, 184, 191n, 208; social, 7, 14, 15, 123, 205, 208; tolerance of, 15, 16, 104, 205
Inflation, inflationary pressures, 45, 47, 55, 60, 72, 76, 84, 93, 94, 188, 195, 207, 212
Infrastructure, 53, 188
Innate, inborn ability, capability, 122, 129, 189, 190
Institutional system, 16, 121

Integration, 54, 63, 88, 110, 115, 117, 187
Intercorrelations, 96, 98, 136, 155
Intercountry comparisons, 10, 182
Ireland: income distribution, 179; standard of living, 57; women's earnings, 104
Italy: income distribution, 182; standard of living, 57

Jamaica, labor share, 66
Japan: development, 203; economic growth, 52; income distribution, 179-181; women's earnings, 104
Jerusalem, East-Jerusalem, 28, 38, 47, 49, 109, 110, 113, 144, 172
Jewish: families, 28, 30, 37, 39, 40, 60, 80, 105, 109, 110, 160, 172-174, 176; population, 23, 25, 26, 29, 30, 33, 34, 36, 38, 40, 42, 47, 48, 50, 59, 60, 62, 75, 79, 83, 105, 107, 108, 110, 115, 116, 206, 107; rural population, 113; sector, 23-25, 27, 33, 36-38, 40, 41, 45, 53, 54, 61, 64n, 101, 205, 206; urban population, 37, 39, 40, 64, 75
Juvenile delinquency, 13, 63

Kibbutzim, 15, 32, 101, 104, 110, 112, 113
Kuweit, per capita income, 194

Labor: productivity, 17, 195: returns to, 65, 67, 206; unions, 73n, 85
Labor force: non-participation in, 167, 168; not belonging to, 9, 17, 65, 68, 70, 79, 81, 114, 135, 136, 139, 140, 145, 147, 151-154, 157, 159, 163n, 165-168, 176n, 206; participation, 48, 60, 61, 81, 82, 84, 97-99, 136-139, 141-143, 145, 146, 151, 154-160, 162, 163n, 207-209
Land holdings, see Agricultural holdings
Land reform, see Agrarian reform
Leisure, 140, 189
Length of residence, stay (in Israel), 122, 130-132
Level of living, see Standard of living
Life: cycle, 123; expectancy, 25, 26, 37, 46, 48, 56, 115, 179, 183, 206
Lifetime income, see Income
Literacy, 37, 49
Literate, illiterate, 37, 49, 115
Linkage, linking (of benefits), 90, 93, 94

Lorenz curve, 11, 18n

Maabarot, 46
Malaysia, poverty, 13
Mandatory period, 23, 26, 37, 47-50, 54, 56, 59, 79, 88, 101, 103-105, 110, 112-117, 186, 189, 205, 207
Manpower: qualified, 84, 87; skilled, 85, 96-98, 110, 189, 207; unskilled (labor, workers), 24, 27, 30, 38-41, 62, 78, 85, 104, 106, 117n, 158
Measurement (of inequality), 7, 9, 10, 185; summary measure, 10, 11
Mexico: inequality by education, 184; labor share, 70
Middle classes, 10, 11, 36, 41, 114, 116, 191, 198
Migration, 187
Minimum: incomes, 90, 193; living standard, 12, 14; needs, requirements, 12, 13, 16, 164, 176n; wages, 93, 188
Modern: economies, 15, 124, 193, 203, 210; sector, 16, 185; societies, 13, 23, 26, 27, 123, 205
Modernization, 23, 24, 46, 61, 107, 117, 206
Mortality (death) rates, 24-26, 46-48, 56, 206; infant, 25, 26, 56, 109
Moshav(im), 32, 110, 112, 113, 118n
Moshava (village), 32
Moslems, Moslem population, 25, 26, 36, 37, 48, 62
Motivation (to work), 64, 133, 148, 189

National: institutions, 23, 101; insurance, 90
Natural: increase (rate of), 26, 43n, 47, 48; resources, 201, 210
Near-poverty: group, 14, 165-172, 174; line, 12, 174, 175, 176n
Netherlands: farm incomes, 112; income inequality, 84
New towns, development towns, 55, 88, 89, 108-113, 162, 166, 171
Non-Jewish: families, 59, 60, 160; population, 47, 48, 56, 59, 83
Non-participation in labor force, see Labor force
Norway: food consumption, 57; income inequality, 84; income distribution, 181, 183
Nutrient intake, 59

Nutritional: level, 8, 17; situation, 25, 30, 37, 39, 45, 202

Occupational: differentiation, diversification, 36, 62, 123, 186, 188, 206; groups, 85, 158, 159, 169, 170; skills, 158, 164, 165, 168, 169; status, 82; structure, 85, 105, 110, 111, 113, 117
Occupations, classification of, 85, 169
OECD countries, 179, 181-184, 189, 191
Old age pensions, 76, 90, 157
Old people, persons, 48, 79, 81, 161, 165, 182, 183, 207, 208
One-parent families, 135, 136, 138-141, 149-156, 158-160, 166-168, 208
On-the-job training, 100n, 122, 124, 131, 133n, 157
Oriental: communities, 30, 37-40, 43n, 48, 62, 105, 107, 207, 212; families, 30, 43n, 105, 107
Overtime (work), 39, 126, 161

Pakistan, income inequality, 180, 191n
Palestine, standard of living, 26
Part-time work, jobs, 38, 124, 139, 147, 159, 169, 171
Pensioners, 38, 65, 68, 90, 151
Per capita income, see Income
Philippines, labor share, 70
Physical capital, see Capital
Population: growth, 47, 51, 186, 201, 210, 211; in poverty, see Poverty; rural, 25, 27, 32-36, 40, 41, 110-113, 115, 186; urban, 27, 31, 33, 36, 40, 42, 72, 78, 96, 99n, 111-116, 179, 180, 186. See also: Arab, Jewish, Non-Jewish
Poverty: abolition of, 12, 19n; absolute (approach, concept), 12, 13, 164, 174, 188; band, 14, 17, 162, 167, 168, 172, 209; budget, 9; causes of, 9, 16, 17, 173; characteristics of groups, 16, 164, 174; defined, 12-14, 19n; groups, 10, 11, 17, 165-172, 174; line, 8, 9, 11-14, 17, 19n, 164, 174-176, 209; population, 162, 165, 174, 183, 213; relative (approach, concept), 12, 13, 164, 174, 209; vicious circle of, 17, 87, 172
Productivity, 50, 52, 53, 111, 187, 188, 202; labor, see Labor
Prussia, income distribution, 185

Public: funds, 94, 95; sector, 68, 88, 89; services, 8, 52, 53, 114, 198
Punjab, poverty, 13

Recession (impact on inequality), 15, 46, 50, 56, 60, 68, 71, 72, 76, 132, 200, 206, 207
Redistribution of incomes, see Incomes
Reference groups, 15, 134n, 137n
Regression: analysis, 82, 87, 95, 100n, 122, 130, 132, 133n, 136, 141, 152, 153, 157, 164, 170, 176n, 185; coefficients, 100n, 131, 134n, 137, 152, 162n; stepwise, 122, 131, 133n, 136
Reproduction rate, 48
Rewards and sanctions, 14, 15, 190
Rights and liberties, 14

Savings, 8, 9, 28, 71, 94, 123, 188
Saxony, income distribution, 185
School: attendance (rates), 124, 211, 212; enrolment rates, 186
Schooling, years of, 50, 61, 82, 83, 87, 100n, 107, 108, 117n, 123, 124, 127-133, 136, 138, 141, 147, 156-158, 163n, 165, 168, 169, 184, 211; see also Education
Second generation, 50, 87, 212
Self-employed, 9, 17, 29-32, 37, 39, 61, 65-71, 99n, 112, 114, 118n, 122, 130, 135, 139, 140, 143, 145, 154, 157, 169, 182, 188, 189, 206, 209, 210
Sex (inequality), 158, 159, 208
Skills, 23, 36, 59, 126, 157, 158, 202, 206; demand for, 188, 189, 208; lack of, 52, 169; scarcity of, 104, 188; supply of, 104, 106, 188, 189, 207, 208
Social: benefits, 55, 76, 93, 95, 99, 100n, 117, 191, 211; changes, 8; ideologies, see Ideologies; insurance (see also National), 193; justice, 13-15, 190, 205; mobility, 72; policy, 8, 12-14, 47, 53, 72, 76, 79, 85, 99, 206, 211; security system, 121, 188, 191, 209; services, 16, 52, 54, 55, 87, 93, 100n, 110, 117, 121, 187, 188, 191, 193, 211; status, 7, 82, 108, 133, 158, 210, 212; structure, 16, 24, 45, 190, 202; tensions, 104, 110, 205; transfers, payments (see also, Transfer payments), 90, 92, 99n, 173, 183, 184, 188, 207,

209-213; welfare bureaus, 90; welfare payments, 8, 16, 21
Spain, income distribution, 182
Standard (equivalent) adult, 10-12, 28, 34, 71, 80, 92, 93, 95, 99n, 111, 150-154, 162-165, 167; consumption per, see Consumption; income per, see Income
Standard (level) of living: defined, 7-9, 12, 13; indicators of, 25, 26, 57, 59, 194, 195; of the family, 144, 162, 209; rise of, 24, 25, 46, 47, 53, 56, 58, 62, 105, 173, 179, 193, 205
Status; see Employment, Social
Structural changes, 9, 52, 61, 202, 204n, 206
Subsidies, 56-58, 76, 87, 91, 93, 94, 121, 191, 195, 207, 211, 212
Subsistence: agriculture, 24; economies, 193, 195, 204n
Surveys: comparability of, 75, 185; consumption (expenditure), 9, 75, 102; family, 31, 34, 37, 40, 68, 71, 92, 105, 113, 116, 118n, 156, 164, 173; income, 9, 65, 75, 76, 99n, 102; savings, 71, 74, 76, 83, 87, 99n, 100n
Sweden: income distribution, 181, 182; per capita income, 195; wife's education, 144
Switzerland: labor share, 70; women's earnings, 104

Taiwan, development, 203
Tax: concessions, 55, 88, 110; exemptions, 94, 153; income, 94, 112, 116, 117, 126, 188; reform, 212; structure, 8, 16; system, 45, 91, 117, 188
Taxes (taxation), 8, 9, 17, 55, 56, 76, 87, 91, 93, 116, 117, 121, 188, 195, 198, 211; direct, 9, 91-93, 100n, 164, 207; indirect, 91-93, 100n
Technological: advance, 84, 85, 87, 89, 206, 207; developments, 85, 89, 193, 203, 209; level, 52, 195, 201, 202
Tel-Aviv, 28
Traditional: communities, 63; economy, 193; sectors, 16, 46, 185, 206; societies, 13, 24, 27, 36, 46, 101, 107, 205-207
Transfer payments, 16, 76, 92, 121, 207; unilateral transfers, 54, 55; see also Social, Incomes
Trans-Jordan, standard of living, 26

Underreporting, 64n, 179, 180, 182
Unemployment, 45, 59, 60, 68, 71, 76-79, 95, 96, 173, 188, 206; insurance, 90; rates, 51, 60, 69, 72, 75-79, 87, 97, 98, 156, 207
United Kingdom: feelings of deprivation, 15; food consumption, 58; income distribution, 181, 183-185; labor share, 69-72; pace of growth, 199; regression analyses, 132, 133; women's earnings, 104
United States: business cycle, 78; food aid, 55; income distribution, 183, 184; labor share, 69, 70; per capita income, 194, 195, 202; poverty line, 9, 10, 12; regression analyses, 132, 133; wife's education, 144; women's earnings, 104
University graduates, 184
Unskilled labor, see Manpower
Urban: families, see Families; population, see Population
Urbanization, 8, 49, 52, 111, 113, 115, 117, 186-188, 194, 204n, 207, 209

Value(s), 63, 64, 194, 203, 204n; judgment, 11; of time, 140; patterns, 62; systems, 13, 63, 189, 190

Wage and salary earners, 9, 28-32, 38, 39, 65-70, 102, 103, 112, 124, 126-130, 182, 193, 206
Wage differentials, 38, 66, 76, 85, 87, 94, 99n, 103-106, 117n, 133
Wealth, 8, 10, 13, 14, 16, 66, 71, 88, 94, 95, 105, 121, 193, 194, 203; concentration of, 55, 71, 188
Welfare: family, 140, 207; ratio, 12; state, 193
West Malaysia, income distribution, 184
Wives: earnings, see Earnings; work, see Work; working, 81, 135, 138-140, 143, 145-150, 153-156, 160, 168, 208; non-working, 82, 138-140, 43, 145-150, 153, 208
Women, 29, 61, 62, 81, 82, 101, 103, 104, 140, 149, 151, 152, 159, 162n, 162n, 166, 209; employed, working, 61, 64n, 139, 140; married, 61, 81, 82, 96-99, 139, 143, 146, 149, 156, 207, 208; single, living alone, 150, 151, 166, 167
Work: ethos of, 14, 62; experience, 66,

85, 121, 124, 126, 128, 133n, 160, 162n, 208; wife's, 126, 135, 140, 156
Workers: agricultural, 32, 33, 102, 103, 111; blue-collar, 29, 38, 85, 103, 169; unskilled, see Manpower; white-collar, 29, 62, 69, 85, 103
World: income, 196, 197, 210; population, 196-198

Youth, 46, 62, 63, 91
Yugoslavia, income distribution, 183